LIBRARY OF
EDUCATIONAL PSYCHOLOGY

THE CHILD IN
PRIMITIVE SOCIETY

LIBRARY OF
EDUCATIONAL PSYCHOLOGY

General Editor : *C. K. Ogden, M.A.*
(*Magdalene College, Cambridge*)

EMOTION AND DELINQUENCY : a Clinical Study of Five Hundred Criminals in the Making. By *L. Grimberg, M.D.*

THE CHILD IN PRIMITIVE SOCIETY. By *Nathan Miller, Ph.D.*

In Preparation

THE ART OF INTERROGATION : a Study of the Interpretation of Mental Tests and Examinations. By *E. R. Hamilton.*

THE SCHOOLS AND THE NATION. By *Georg Kerschensteiner.* (New edition.)

THE PSYCHOLOGY OF THE INFANT. By *Siegfried Bernfeld.*

AN INTRODUCTION TO CHILD PSYCHOLOGY. By *Karl Bühler.*

THE CHILD IN PRIMITIVE SOCIETY

By

NATHAN MILLER

*Ph.D., Assistant Professor in the Department of
Sociology at the Carnegie Institute of Technology*

PUBLISHERS
BRENTANO'S
NEW YORK
1928

PRINTED IN GREAT BRITAIN BY THE DEVONSHIRE PRESS, TORQUAY

CONTENTS

THE CHILD IN PRIMITIVE SOCIETY

CHAPTER I

INTRODUCTION

A SOCIETY has been defined as "a group of human beings living in a co-operative effort to win subsistence and to perpetuate the species."[1] This tendency among men towards association has often been termed the gregarious instinct. It is probably a characteristic developed in the course of organic evolution and taken over into the sphere of societal evolution along with the other broader characteristics that man has acquired as part of his animal inheritance. At all times and in all places men have been found binding themselves together more or less willingly into groups, larger or smaller in dimension, temporary or permanent in character. The individual living the lone life, such as the recluse, the hermit, the ascetic, the ostracized—these have always been considered as aberrant from the normal type of humanity. The individual has ordinarily been set securely in his society, and his individuality has been moulded inevitably by the nature of the folkways and the mores of his people.

It is the sociologist's task, primarily, to examine the nature of these objective and historical wrappings, produced by the social existence, which serve to encase the individual. It is the psychologist's task to consider the personal and subjective impacts of society upon the individual's behaviour and attitudes. The sociologist is confronted with difficulties at the outset. The way must be paved by a classification of groups and group life, such as the blood- or kinship group, the sovereign or territorial state, the culture-area, and the like. In addition, a cross-section of any society will reveal co-existing institutional forms, such as the family, the cult, the state, the economic structure, and the like. These are all conjoined and interrelated and there is a tendency to consistency between these various institutions in the light of the cultural history of the particular group in question. From this point of view, at least, society is organic in nature, since each individual in it reflects the nature and construction of the entire society.

The most valuable scientific results attained thus far in the study of the complex field of society have doubtless been secured by the use of the anthropological and culture-history approach. This has consisted in drawing upon the immense body of facts collected by trained observers and travellers among the peoples of simpler cultures. In this field of comparative ethnography, the social nexus is not so vastly complicated and the treatment can be rendered more objective. Besides, the groundwork toward an understanding of the sweep of social forces can be apprehended the more easily by this method. This was the technique employed by pioneers like Herbert Spencer, Julius Lippert, W. G. Wilken, Sir James Frazer, E. B. Taylor, W. G. Sumner, and others. By drawing upon the materials descriptive of the simpler and the historical cultures, the first inklings of the social processes and forms have been secured, free from theorizing and prejudiced conjecture. The present essay is an attempt to follow this method in the study of the sociology of the child.

The emphasis in this treatment is thus laid upon the position of the child in the primitive, less developed societies reaching back as close to social " origins " as is possible. Here conditions are less involved, and the prejudices that the investigator carries with him are dissipated because of the objectivity presented by the strangeness of a primitive culture. The position of the child in all society will be rendered clearer by the inspection of the rôle he plays in the simpler culture. As will be appreciated further in this study, the " primitive " in the relations of the folk to the child still remains the prevailing attitude to the child and his function in the more developed, contemporary social life.

The objection has of late been vigorously raised by anthropologists that an unbroken parallel course of development for all societies cannot be traced, and that each group has rather had its own particular culture-history determined by the circumstances of the environment. In many instances, this school avers, the diffusion of culture from certain centres has played a larger part than parallel development. It is not necessary, however, to subscribe rigidly to the doctrines of the evolutionist school in order to be convinced that certain broader lines of development are discernible which have involved all groups in their culture-history. Such a universal condition must be the relation of the child to the parents and the elders in so far as the child occupies the position of the perpetuating organ of the folk-life, with its mores and culture-equipment. The unusual deviations and the sources of particular customs with regard to the child are of less consequence certainly than the fact that all societies, especially in the first stages of development, have treated the child with the same concern and adopted more or less consciously a type of training and preparation for life for the child. And it is also maintained that the modern state of affairs as regards the attitude toward the child can be definitely related to and made dependent on the position occupied by the child in the simpler societies.

There is another difficulty or precaution to be kept in mind throughout this study. The picture of any class or division in society is apt to erase individual distinctions. Individual differences are altogether too subtle and, in the state of modern psychology, often not susceptible of direct recording. Hence, the essentially vital developments in the social field are unassignable to individual actors or participators. In the grand sweep of events the variations produced by individuals are often engulfed or absorbed by the general movement. In addition, in the primitive society, individual differences are of small moment, as the person is completely lost in the strict solidarity of the folk. Sameness and conformity subdue marks of individual variability. It is the child as a representative of a functional class in society of which we treat here rather than individual children.

The sociologist is forced into the study of the more objective phenomena of society, such as custom, institutions, beliefs, lore, language and the like. The outward behaviour of the individual, at least, is completely moulded by these aspects of his folk-life, so that in his methods of food-getting, his family and sex life, the practice of his cult, and even the usual expressions of vanity and self-indulgence, he is hardly to be distinguished from his fellow tribesman. To the psychologist is left the important study of individuality and its expressions as in art, invention and innovation. We are rather concerned with the massive social forces which in the earlier stages of society have almost completely enmeshed the individual actors—in this case, the children.

This essay upon the place of the child in the history of society will serve, perhaps, to reinforce the point made, that the social heritage definitely colours the life of the individual, shapes his behaviour and in part creates his character. The purpose here is not to enquire into the inner processes of learning, habit-formation and acculturation in the child himself, but our aim is rather to examine the social milieu as it impinges upon the child—in other words, the customs and institutions which emerge as the educational systems of society later in the course of development. The purpose is to delineate the gradual trimming or fashioning of the child's socal existence by these social forces. The folkways as receiptive adjustments to the fact of the child as a newcomer into the tribal life are to be considered, and also the processes by which the child assumes his cultural heritage.

It is important to include within the scope of a study of society not only the objective facts of the texture of society and its component parts, but also the views, opinions, rationalizations and beliefs of the people as to the worth and meaning of their habitudes and institutions. Very often a divergence appears between the actual facts and the opinions or myths set up for their justification. These myths frequently take the form of the proverbial folklore and traditions. We are too apt to call these " superstition." Nevertheless, it is important that these bodies of beliefs be regarded as facts in themselves—that is recurrent, usual social phenomena. They have played a large part in the history of culture. Fallacious and illogical though they may seem, they are a product of the social life, have reacted on the subsequent development, and must therefore be taken into account.

The importance of the study of the child in culture-history is due to the fact that we are attempting thereby to lay bare the mechanism of social heredity. In the simpler societies, at least, the child has been the main organ or instrument in the perpetuation of culture. Short of the acquisition of a written language, a device which few of the peoples here to be considered have attained, it is only through the child that the continuity of the culture may be preserved. The folkways and mores surrounding the child and the younger generation will present a picture of the genetic movement of culture. An interpretation of the manner in which social forces acquire that inclusive and pervasive force over the individual which we have already mentioned will be presented in this consideration of the sociology of the child. The personal basis of the mechanism of social heredity is thus our main consideration in this essay.

The child, in the life of society, as well as in the organic life, is also the element of refreshing and revivifying novelty and variety. The offspring differ from the parents in many ways. This is a law of life. To what degree this also holds for the folk or cultural life will be another object of treatment in what is to follow. Unfortunately, the history of the major stages of society enshroud in doubt and darkness the originator of changes. In comparison with the insuperable forces of the past which lumber perseveringly along, the fact of change appears to play an insignificant part. The relative insignificance of the child as a variant in the social life has important consequences for society to-day.

This problem is not of academic interest alone. The purpose of society, if we can speak of any such thing, is the enrichment of individual opportunity and welfare. Men tend to fall into the social mode of life in pursuance of the basic ends of life, such as self-maintenance and self-perpetuation. But inevitably the suspicion arises from a study as the present that a developing society tends to override the individual in the attempt to produce an unerring conformity. Above the stiff unyielding cohesion of the child to his social heritage, individuality giving rise to variation plays an insignificant part indeed. The masses predominate. The child sinks into the mass-expression of life in the manner to be described in the course of our survey.

Social phenomena, which include tools, arrangements, ways, institutions and beliefs, are adjustments to the life conditions presented by the environment. In the past, the necessity for preserving intact the results of the folk's history which has taken the above forms has greatly curtailed individual expression on the part of the child. The forces making for conformity have had a greater survival-value. To-day, however, dullness, sameness, crude conformity and mediocrity appear to be too great a price to exact of the child. Still, the " primitive " strain in our educational systems and the attitudes toward the child developed by the simpler culture prevail as actuating motives. The future calls for more originality and diversity, and for the freeing of the rich promise held out by the innate differences in ability and talent that lie hidden in the make-up of the child.

CHAPTER II

PRIMITIVE NOTIONS OF THE CHILD

MUCH speculation has surrounded the topic of the nature of early societal organization. A plethora of terms to indicate the primitive, original human group has been coined, such as gens, phratry, tribe, class, sib, clan, family and horde. The usual picture is drawn of a beast-like collection of human beings sullenly and suspiciously banded together for the moment, half out of fear and half out of desire for mutual protection and warmth, and the chance to despoil other members of the horde.

It is not necessary here to attempt to clear this terminology of its hazy overlapping and indistinctness. This much can be said with certainty, however, that the tie that bound the original human groups was primarily organic, and possessed by man in common with the higher mammals ; the bond, namely, between mother and child—a definite and obvious relationship founded securely on physical urge and compulsion. This relationship is the germ of all subsequent social concepts. The fact of the organic dependence of the child upon the mother lays the groundwork for all the complex divisions and categories of societal experiences that have followed.

The most primitive social structures in regard to which we have a sufficient body of data appear as loosely aggregated bodies of persons who consider themselves related through a common " blood-tie." The obsession with blood runs through primitive society in an amazing manner. This blood-tie is no doubt drawn as a fiction upon the relationship

8

between mother and child, which apparently seemed to primitive man to inhere in the possession of a common blood. The mother's blood makes the child.[1] All societal fictions are built in this way upon analogy with the apparent facts of organic phenomena. The idea of the common blood as the basis of kinship is thus the typical organizing thread of the most undeveloped societies. It must be understood, however, that this concept is vaguely demonstrable in these stages of society because of the paucity of experience and knowledge. Simple proximity, therefore, may often be indistinguishable from this supposed common blood-tie. The exigencies of the struggle for existence bring together individuals to whom the blood-tie becomes merely the social expression and bond of common needs and common experiences. Mere proximity becomes confused with the customary kin-tie.[2]

If there is any grouping on a different principle preceding this kinship idea, it is lost in the vagueness wherein lie all social origins. Such a society may be said to be in a relatively " promiscuous " state.

Social division within the kin-group is extremely lax. Beside the pervasive feeling of a common descent from the real or mythical kin-mother and a partaking of a common blood, there is only a scission between young and old. This fact is based on the obvious physical differences between generations. There are the mature and old who come to assume authority over the young and weak. This division is based on force and physical strength, like many other societal forms. The child is related among these folk to its generation-group. There is no possibility, as yet, of attaching the child to any narrower allegiance or property-relationship, because these did not exist. The kin-group as a whole embraced all its children in a communal fashion. These small atomistic groups had common interests and rights in their children. The children could be related rather indefinitely through mother-descent. This is the basis of the so-called matriarchy or mother-family.

It is profitable to examine the mores of these societies with respect to the child, his function and his place. The mores are notions and rationalizations which a people will unconsciously assume in justification and explanation of the current social practices or folkways under which they live.[3] These ideas may seem strange and outlandish. Taking into account, however, the meagreness of the folk's experience, this strangeness vanishes. It is quite impossible to expect the primitive man to possess a compact body of theory on life, including the subject of the child. The aborigine meets his problem with a direct, flesh-and-blood reaction. He is given neither to abstract thinking nor useless cogitation. He would rather sleep. In the earliest stages of societal development, the ideas of men are inconsistent because they are never verified ; and society lumbers along, carrying with it many of the old ideas even in the midst of entirely new conditions. Thought always lags far behind fact, or is used to justify what has long existed and is even decaying.

Thus the child among these groups is identified with that which is immature, unfashioned, unripe, weak, negligible, pitiable, incomplete. Traces of this idea often remain the dominating abstract conception of the child in societies even more advanced. This notion may easily be discovered by examination of the vocabulary and linguistics of primitive man, where many an outworn, obsolescent usage lies frozen and preserved.

Thus, a Bantu tribe in Africa, the Mukuni, use the word *bana* (literally, " children ") in a derived sense to convey a general depreciative meaning, translated variously by " come, come ! ", " nonsense ! ", " dear me ! ", etc. The Basuto, in speaking of an older person say, " my father, my mother "; of an equal, "my brother "; of inferiors, "my children ". In scanning the Kafir vocabulary, one finds the following : " *ubu-Ncinane* : smallness, littleness, insignificance ; *ubuncinane* : my childhood ; *uku-Teketa* : to do like a child ; to condescend to children ; *i-Teketeka* : any soft, jelly-like substance ".[4] Where such glosses are unavailable, the word for child is a simple descriptive of some physical feature or habit, as among the Yoruba of the Slave Coast : " *omo*, child is literally ' suckling ' and comes from *mo* or *mu*, to drink, suck, as does *omo*, or *omu*, breast, udder ".[5]

Yet in the social sense the child does not " belong ". Before official ceremonial induction into the group (which comes usually with maturity),[6] the child is a nonentity. Thus, the Thonga in South Africa conceive of the child as less than a human being ; a *shilo*, " thing ", or *khuma*, " an incomplete being ".[7] Among the Omaha Indians, for example, " when a child was born it was not regarded as a member of its gens or of the tribe but simply as a living being coming forth into the universe . . . it was hardly distinguishable from all other living forms into its place as distinctively a human being, a member of its birth gens, and through this to a recognized place in the tribe."[8] In Borneo the little child has no name but is called indiscriminately by an appellation best translated by Thingumybob ; and to the West Australian, the uncircumcised (i.e., immature) boy is " all the same dog or other animal ".[9] The Winnebago Indian does not doubt for a moment that the early years of his life are identical with an unconscious condition occurring in mature life ; that is to say, utterly futile, like sleep.[10]

These groups are in different stages of societal development. While it is not asserted that they have all passed through the same course of evolutionary development, yet there are larger aspects of needs common to all human-kind which attain to social expression. The notions as to the child do possess a remarkable similarity among the most widely separated peoples where direct contact is inconceivable. The mores of more highly developed peoples, such as the Thongas, preserve at the same time, ideas that are perhaps outmoded. Yet they hang on as signs of former conditions. A moment's reflection will discover a depreciative attitude toward the child lurking behind even modern language and belief.

Additional light may be shed upon these general notions of the child by considering the ideas held as to his origin. Whence comes the child ? In this connection we invade that precinct of primitive belief in which every-day experience and observation is projected into the unknown. Man has always tended to clothe the mysterious, unknown forces of nature with the characteristics and motives he alone possesses. The science, i.e., the ordered body of knowledge, is indistinguishable from the religion of the primitive man. Both run true to the animistic belief in projecting into the animal, the plant, and even the inanimate clod a moving spirit or life. Where experience is foreshortened, and there are no means of recording it, data are necessarily meagre and scanty. Hence a " spirit " is seen in all things. A completely animated imaginary environment is thus formed, and all that is fortuitous and otherwise inexplicable in life is traced to the workings and machinations of this potent " spiritual " environment.

Death is not considered inevitable or usual by primitive man. The " life " or shade which animates the individual evidently has left the body in such a state. The evidence drawn from dreams, echoes, reflections, temporary unconsciousness and the like are sufficient to convince him that the intangible spirit has left the body and is flitting about in the neighbourhood invested with malignant potency because of its insubstantiality and nebulous form.[11]

The ancestors of the tribespeople are supposed to inhabit

this realm of disembodied ghosts. The actual form of this imaginary, projected world and of the figures in it depend closely upon the extent to which the group has developed in its industrial organization. This is natural because the cult of the folk is derived as a projection, often in an idealized form, of actual life-conditions and environment.

This cult, i.e., the body of religious beliefs and organizations is, however, in a simple society, often removed from the impact of ordinary life-experiences ; hence it is slowest to change of all the cultural forms. It is difficult to verify or test these ideas ; hence they linger on. Only slowly are changes felt in the general ideas of the imaginary environment. Hence the anomalies which may appear here below. The actual ghostly inhabitants depend in good part on the memory of the primitive man and often lapse where a recorded language has not yet appeared ; but the underlying conceptions of the spirit-world remain in the folkways and are transmitted to the child. As the group increases in numbers and a definite political organization appears, the stress towards passing on these beliefs becomes stronger. The specific ancestral spirits give way to conceptions of a few glorified and half-deified figures.

To the primitive mind, the child apparently has his origin in the limbo of the traditional ghostly environment. The exact nature of this inter-world immigration reflects various forms of the religious beliefs and cult-apparatus of the group. The believers in simple ancestral reappearance are aptly illustrated by the Bambara of Central Africa, who claim to be able to recognize some physical mark, as a tattoo on the back, stomach or arm as evidence of the re-emergence of an ancestor who was similarly marked.[12] This usage is explained thus by Tauxier, in relation to the neighbouring Mossi people ; " At the bottom of this concept is the idea that it is always the same who return to this deplorable farce

of life ".[13] To make no mistake about it (and incidentally
to justify their belief), the Gold Coast natives proceed thus :
" On the death of an infant, the grave-digger makes a small
mark with ashes on his cheek or his forehead, and when this
child is born again he will have the same mark on his forehead
or cheek. Others, instead of marking the child with ashes,
fold his little finger, and when he is re-born his little finger
is bent ".[14] In Northern Rhodesia, the child, that is, the
ancestral spirit on another life-jaunt, makes its identity known.
The child is placed at the mother's breast while the names
of the forebears, so far as they are known, are repeated. If
it begins to suck at the mention of a name they are satisfied
as to its identity.[15]

The theory of social evolution, like that of biological evolution, is inadequate unless we are able to trace an unbroken
series of well-defined stages which are amalgamated or joined
together by intermediate transitional developments. The
old ways may be gradually transformed. But each human
society varies, it may be but an iota, from its next-neighbour-
ing or equally-developed society. So in the following stages
the folk attempt to trace no longer an exact reappearance
of the ancestor in the child but rather a new physical frame
equipped with or sent forth by the old ancestral spirit. Thus,
among the Akamba negroes, " the spirits of departed ancestors
are supposed to create and shape the child in the woman;
they decide whether it shall be a boy or girl, dispute about
the matter and forestall one another. In fact, the spirits of
the deceased long to have another body and so pray to the
deity, *Emai*, to grant them this wish."[16] It is believed by
the Yukaghir of Siberia that the spirit takes possession of
its new body while the child is in the womb.[17]

The logic of primitive man is apt to be vivid and relentless,
in the anthropomorphic manner. On the Congo, the Bakongo
believe that the spirit, dressed anew as the child, may be that

of a living person. "If the child is like a relative, it is thought
to have the soul of the person it resembles, and that person
being now soulless will soon die." At all events a spirit
has returned because the "child speaks at an early age of
strange matters the mother never taught it."[18] The ancestor
no longer reappears bodily, perhaps, but merely infests the
infant; provides the spark of life or identity in a vague
manner. Among the Kaonde of Rhodesia, "the departed
soul (*mukishi*) when it reincarnates itself . . . does not
enter the womb, but sends off an emanation of its eternal
self; and itself remains as before".[19]

Where totemistic practices prevail, the group holds to a
belief in a personal connection with certain animals which
are closely related to them, often as forbears. In more
isolated cases, vegetable life, particularly trees, occupy this
same position. The totem-animal or plant carries with it
fetishistic powers—the inexplicable and dreaded powers
which come originally from contact with the spirits. This
is probably due to the fact that such animals or plants have
had contact with the corpses. There is no reason for endowing
extremely mystical origins to totem-practices as some investigators have done. The totem is revered and dreaded
only in virtue of some close relationship with the ghostly
forbears. Hence it is not unusual to find the thought that
animals impregnate women, or themselves turn into children.
Biological species do not exist as yet to the primitive man—
the animal possesses likenesses to man that are more striking
than the differences and hence there is no reason that they
also should not possess a soul, spirit or shade. This is true
of animals that are semi-domesticated, or are friendly to
men and live near them. In addition, the greater strength
and keener senses of animals are much desired and admired,
and there always exists the tendency to appropriate these
superior qualities to man's use if possible.

This connection of the child with the totem is well illustrated in the beliefs of the Australian natives. When a woman conceives, it is believed that the spirit of the totem of the neighbourhood she is in has entered into her. Hence the child's totem may be determined by its place of birth. This may be a gum-tree or even some prominent natural object.[20] The following illustrates the realism of primitive man, which seems to refute all the elaborate theoretical ideas attributed to him. These people say that babies " in their original condition are full-grown, but in their passage into their maternal homes take the form of a curlew (the spurwinged plover) if a girl, but of a pretty snake, if a boy. . . . When at night the blacks hear the curlew crying out, they will say, ' Hallo ! there's a baby somewhere about ? ' In the case of a boy, the woman will probably be out hunting, and suddenly sing out that she sees the snake in question, and as often as not, run away ; her mates, even she herself will perhaps join in looking to see where the serpent has got to, and turn over rocks, leaves and logs in their fruitless search—it can nowhere be found and this is a sure sign that it has reached its destination, and the future mother knows now that she is pregnant."[21] Among the Central Australians, the breeding-grounds are localized near certain stones, so that if a young woman does not wish to have a child, " she will carefully disguise her youth, distorting her face and walking with the aid of a stick. She will bend herself double like a very old woman, the tones of whose voice she will imitate, saying ' Don't come to me, I am an old woman ' ".[22]

Other Australian tribes trace entering child-spirits to the foliage of certain trees. West Africans have " bush-souls " in leopards, fishes, tortoises, etc. In Siberia, the Kamchadales believe that the spider carries the child's soul. In Guatemala, the snake was thought to bring the infant.[23] A most characteristic human trait is supplied by the lowly

Semang of the Malay Peninsula. The tendency in all
societies, particularly where extended scientific knowledge
has not been developed, is to ascribe human traits to the
rest of the universe. These people believe that children are
transported by (no longer actually identified with) certain
birds who have fetched them from soul-trees in another
world. But the souls of *animals* and *fishes* are conveyed in a
somewhat similar way—that is through the eating by the
parent animal of certain fungi and grasses.[24]

A tendency arises to classify and order experience, and
thought as such becomes recurrent and predictable. This
is the beginning of science. The above attitudes toward
the child thus become amalgamated, and beliefs arise of
pools or reservoirs from which children are supplied to the
world—of souls waiting to be born. To take one instance :
On the Upper Congo, each family had its " factory " or
" warehouse " in the bush, in a forest, or on an island ; it
may be a creek, or a Bombax cotton tree where the disembodied spirits supplied the family with children.[25] The
Daly River aborigines in Australia possess a hill called *verak-
yinda*, i.e., the place of the children. Here, it is held, there
exists an old man, a watchman who regulates their births—
that is, their order of appearances in the world ![26]

The station of the child in primitive thought will perhaps
be made clear if we pass from this consideration of his connection with the ancestral background as the source of its existence and take into consideration the child's connections
with the aleatory element in general. This is the element
of the unknown and unfamiliar. All that is unexpected,
otherwise inexplicable, unforseeable, dependent on chance
—in short, all that is not easily assimilated to the ordinary
affairs of life and stock of knowledge of the group enters this
category. All such events take on a mantle of irritable
malignancy. Thus, all the reactions surrounding the advent

of the child, such as conception, the development of the embryo, and childbirth, are immersed in this element of unpredictability and strangeness. In all such cases, one must toe the line of tradition with care, lest all the potential calamity of this period be heaped on one's head. Sickness, famine, drought, want and storm are usual evidences that the inhabitants of the spiritual world are displeased.

To avoid these dire consequences the woman at childbirth is segregated from society, for fear of contagion ; she is frequently isolated, in a separate hut, and is not allowed to return until the danger is safely over. Even then, she is only admitted after passing through ceremonial " purifica- tion."[27] Everything with which the woman has come in contact must also be isolated under magical charms.[28] Everything connected with the child is likewise " unclean ". It is believed that the child is fresh from the spirit world, as we have seen, and hence must be rid of evidences of this contact to be received into this world of work-a-day life. In the Kafir dictionary we find, for example, the word *i-Hashe*, which is defined as " originally, the natural impurity of new- born infants, believed to be from an external swelling, of which they are to be purified by enchanted medicines."[29]

Childbirth remains a dangerous event because it is the point at which the imaginary environment intrudes directly upon the ordinary world. For example, the Marshall Islanders, at the first signs of birth pains, start a fire which is kept going for the entire period of confinement ; under no circumstances may it be extinguished. This fire is to keep off the evil spirits who throng about at this juncture, and is lighted by a medicine man with proper exorcistic incanta- tions.[30] Among many peoples the men studiously avoid all contact with the house and its utensils.[31] After the birth, mother and child are purged and purified of the accretions of " uncleanness " of birth. This " uncleanness " is often closely allied to the " holy " in the development of religious thought and feeling.   Among more highly developed peoples similar observances have been practised.   Thus, in ancient Greece, the child was " purified " five days after birth ; in Rome, the " lustratio " which consisted in sprinkling the child with a branch of laurel or olive tree dipped in water, took place nine days after birth in the case of a boy, eight days after birth in the case of a girl.   In China, the child was similarly " washed " three days after birth.[32]   The preparation for the worldly life in all these cases seems to include the laving-off of the touches of the other original home of souls.   The attendant circumstances of risk to life and that of human interest serve to reinforce the gravity and ceremonial importance of the arrival of another " spiritual visitor ".

From the foregoing one might expect unusual perturbation at the approach of this event.   But such is not always the case.   Births are very frequent.   The women are kept to their tasks up to the last day.   As some justification can easily be found even for the most futile and detrimental conduct, so this practice has been rationalized by the Cahuilla Indians in California as follows : " It is best for an expectant mother to have plenty of work to do during the nine months so that the child will be industrious and strong."[33]   The actual process of birth is not protracted.   In regard to the Fijians, it has been observed : " Cases are recorded in which a woman has gone out in the morning in an advanced stage of pregnancy, and has returned in the evening with a load of firewood on her back and a new-born child in her arms."[34] Nansen relates the case of an Eskimo birth which occurred on a journey : " While the labour continued, the husband stretched himself on the rock and fell asleep ; but presently they awakened him with the joyful intelligence that a son had been born to him. . . . Ernenek accordingly (that was the husband's name) expressed his satisfaction by smiling on his spouse and saying 'Ajungilatit' (Not so bad for you). With our new passenger we at once proceeded on our journey."[35] Likewise, among the California Indians, a child may be born while the tribe is journeying. The woman "will stop by the wayside for half-an-hour to be delivered, and then overtake the party who have travelled on at the usual pace."[36]

Ideas as to the child acquire a closer clutch upon the actual circumstances of life as we come to consider the relationship supposed to obtain between the parent and the child, in its widest sense. Particularly illuminating are notions of the pre-natal influences exerted by the parent upon the child. There is certainly still extant in all strata of contemporary society a wide-spread belief in the potency of pre-natal in-fluences in affecting the child physically and even mentally. These beliefs were all the more vivid and universal in the societies of which we chiefly treat owing to lack of experience and organized knowledge of the processes of the development of life. Coupled with this was an unshakable faith in the system of sympathetic magic—that is, provoking like results through the employment of like means or the working of apparently similar forces. This form of belief was applied notably to the conduct of the pregnant mother as it affected the welfare of the child. The profound biological relationship of mother to child formed the basis of all social organization ; and in the most primitive groups, this relationship was recog-nized to have force even before the child had started on its fully independent career. Thus, in a sense, the social heritage of the child began to impinge upon him, at times, before his birth. This perhaps typified a linking or merging point between the organic and societal form of hereditary influence.

It is no devious reasoning which convinces the Bakitara

of East Africa, for instance, that the pregnant woman must abstain from eating hot food or drinking hot water lest her child's hands should be scalded and show white patches.[37] The Kafir mother " avoids eating buck lest her baby be ugly ; she does not eat the underlip of a pig lest her baby should acquire a large underlip."[38] The Ila-speaking people taboo her consumption of goose lest the child develop a long neck and even forbid her sleeping in the day-time lest the child become dull and stupid.[39] To choose a few more representative cases : In the Admiralty Islands, certain roots are ruled out of the diet lest the child become long and thin ; other bulbous roots would make him stout and short, while consumption of pig's flesh would bestow on him bristles instead of hair.[40] In the islands of Torres Straits, flesh of the sole-like flat fish is said to cause the child in the womb to develop weak eyes and a mis-shapen nose ; the eating of another fish causes the flesh of the child to become wrinkled like that of the old ; while the use of octopus-flesh will cause the child's hands, mouth and fingers to become malformed.[41]

The relation of mother to child is easily understood, as a patent biological fact, and much is read into it. The connection of the father with the child has, however, been an uncertain, vaguely understood notion until comparatively recent times. To attain to a degree of definitiveness in the modern sense of the male progenitor has been a slow development. In the simplest societies, this genetic connection of the father to the child was practically unknown in view of the relatively unregulated marital relations. Sex relations were hardly durable enough to enable the creation of a more definite parental tie than the attachment to the mother. The ideas relative to paternity have developed in response to the general evolution of society. Biological knowledge slowly accumulated to men in large part through experience with the domestication of animals. At the same time the concept of the " father " in the artificial, cultural sense was evolved as an adaptation to the increasing economic contribution of the man in society. The effects of this reacted upon the mores in exaggerating the importance of the man in his relation to the child. The peak of this development was reached in the patriarchal society where the male predominated ruthlessly—one might almost say, boisterously. Theoretical assumptions in the mores were invoked to complete inadequate biological notions and to explain the man's power which had been won solely by dint of a superior influence in the economic life of the times.[42]

The idea of " no paternity " lingers, however, long beyond the acquisition of sufficient knowledge to establish a premonition at least that the child bears a definite imprint of his father's features and general make-up. The intolerance of the established folkways and of the mores built upon them prevents recognition of such facts. Thus, among the Akamba of Africa who have apparently reached the stage of domestication of animals, the matriarchal system still prevails. It is believed that the woman's experiences during pregnancy and even her mental life during that period are not without influence on the child. " The father's sayings and doings, on the other hand, seem to have no effect on the child."[43] Gradually the idea creeps in that the father has some connection with the child, as among the Ila people, who believe that diseases in the father at least affect the course of birth. The idea of sympathetic magical transference of the father's conduct upon the welfare of the child strikes a high note of this development in the ideology of paternity. Thus, Du Chaillu reports that the Shekiani in equatorial Africa, believe firmly that " should the husband of a woman with child, or the woman herself, see a gorilla, even a dead one, she would give birth to a gorilla, and not to a man child."[44] There is thus an ambiguous connection set up between father and child, a relationship so indefinite that it can be shared as well by a gorilla.

Unmistakable faith in an extremely intimate bond is revealed in the mores of groups whose experience in animal domestication or allied advances in material resources is of longer standing. It then becomes incumbent upon the father to abstain from certain actions lest they injure the unborn child. Thus, among the Dyaks of Malaya, " the husband of the pregnant woman, until the time of her delivery, may not do work with any sharp instrument, except what may be absolutely necessary for the cultivation of his farm ; he may not tie things together with rattans, or strike animals, or fire guns, or do anything of a violent character—all such things being imagined to exercise a malign influence on the formation and development of the unborn child."[46] Chandless, an explorer on the Amazon River, on one occasion could not induce two of his native porters to row more strenuously ; one said that he had left his wife pregnant, the other that his wife was at home with an infant. Their actions had to be tempered if their young ones were not to be injured.[47] Paternity implies a mysterious connection with the child, typical of belief in sympathetic magic. This signifies that the actions of one of the closely-connected persons is bound to have an effect on the other as if the latter had actually acted. If the father handles sharp weapons or ties a knot or smokes, it is tantamount to the child's acting in the same manner. Inasmuch as these actions are bound to injure the frail child or hinder its easy birth, it is evident that the father must desist from such practices before, during, and after the confinement, until the infant has grown in strength and has overcome the dangers of its transition into the worldly arena.

This movement in culture-history reached a dramatic point in that exotic flower of the folkways, the " couvade."

Its strangeness has attracted undue attention and imaginative explanations have sometimes been given ; yet it may be viewed simply as an outgrowth of this development in the notion of paternity. It is a clear and striking episode. The father takes to bed, simulates the pains of childbirth and otherwise comports himself as though he instead of the woman were being delivered of child. The usage is widespread. It has been observed among the West Africans, in Micronesia, many Melanesian tribes, throughout the Indian archipelago generally, in the Philippine Islands, and among the Ainu of Japan. In its fullest form it was found among the Caribs of the West Indies and still persists among Indians of South America.[48] The lengths to which the couvade may be carried out is well illustrated by the Jivaros of Ecuador, among whom the " woman has to undergo all her parturient troubles outside the house, exposed to the elements, whilst the husband quietly reclines in the house, coddling and dieting himself for some days, until he has recovered from the shock produced on his system by the increased weight of his responsibilities as a father."[49] This is an early instance, evidently, of a dogma flouting the bare facts of life—of a rigorous carrying out of the implications of a belief at the cost of the neglect and jeopardy of other persons, more critically concerned. The emphasis in society often tends to fall upon a stupid consistency and conformity at all costs.

The importance and singularity of this custom has been over-stressed. The couvade is merely one of the manifestations of that movement from the loosely-organized matrilineal system that culminated finally in the patriarchal organization of the family and social life. It is a step in the evolution of the idea of " paternity ", later exfoliating into the extreme father-family of the nomadic culture-groups of antiquity. Yet it is objectionable to maintain that this is the " very sign and record "[50] of this momentous change in the history of culture. The couvade reflects a stage of development in which the paternal tie appears to have become an extremely intimate one. Von den Steinen, with Brazilian natives in mind, offers linguistic evidence to show that the " child " means the " little father " and this term is applied to the daughter as well. The child is thus a miniature, or part of the father.[51] One of the natives actually explained the fiction of his " giving birth " in the couvade, as a step taken " in order to regain the strength he had lost in becoming a father ; for that reason he took to bed and acted the convalescent."[52] The custom may last on into the developed patriarchy where the notion of paternity is no longer so novel as to require a performance like the couvade to impress it upon the tribe-fellows. Weeks unearthed such an instance on the Congo. There, while the man is observing the food prohibitions, he is said to be in a state of *liboi*, a noun derived from the word *bwa*, to be confined, to deliver of a child. " It is probably a remnant of *la couvade*."[53]

The variations in the actual conduct of the man are first of all an imitation of the mother's action. It is clear to the primitive man that to have a child it is necessary to be temporarily ill. Most social fictions are developed in imitation of the observed facts of physical life—hence, it is not surprising that " paternity " should come to be demonstrated originally as a play-acting of maternity. Language, or abstract, legalistic thought had not yet developed upon a thorough foundation of long, recorded experience to enable the connection of father with child to arise, sociologically, in any other way. These practices are therefore intensely realistic, in response to the actual beliefs entertained. So it is also that the man's actions may be very effective in alleviating the pains and labour of the woman as well as the child. In the Torres Straits islands, a husband was told that his wife was in travail ; whereupon he went into the sea and kept diving in order to relieve the

c

pain of his wife. This he had to do continuously until the child was born. In somewhat the same manner, in New Guinea the man takes off his arm-bands to relieve his wife in case of protracted parturition.[54]

The manner of establishing this notion is thus extremely graphic and dramatic, but the ideas of paternity so grounded only developed slowly and even imperceptibly in the nature of the evolution of social forces. The idea of the father's connection with the child took on a definitive aspect at an unequal rate in various parts of the world. Its full development transcended generations of men. The couvade is a vivid illustration of the adjustments made in the folkways and in the beliefs of men in accommodation to the critical event of the advent of the child. It is the purpose of the preliminary chapters of this work to consider further these adjustments of the group to the fact of the child in its midst. Significant for our purpose, too, is the fact that these adjustments in the ways and beliefs of the folk are transmitted to and preserved by the children, or the younger generation. The later chapters are to be devoted to a consideration of this aspect of the child as the heir and legatee of society.

CHAPTER III

THE BURDEN OF CHILDREN

THE chief force which serves to determine the outlining features of societal life is the limiting support of the natural environment. The whole tendency towards group-life lies in the attempt to make a superior adjustment to life-conditions as represented by the topography, climate, flora and fauna or the land. Animals become adjusted through keener, fine organic equipments and sense-developments. These are preserved as adjustments in the struggle for existence and become the basis of new animal types and even species. But in the case of man a new level of adjustment is struck. It is " social " in the sense that men rather deliberately band together and slowly select out ways of life that prove of greater efficacy and survival-value. Except in a very subtle way, man does not acquire claws, or fur, or a proboscis, or protective colouration. His expedient lies in the unconscious concurrence in mental adjustments originated by outstanding individuals. These adjustments are perhaps not as fortuitous as those in the animal world. Man *seeks* to adjust to the environing circumstances. It is the economy of " thought ", as highly typical of this mode, that forces men into group-life where in a loosely co-operative way they can subsist more securely and reproduce their kind more abundantly.

Social phenomena are thus devices born of attempts to adjust to the given plan of life in the typical human way, i.e., an unconscious co-operation. In the simplest societies the folkways are extremely undeveloped ; feeble, halting, uncertain and often mere blind, rash reactions to the pinch of circumstances. In the degree that society develops, to that degree do its adjustments become more consciously felt. The successful adjustments are carried along by tradition. Then it becomes possible to elevate the group from immediate contact with natural forces. This has occurred in the main through the appropriation of animate and inanimate energies from nature, and their harnessing to do man's will and so contribute to his food, clothing, and shelter and the satisfaction of his demands for social distinction.

This is the process of societal evolution. The general tone and temper of all societies is moulded by the relationship of numbers to land—of mouths to be fed to the available food supply. At all times, the stage of life upon which man seeks self-maintenance and self-perpetuation, is limited in dimension and capacity of satisfying these desires. Within the set conditions, the group seeks a workable, comfortable arrangement. This can be effected by either of two methods : by the elaboration of more effective methods of food-getting, or by a decrease in numbers. The former method has been more consistently followed. As man has gained more knowledge of the world about him, painstakingly and pragmatically he has developed the arts of life which have enabled him to support greater numbers. At the same time there has been in operation the more sporadic, fitful policy of limiting numbers where newcomers tend to imperil the habitual levels of living already attained by the society in question.

There arises a blind attempt to preserve a standard of life. The menace of over-population reveals this aspect of life in society, which is its very *raison d'etre*. Men struggle desperately for the maintenance of life itself in the uncertain, dim beginnings of cultural development. But they are concerned just as insistently in the developing, elaborating groups, with the protection of an habitual mode of life—a certain level, kind, or degree of food, raiment, housing and varying expressions of individual worth and vanity. The effort to preserve the customary standards impels men to limit population-growth. They are often unwilling to forego the crudest, simplest refinements developed by the group. The standard of living amounts, in affect, to the insistence upon the acquisition and preservation of standardized notions of "good-living" before men are ready to jeopardize them by having children.[1] That is because a steady increase in numbers would call for a profound readjustment in the ways of life—either a deterioration in the customary level, or an incitement towards wresting more support from the environment through further development of the arts of life. These alternatives do not generally appeal because both connote distress. Men fasten themselves irretrievably to the customary ways of life and for long this same inertia prevails against further improvements in food-getting, development of tools, and accumulation of capital.

In the simpler societies here dealt with, the level of economic development is low. It is fixed, and little effort is expended in its elaboration or improvement. Because men cling desperately to standards, the desire for change is feeble and intermittent on the whole. The element of foresight is practically lacking. The "dead hand" of the ghostly ancestors weighs heavily. It guards jealously the preservation of old methods and ways. The standards of the dead become the standards of the living and impede their betterment.

These primitive men have no "population-policy". The strain of adjustment to the environment is of course felt by individuals. They react in limiting their numbers only as the threat of dearth or actual impoverishment sharply impinges on them personally. Bodily discomfort and personal inconvenience are often a sufficient motive to bar the child's entrance into the world. This fact explains the intermittent occurrence of infanticide and abortion among primitive

peoples. After society has reached a certain degree of development, however, the social compulsion becomes prominent. The individual's notions become coloured by the group. The adherence to a standard of life incites the very same practices which personal bodily discomfort on the part of the woman would alone have worked earlier. The parents snuff out the life of the child as a personal, individual reaction. Yet the accumulating force of all these individual instances goes to make a social reaction which can only be observed afterward. Social forces thus originate in individuals but very soon transcend them, and, viewed broadly, acquire a significance over and above the agents that set them forth.

Primitive man often feels this press of population very keenly. The child must enter the world only when his presence will not crowd or necessitate unwonted economy. More than " elbow room " is needed to induce his progenitors to take the trouble of caring for him in his infancy. If he is likely to become another *bouche inutile*, his career is summarily checked while yet in the womb. That abortion and foeticide are commonly practised among these people is a conclusion forced upon us by the abundance and extent of the evidence at hand.

Before passing on to illustrative cases, however, it is interesting to point out the apparent divergence between belief and action—the divergence in manner of approach toward flesh-and-blood problems and the vagaries of beliefs and " superstitions ". In the last chapter we have observed the widespread belief in the " spiritual " precedence of the child, as the reappearance of former disembodied souls. Yet in the practices of abortion here to be described, this attitude is forgotten and decisive overt measures are taken. That is because men react primarily to inner, personal motivations, and these often disregard traditional views. This has been true to some extent in all ages, although for our present purpose it is interesting to record such behaviour only in so far as it becomes usual and customary and constitutes a folkway constraining men to this one mode of action. From this aspect, it can hardly be said that the practice of abortion has at any time taken on the proportions of a folkway. In a sense it has appeared as a defensive reaction to stringent needs, irrespective of the beliefs held as to the origin and place of the child.

Among the Congo people, abortions are frequently procured even though the practice has come under the social ban, and so recourse is had to it secretly. This, however, does not seem to diminish the frequency with which it is resorted to.[2] Among other peoples the practice is more usual, the girl being abetted by her mother who conducts her to a woman, professional in these matters.[3] Among other primitive peoples, as among the Bontoc Igorot of the Philippines, " no effort is made at secrecy and its practice is no disgrace ".[4] Like comment has been made of the now extinct Tasmanians and the Ainu aborigines of Japan.[5] The natives of Kamchatka, according to older accounts, used a variety of means, both internal applications and violent physical manipulations of the body to procure abortions. This is substantiated by more recent reports.[6] This unusual *sang-froid* may be related to the harshness of the climate and the comparatively raw struggle for existence, which discourages the slightest increase in numbers. Foeticide is widespread in Micronesia and Polynesia.[7] It is rather notable that one observer declares that the rapid increase in the practice of abortions in recent years is to some extent the result of missionary influence.[8] This may perhaps be the unfortunate reaction upon the natives of the attempt to grasp higher material standards of life inadvertently introduced by these outsiders. Among the larger islands of the Pacific, in Melanesia, more evidence may be easily culled.[9]

As we approach the Asiatic continent and study peoples possessing more effective tools and processes of food-getting, the abortive practices fall into comparative desuetude. The crudest methods come into use as the knowledge of the older medicinal methods fails.[10]

The American Indians had resort to abortive devices also. Charlevoix in his day, and in characteristic language, was moved to remark with regard to the Indians of Canada, that " the use of certain simples, which have the virtue of keeping back in them the natural consequences of their infidelity is familiar enough in this country."[11]

Both medicines and violent methods were commonly used on the North-west coast of Oregon, among the Indians of the South-west, and in the wilds of Brazil.[12] Like information is supplied even from the more remote Easter Islands.[13] The Paraguayan Indians defended their " right to procure abortion and kill the newly-born whenever they willed it. They claimed a right to the life which they had given."[14] Thus man finds adequate rational justification for practices imposed by the conditions of life.

These instances are typical of the uses of abortion as a method of redressing the probable distress to be caused by increasing numbers in the population. The need to employ this check arises only when inconveniences are personally felt.[15] With progress in the arts of life, however, abortion becomes frowned upon and is henceforth perpetrated in secret. This is pre-eminently true if the practice is motivated by the mere caprice or will of the woman at a time when additional children would no longer endanger the food-supply or the beginnings of a standard of living. So, taking up the Kafir dictionary of Kropf, we read, " *Qomfisa* . . . to cause or help to procure abortion. (It was looked upon as a crime, for which payment had to be made to the chief, who lost by this practice one of his subjects)." The mere desire to

retain youthful appeal or the shirking of an arduous physical
burden was not sufficient to counteract more fundamental
aspects of societal development.

These conditions probably coincided with the growing
importance of the male in family and societal life. The
superior economic support furnished by domesticated animals
and plants was first introduced, or at least developed, by
the men. It became possible to support greater numbers by
this series of more able adjustments to the environment.
The men, now, in addition, earnestly *desired* children.[16]
Abortion became decidedly taboo and contra-mores in a
society shaping itself under the growing power of the man.
The life of the child was *his*, and as the wielder of economic
power also determines the basis of beliefs, or mores, the
procuring of abortion henceforward became a *theft*. Thus,
among the Wasongola of the Congo region, the woman must
conceal the deed of abortion from her husband, who, if he
became aware of it, would return her to her father with
claim for material reimbursement for the damage done.[17]
This is quite a serious misdemeanour : among the Baholoholo
near by, in case of abortion, the man drives his wife from his
hut, cuts her arms, thighs, abdomen and her entire body ;
cuts off her hair, covers her with cinders, and then, bloody
and bruised, clothed only in an antelope skin, she is sent back
to her parents—and often in addition recompense is claimed
for the life she has frustrated.[18]

Among the Jakun of the Malay peninsula the husband,
upon discovery of the attempt at abortion, " had the right
of giving his wife a sound drubbing with a club, and if in such
a case he killed her, he was not brought to justice for doing
so."[17]

Supernatural sanction is constantly brought to bear to
bolster up the folkways developed by the powerful ones in
society. The whole terrifying threat of the malignancy of

the spirit-world is let loose upon those who tend to dispute the power, and threaten the interests of the predominant sex, class, or group. Those who stray from these beaten paths of custom become tainted with moral iniquity. Thus, in Rhodesia, " abortion is regarded with horror, the woman is in a state of uncleanness and a distinct danger to the community ".[20] It is interesting to observe the ease with which the interests of a sex or group (in this case the men presumably) are also assumed to be the interests of the community. The woman is an " evil-being " and must insulate herself from the dangers attendant upon unworthy acts. If the abortion is actually carried through, some insurance against the revengeful depredations of the injured spirits must be taken at the same time, for in the light of the notions held as to the spiritual origin of the child, as noted above, this act is a direct mutilation or attack upon an inhabitant of this ghostly environment who is about to move into the worldly scene. So, in South-west Africa, " during the act of abortion, a goat is killed by a woman-magician, with the blood of which the road is sprinkled (the procedure must take place outside in the bush) because the road has become unclean ".[21]

Another aspect of the recourse to abortion is confirmatory of the view that the practice has rarely become an ordinary usage or folkway. This is its use as a desperate resort, rather, to bring the person back into conformity with customs which have already been transgressed. Most often it is a corrective usage in such cases when the child will come into the world of a proscribed or forbidden relationship. Incidentally, the occasion of the use of abortion will, therefore, often give an indirect picture of the make-up of the society and its mores. Thus, abortion is used to destroy the fruit of the relationship between a free girl and a slave, among the Suaheli, or between a native and a professional prostitute, as among the Wadschagga—both cases of peoples more advanced in culture-development.[22] Thus, an "immoral" expedient is used to preserve a "moral" status. This also indicates the growing ostracism of the user of the device of abortion in the developing society.

There have always been more capricious incitements to this action, such as the desire of the woman to preserve youthful attractiveness, or to pique or hurt her spouse. Those motives fluctuate around the evolutionary development sketched above, and must be considered of subsidiary importance in the sociological study. One of the most frivolous causes is that moving the Akamba women in East Africa : " When the dances of the young people are at their height, the desire to be able to take part in this recreation will, by itself, be sufficient to induce a pregnant girl to try to free herself of the unwelcome burden which begins to weigh down the body."[23] Codrington, in speaking of the Melanesians in general, lists the following minor causes : " If a woman did not want the trouble of bringing up a child, desired to appear young, was afraid her husband might think its birth before its time, or wished to spite her husband, she would find someone to procure abortion."[24] Among widely-separated peoples in various stages of development, this measure is used deliberately to annoy or disappoint the " man whom she hates or quarrels with . . . "[25]

Often the child will mean an extra burden to the wife, hindering her in the manifold duties and work which she has to perform in the primitive society. The Fuegians, a very backward group, fear to be incommoded in their huts and canoes by the newcomers. The Australians use abortion because their nomadic life will not permit of their being able to carry more than one child on their constant marches.[26] Among the Akamba of East Africa, again, " the woman has much to do in preparing the fields for the rains, sowing, etc., and she is therefore quite naturally anxious to free herself from a burden which hinders her in her work."[27]

Where domesticated animals have been introduced, the burden of heavy labour slips from the shoulders of the women. Then the prospect of the child as a burden no longer serves to instigate this extraordinary device of crushing the developing life. Again, the elaboration of the economic arts allows of greater numbers and the growth of " moral " concepts. Abortion, as we have seen, came under the ban of social disapproval, and thus became " immoral ", originally, as an economic misdemeanour. It became a nefarious, reprehensible practice only as men learned to win a steadier and larger support from the environment. Many of our vaunted moral standards have like roots in the bare struggle of men in groups, to provide greater and more varied sustenance. This is, of course, no prejudice to the refined ethical strivings of more complex and highly developed societies.

Infanticide is another means of restoring the equilibrium between human numbers and natural resources. Here again, as is the case with abortion, the practice is undertaken as a " primary and violent act of self-defence by the parents against famine, disease and other calamities of over-population, which increase with the number which each man and woman has to provide for ".[28] In the recurring lean periods of destitution, when the country is in drought or ravaged by pestilence, additional mouths are vexing encumbrances. In this way, the practice of infanticide may vary in extent with such conditions of privation. Nevertheless, we must include infanticide among the ordinary folkways of our simpler societies; for there is nothing to hinder the primitive man from doing away with the child, since it has not yet acquired any measure or form of status, or bonds in the group. It is a stranger from other parts, and it is wholly within the discretion of the parents to write " Finis " upon its social career before it has acquired any " rights " to its life in the tribe.

The practice may become habitual and part of the expected, i.e., part of the folkways. It is at times entered into with a feeling of relief and looked upon as a fortunate occurrence. Hence, as habitual behaviour comes to influence custom, and this in turn to colour feeling and resentment, so infanticide, repulsive as it may seem to us to-day, is carried out automatically and without any qualms.

The instances are legion.[29] The cases are here cited to illustrate the usualness of the practice. Thus, among the Kuni of Africa, " there is not a woman who has not killed one or several children. It is a cruel custom which all the women have to follow because, as they say in Kuni, *kufamai tsi Koakoa doka*, such were the customs of our ancestors ".[30] The practice was quite common among Australian native women who were always living on the edge of want. " In the laws known to her," says Smyth, " infanticide is a necessary practice, and one which if disregarded would, under certain circumstances, be highly disapproved of ; and the disapproval would be marked by punishment."[31] Infanticide may be arranged in advance, as in the islands of Torres Straits, where the parents would agree on such a disposition of the child before its birth.[32] In Fiji, the extent of infanticide " reaches nearer two-thirds than half. Abominable as it is, it is reduced to a system, the professors of which are to be found in every village ".[33] According to the missionary, Ellis, the Polynesians were given to the practice of infanticide to this extent : " We have been acquainted with a number of parents, who according to their own confessions . . . had inhumanly consigned to an untimely grave, four or six or ten children . . . three females had destroyed not fewer than one and twenty infants. One had destroyed nine, another seven, and the third, five."[34] In America, the custom was not unknown. In the Chaco of Paraguay it has been related that " the child is simply buried, there are no rites connected with it, and no mourning attached to it beyond the death-wail of the mother ".[35]

The disposal of the child occurs most often because of its burdensome annoyance to the living. The situation among the poorest groups is well summed up in the Australian example. " It seems to have been the custom to kill many of the children directly after birth, to save trouble and privations in time of drought, when long distances must be travelled in the search for food and water, and it would be difficult in the fierce heat to transport a number of young children over a dry journey of twenty miles and often more. . . . An Australian never looks far enough ahead to consider what will be the effect on the food supply in future years if he allows a particular child to live ; what affects him is simply the question of how it will interfere with the work of his wife as far as their own camp is concerned." A rationalization is given. There is no human society however poor and backward that cannot supply explanatory ideas, which often seem beside the point. The native women plead that they cannot suckle and carry two children together. But it is probably the additional hunting required that explains the gruesome practice, according to our authority.[36]

This pressing material interest may overcome the personal feelings of the mother, as among the Samoans. The husband, if he thought the infant would interfere with the work of the wife would forcibly take the child and bury it while the woman would bemoan its fate for months.[37] Imperious necessity lays the basis for the practice among such widely separated groups, in addition, as the Polynesians of Hawaii, who " are unwilling to cultivate a little more ground, or undertake the small additional labour necessary to the support of their offspring during the helpless periods of infancy and childhood ", and the Paraguayan Indians, to whom " a large infantile population would be a serious hindrance."[38] Among peoples more advanced in cultural development poverty still is the cause for infanticide and the formal exposure of infants, as in China and Japan. In ancient Athens, the poor exposed the newly-born in baskets at the market-place in the hope that they might be picked up by strangers.[39] Even to-day occasionally the practice remains as a desperate expedient of the poverty-stricken, as is illustrated by occasional notices in the press. In the simpler societies the practice is customary because the woman's contributions to the labours of self-maintenance preclude the rearing of children. The cry of " Woman's place is in the home " is therefore not very ancient. It is only with the gradual emergence of man's superior economic productivity that woman's place in life was reduced to the hearth and the nursery.

There is another occasion for refusing to admit the immigrant human soul to another earthly birth and span of years. This is on the occasion of the death of the mother in child-bed, or immediately thereafter, in case the child cannot be taken care of by others. Short of the pastoral economy, there is no artificial food for children and the other women are too burdened to suckle these infants. In Australia the infant is buried alive with its mother or killed and burnt with her corpse.[40] The Semang of the Malay peninsula wrap mother and child in one shroud, the child being placed on the mother's breast with its face downwards.[41] Among the Nishinain of California, custom provided that the relatives destroy the very young infant on the death of the mother. It is expressly added : " We must not judge them too harshly for this. They knew nothing of bottle-nurture, patent nipples, or any kind of milk whatever than the human."[42] Among the more backward Amazon natives, such a child is simply thrown to the wild dogs, or buried alive with its mother.[43] Among the Chiloctin Indians of Canada, the death of a mother during delivery leads to burying the child in its cradle with the mother.[44] In the Paraguayan Chaco all posthumous children are killed. Indeed, infants are murdered should either father or mother die at the time of birth.[45]

However, after the domestication of animals has been introduced or where that stage has been reached, alleviation of such " savagery " becomes possible. There is an additional source of the food supply. The Kuni of Africa are an example in point. If the mother dies in child-birth, the child is still destroyed ; perhaps through dread of meddling with the " spiritual " aura surrounding the child, fresh from the imaginary environment. But it is of interest to note the various alternatives open as soon as material development allows them to appear. If the mother dies but a few days later, the child is kept and given to another woman to be nursed, fed artificially and adopted by another family or even sold by the father for an axe or a knife.[46] So also, among the natives of California, infanticide was materially reduced as soon as the missionaries began to dole out double allowances to the native mothers.[47]

The preceding material has attempted to portray the direct-ness, even brutality, with which the menace of over-population has been met among these peoples. Abortion and infanticide are keen-bladed knives that trim off the threatened excess of children with their demands for food and care. One must be fed and cared for before taking up the additional burden of others. These devices are exigencies entered upon to meet each case as it arises and although often grown to the proportions of a recurrent custom, yet we can hardly include them among the more settled aspects of a "population policy". They will always remain in the nature of ultimate resorts, expedients, subterfuges or palliatives undertaken in individual instances. It is difficult to unearth any element of prevision, plan or policy. With few exceptions this is certainly true of the simplest peoples, with whom most life-practices are almost entirely instinctive and immediate.

A definitely formulated " population policy " is produced only after a long uninterrupted experience of the group, which has been impressed by the need of a constant check on population growth. Measures of birth-control had been used long before Malthus startled the dawning nineteenth century with his memorable disquisition on the depressing tendency of population to endanger standards of life. Evidence is not abundant in testimony of birth-controls employed by primitive man, because in the very nature of the case, he is not liable to forego any of the instinctive urges or apply the restraints and cares implied in the notion of a control of births. It requires a mighty, potential source of pain to deter him. Yet we can discern here and there a tentative attempt at spacing-out births in point of time. Among some groups where its function is known there are limitations on sexual intercourse by parents for longer or shorter periods after the birth of a child. This predicates the fact that some inklings of the notion of paternity have been gained. As experience attests to the value of continence, a taboo arises which works against those who fail to practice it. Furthermore, these prohibitions are distorted into the language which alone can prevail upon primitive man : they are enforceable with all the magical malignancy of the spirits hovering about who can wreak all evils upon those who do not heed the taboos. In this manner the cult of the group moulds moral precepts and " commands ".

Thus, among the Bakitara, women often lived apart from their husbands for two years after the birth of a child lest they conceive again. In Dahomey, the natives abstained until the child was weaned ; often a period of two or even three years in the Congo region until the child ran about. Among the Mandingo of Liberia, the period is " three years after the birth of a girl-child and for four years in the case of a boy ", and among the natives of the Gold Coast two years.[48]   In Fiji the male is actually banished to a hut to live a life of celibacy for the duration of the suckling period of the child— varying from twelve to thirty-six months.[49]   Among the South American Indians, the Abipones were said to practice continence for three years until the child was weaned, and among the North American Indians, the Jesuit priest Brebeuf remarked of the Hurons, that " in marriage a man will remain two or three years apart from his wife, while she is nursing."[50]

Nor is this an unusual measure to judge from the shame and ridicule which is heaped upon the heads of those who do not follow these ideas of periodical continence. Ridicule is a common social force making for conformity. In New Guinea, if a second child is born before the first can walk the parents are ridiculed by the rest of the village.[51]   In the islands of the Torres Straits, " if the husband or wife had a quarrel with someone, they might be taunted with having a large family . . . and they would be greatly ashamed and decide that the next child born should die . . . ."[52]   As a matter of fact, the common and usual explanation given among these peoples for following this custom of abstinence is that the failure to do so will cause the youngest living infant to " sicken and die ".

In New Guinea, " cohabitation should not be resumed until the child can toddle about, if it is resumed before then the child will sicken and die."[53]   Among the Wagogo of Africa, the man insures against this contingency by giving his child medicine before he breaks the interdiction.[54]   The Australian native woman gives the case away in even more naive fashion : Smyth asked a mother why she had dashed her infant's life out against a tree. On being probed, she pointed to a child of two years of age : " Oh, too much young fellow Jimmy ;

no good two fellow pickaninny."[55] The realities of life are too direct to the women to necessitate attributing such actions to the dictates of the spirit-world, according to the beliefs of the more developed patriarchal group.

The spacing-out of births reaches unusual extremes of planning and foresight and becomes securely implanted in the mores through the force of ridicule and ghost-fear. Particularly did this become apparent on the smaller islands where living space was rather cramped. On De Peyster island, near Samoa, only one infant was allowed to each family. Only under special circumstances " and by paying a fine a second might be allowed to live."[56] Here the custom has apparently hardened into law. On the small island of Yap, likewise, the man is prohibited indulgence even with other wives or prostitutes until the child can run, and often until it is able to speak. " Otherwise it will fail and sicken."[57]

An interesting case illustrative of the social standing of parents using this birth control is that of the Cheyenne Indians. Grinnel relates : " It was long the custom that a woman should not have a second child until her first was about 10 years of age. When that period was reached the man was likely to go with his wife and child to some large dance or public gathering, and there, giving away at the same time a good horse to some friend, to announce publicly that now the child was going to have a little brother or sister. To be able to make such an announcement was a great credit to the parents. The people talked about it and praised the parents' self-control."[58]

The Malthusian menace certainly does present a drear, drab prospect of continual resort to heroic measures to ward off the incessant onset of children. It is all that these more primitive groups can do to preserve the crude customary standards of life that have already been evolved and which cannot support more individuals. There is, however, another side to the problem which is more enheartening in that an element of choice or discretion is added. Now a selective note may be introduced. Not each head is cut down as it emerges at an inconvenient time, but in the light of some standard, only certain ones are so disposed of. These criteria are to begin with, highly capricious but become more "rational" in the sense that developed considerations and evolved desiderata habitual to the group are held to judge the fate of the child. Later, more developed societies may add a degree of rational judgment in this choice as the body of knowledge increases and individual motivations decrease in importance. The extreme point of this development is to be reached in "eugenics" where scientific data and judgments are to control the birth-rate of a people. At any rate, a qualitative aspect of the problem of numbers makes itself felt feebly and sporadically even among the simpler peoples of this study. It is no longer simply the fact of an additional individual but the particular kind or sort of child which determines its fate—life or death.

The birth of twins presents the double aspect—the quantitative press of numbers, and the possibility of selection among births. If the prospect of an additional child is often perplexing, the appearance of two at once clearly makes the problem doubly acute. The difficulty of providing for such a calamitous increase in population is very often the sole motive for doing away with the twins immediately after birth.[59] In addition, the appearance of such an unusual phenomenon is evidently a stroke of "luck": it sets up a great uneasiness and perturbation as one of those fortuitous, mysterious happenings outside the usual experience of men. The hand of the ghostly and ancestral is seen therein just as it shows itself in a plague or in a terrific storm.

Among the Makonde of East Africa, therefore, such a predicament was to be avoided at all costs by " all sorts of

charms ".[60] Among the Akamba the twins were killed at
once " as something unnatural which might bring bad luck ".[61]
Plural births are the work of powers that bode ill and the
fault may be ascribed to the mother who is deemed unclean.
She is compared to a pig or a dog (as on the Niger River),
and is sacrificed or segregated for the rest of her life. She
may be accused, also, of adultery through such circumstantial
evidence. " No greater insult can be offered to a woman
than to call her ' twin bearer ' or to hold up two fingers to
her."[62]

Among the Ba-Thonga of South Africa, the birth of twins
is a severe blow and such defilement of the woman can be
removed only by a qualified medicine-man. No visitor is
allowed in the isolation hut where the woman is kept and
friends may speak only from a distance.[63].

More often where conditions are a bit more beneficent and
the ills of life do not constantly hang as a pall of dread and
fear over the folk, one child of the twins may be spared.
Obviously there is more likelihood and opportunity of exercising some choice in the case of plural births than there is in
the case of single ones !   One child may be killed in line
with the preceding argument as an unhappy burden, but
there is even then opportunity to choose the one who is to live.
In addition, the motive for preserving only one where it might
be possible to support the two comfortably is in order to
readjust matters to the normal condition of parturition else
both mother and the children will die of " uncleanness ".
However, this motive is introduced probably after the act,
as a rationalization of the possibility of saving one child,
where the material conditions will allow it.

Where the choice is left to the mother, the girl-child is apt
to be preserved.[64] In such cases girls are valued because of
their greater prominence under maternal filiation, where
descent and personal property, the name, and status descends

on the female side. More frequently, however, the male child is preserved while the female is killed, probably a reflection of the father's power under the later system of male societal control. The bulk of the evidence leans in this direction also, because the father is more apt to choose one and be less swayed by sentiment than the mother.

A less developed, simpler group is that of the Bontoc Igorot where mere instinctive caprice or sentiment prevails. They choose the quieter of the two, or if both are equally peaceable, the larger one. Among the Ipi of New Guinea, the weaker of twins is buried alive.[65] In order to deceive the spirits of the murdered child and the possibility of its striking back in resentment, a piece of wood roughly carved to represent the murdered child may be placed beside the living twin " so that it might not have to wander about, and feeling lonely, call its companion after it ".[66]

It has always been considered audacious to tamper with such divinely-appointed matters as twins, but man's craft can comfortably thwart the results of his superstitious inertia and allow the two—clashing fact and belief—to exist side by side in peace. One may, as we have seen, believe that the ancestral soul returns in the guise of the newly-born. Yet the realities of life lead to the killing off of excess children. Expiation for this meddling with divinely-appointed events can be made in some shrewd bit of self-deception as maintaining that the spirit has been beguiled into making an ill-timed appearance or that something has slipped up in the economy of the other world—not in this one !

Clear instances of the practice of a negative " eugenics " are reached when no longer content with killing a child because it is one more, or one of two more, it is sacrificed because of the peculiar manner of its debut into the world. Above all, the birth must be *comme il faut*. Thus, among the Masai all must be in the orthodox fashion, for children " who cry in their mother's womb, or if at birth . . . present their legs first, or are born with teeth . . . blind or badly deformed . . . left-handed, albinos ", etc., are marked for expeditious cutting-down at once.[67] A deformed child is a devil : its mother is beaten and its father despised by fellow tribesmen. Certain unpropitious dreams about the time of birth are often sufficient cause to mark the infant for destruction, no matter what the actual appearance may later turn out to be, for the spirits have given their warning.[68] We can thus discern a stress towards strict conformity at the very outset of the child's life : tests of customary appearance and behaviour at birth. These people are wary of harbouring dangerous abnormalities which cannot be understood and which often are hard to support.

Deformed children bring down evil consequences if allowed to live. The rain ceases to fall, famine or starvation sets in, and the people will be plagued endlessly. A monstrosity, or a child that is deformed or crippled is therefore strangled at birth.

Krapf cites an extreme case. " A woman in Muelle . . . had given birth to two children one of whom had six fingers but neither nose nor lip. The parents took the mis-shapen child to the chiefs . . . that it might be strangled and buried in the wood. . . . "[69] Among the Akikuya of East Africa, " an ill-omened child is either suffocated by the mother or is put into fallow land, and grass placed in its mouth and nostrils ".[70] (To have put it in cultivated land would have ruined the fertility of the soil.) Among the Hausa, the deformed are immediately thrown into the river, and in Borneo they are ripped in the throat. Among American Indians, no mis-shapen child was generally permitted to live.[71] So strong was this feeling against abnormalities among the Pima Indians of Arizona that " they tried in recent years to kill a grown man who had six toes ".[72]

A particularly unfortunate being is the child whose upper incisor teeth appear first, for it is then thrown into the bush or into a stagnant pool or to the hyenas ; were such children to live they would bring down misfortune upon all the tribe.[73] Among the Marioris of the Chatham Islands children who cry during birth are doomed. Skinner reports that on one occasion a Mariori child was born during the night and . . . on inquiring for it the following day it was reported that it was a *tamaiti-tangi* (crying child) and had been destroyed before sunrise. " He later saw the body of the infant, crushed beneath a huge piece of rock."[74]

From such an intimation through fear of irregularities, these peoples may attain to a rough and ready system of purposeful elimination of children deemed weak and hence unworthy of further care. This is markedly apparent in a fighting society where strength and powerful physique are admired, as is well illustrated by the ancient Spartan custom of exposing all weaklings on mountain-tops or throwing them down precipices. If found and adopted, such children could never become citizens of the state.[75] Even among the pre-literate natives of New Guinea, the stronger child " would get the larger share of nourishment, the weaker one would become proportionately puny, therefore it was better to bury it that the mother might rear one strong, healthy boy rather than two weakly lads who would never become fighting assets of their tribe ".[76] The Papuans killed the crippled as they were averse to doing anything which meant arduous care and anxiety.[77] There are also African and Australian parallels.[78] Among the Indians on the Amazon River, the child was exposed to a test for the right to survival, as all infants immediately after birth were submerged in a stream (probably for purification), but the deformed children were never pulled out again.[79]

The most insistent and direct impetus toward infanticide

among the peoples of a comparatively undeveloped society is the dread of pressure of additional children upon the meagre food-supply which their simple tools can win from the surr⌒undings. Incidentally, in the carrying out of this attempt at self-maintenance and the maintenance of a groping standard of life, choices may be exercised as to the sort of child which is to pay the penalty of an ill-timed arrival. The primitive point of view in this connection may appear preposterous and foolish, yet following out these delusions, these people have unknowingly come to exercise a measure of eugenic selection, often very salutary to the tribe as a whole. Motives and purposes are not always as significant as the end-results in society. The brutal unfeeling nature of these usages was often phrophylactic and the child that did escape the various pitfalls described in this chapter was able to fit into the strenuous stride of the simpler society. We must not forget that if ethnographers fail to report the use of these clumsy birth-controls among the most primitive tribes as the Veddas of Ceylon, the Fuegians of Patagonia and the Bushmen of South Africa, it is because nature itself is doing the blue-pencilling and maintaining an " optimum " number with regard to the food-supply in her own effective way.

The necessity for the employment of these crude measures rapidly disappeared with the augmented food-supply which was developed through the domestication of animals and plants. Abortion, infanticide and child-selection became " immoral ", because inexpedient and unnecessary, *pari passu* with this development. " Humane " feelings were allowed their sway and encouraged and children became a boon in life—both in the worldly scene and in the imaginary environment beyond and about this life. To this aspect of the desire for children we now turn in the following chapter.

It is instructive to note at this point, however, that again, in our own time, the agitation for universal recourse to birth-control has become widespread. This movement is motivated by a desire, mainly, to preserve extremely artificial and refined standards of life which have always been threatened by a surplus of children. At the same time, the devices to be employed are not the crude, violent strokes of the primitive man but applications of ordered experience, or science which the more highly cultured society of to-day has been able to amass in its unbroken course of development.

CHAPTER IV

THE DESIRE FOR CHILDREN

THE desire for children reaches an extreme development in
primitive society. The child is a boon and good fortune in
many ways. Material progress and ease in this life, security
and peace in the next life, are dependent upon having children.
Only in this way can we understand the poignancy which
characterizes the longing for offspring among those peoples
who can support infants and are not compelled to do away
with them as dead-weights in the struggle for a livelihood.
Primitive man will condescend to the most nefarious practices
to attain this priceless concession, which it is within the power
only of the spirit-world to grant him. The position of woman
answers in the main to her ability to bear children and thus
grant the coveted desire. Even as the possession of children
is considered by primitive man as the greatest fortune, so,
on the other hand, the barren woman is the most despicable
of humans, and the childless man the most ridiculous and
disappointed of individuals in the eyes of his folk, and inevitably in his own estimation.

The instances expressive of the desire for children are
legion. A few striking and characteristic cases will suffice.
Thus Smith and Dale, speaking of African negroes, declare :
" To have children and many of them is one of the great
ambitions of our natives. . . . He who fails in this respect
is regarded by others and he regards himself as something
less than a man. . . . To avoid this indignity, it is incumbent
on every man to try every possible means to have children.
. . . If no favourable result follows he has to reconcile himself

to disappointment and to the jokes, if not contempt of his fellowmen and wives."[1]   Of the West Africans Wilson says that " they would give any price for the ' child medicine,' and it was really heart-rending to hear the earnest entreaty and see the tearful eye which bespoke the intense desire for offspring."[2]

A surprising instance of the extreme development of this wish is revealed in a literal translation of a Sarawak cradle-song of Borneo.   According to Low, the women sing to their children : " Would that thirteen sons and seventeen daughters be born unto you ! "[3] In Polynesia, also, children are prized and redound to the glory of the women as a duty done. One of the commandments of Fijian ethics has it that " the wife who has born children has fulfilled her mission, and she pleases her husband best by ceasing for the remainder of her life to please other men ".[4] Among the lowly Igorot of the Philippines it is said that they love all their children and say when a boy is born, " It is good," and if a girl is born, it is equally " good "—it is the mere fact of a child, irrespective of whether it is a natural or legitimate child, which makes them happy.[5]

In the cattle-raising stage of culture-history the provision for the support of children becomes considerably enhanced and therewith the desire for offspring is accentuated. Woman's part in the arts of life sinks in importance, and with it her social influence, until in the full patriarchal group she loses her position as a contributor in the struggle for existence and becomes of worth primarily as an agent to satisfy the deep desire of the man for children. Women are assimilated to other objects of personal possession as a peculiar kind of income-yielding property and are usually purchased for a bride-price. In the measure in which she is prolific is her position as wife secure. If she fails in this paramount duty the man has purchased a deficient commodity—he can return her to her parents and demand the bride-price in return ! But if the woman has borne a quota of children, often merely one child, then her consort loses the right of demanding back the cattle or other goods which were expended for her services. The woman's primary destiny on this stage of cultural development is to bear children. There is nothing to prevent the man from taking more wives if he can afford to do so.

Among the Bagiririni in the Sudan, in Africa, a wife was expected to present her husband with at least five children. That accomplished, she was at liberty to return to her parents' hut if she desired, the children always remaining with the husband.[6] If the wife were to commit adultery (which was considered a species of theft), the man lost all right to reclaiming the bride-price among the Ama-Xosa if she had borne her rightful spouse children. Love is not to stand in the way, as the Ila peoples expressly state, for if the beloved one does not give birth to a child, she is not cashiered, but another house is built for a new wife who will be secured to bear the man children.[7] On the Upper Congo, the barren woman will take her sister to her husband that he may have a child by her. " This is called *boko loboja*, to give one in place of . . ."[8] The moral standards implied in these ways are outlandish and extremely lax in the light of our cultural attainments, yet they portray the reality and fervidness of the wish for offspring and the measures taken for its fulfilment. In this light, these folkways are " right " and become encrustrated into commandments with the sanctifying force of the spirits and the ancestors.

The practices undertaken to secure the benefit of children recall the primitive conception of the origin of the child in the unsettled sphere of the brooding ancestral wraiths. The birth of a child is a concession that must be secured through inveigling or beseeching the ancestral spirits who have apparently been piqued by the waywardness of men. Prayers are constantly arising on the African continent to the local spirits to bestow upon men the great boon; fetish-objects and doll figures are being prayed to to bring about the great blessing of children.[9]   In Borneo it is common to slaughter a pig for this same purpose, make part of it into a lotion with water, which if consumed would be sure to bring the desired result.[10]   Elsewhere, phallic figures are worshipped. Among the Zuñi Indians of the south-west the following method of insuring a future addition to the tribe was observed : " Previous to the birth of a child, if a daughter be desired, the husband and wife proceed together to the ' mother ' rock, and at her feet make offerings and prayers, imploring her to intercede with the great father, the Sun, to give them a daughter. . . . Should a son be desired, the couple repair to the shrine above, and here, at the breast and heart of the ' father ' rock, prayers and plume sticks are offered that a son may be given them."[11]

The passionate longing for children is strong enough to subdue the quakings of heart and personal anxiety usually experienced when face to face with what appears to be the unusual and inexplicable in life.   As we have seen,[12] the birth of twins was apt to cause sinking of the heart as a dire visitation of "spiritual" malignancy.   Noteworthy instances, however, prove the emphasis of desire for children, in that twins are cause, rather, for rejoicing.   Their appearance is the signal for great festivity and merriment.   This is truly the case when both are males, in the more developed groups, as this is evidence of great fortune and tremendous virility on the part of the male.[13]

Among the Baholoholo of the Congo watershed, such an event " inspires a most intense joy; in fact, this event is regarded as a very splendid favour of superior powers."[14] Thus, the superior supporting power of a higher economic development of a people rides again roughshod over ancient superstitions and fears. It germinates a higher degree of humanity and " ethical " conduct. Plural births no longer need give rise to death-dealing cruelty and savagery in which the literally " poor " primitive man must wallow. Man's moral development stands on a rising ability to care for this life as well as ward off the dread of otherworldly demands.

But there is still the marginal province wherein the sway of the unaccountable is apt to wreak depredations in the life of the primitive. The spirits jealously begrudge the mite of prosperity or joy which may fall to man's lot. The native is constantly apprehensive lest his good lot be snatched from him and he be pinioned underneath the power of the spirits again. Hence, defence measures must be assumed against the possibility of such onslaughts which will probably take the form of the " ills of life ", sickness, disease, famine, want or old age. Man must appear miserable to conceal his temporary fortune. For this reason he is adverse, for one thing, to revealing the number of his children. Hence, as Weeks reports : " . . . the native has a very strong superstition and prejudice against counting his children, for he believes that if he does so, or if he states the proper number, the evil spirits will hear it and some of his children will die ; hence when you ask him such a simple question as, ' How many children have you ? ' you stir up his superstitious fears, and he will answer : ' I don't know '."[15] That this fear is a part of the general fear lest his prosperity be disclosed is illustrated by the Akamba people, who consider it just as unlucky to count their cattle as to reveal to others the number of their children.[16] It is evident that prosperity hangs on a slender reed, and must not be boasted of and is to be enjoyed in utmost privacy, if at all.

We can now understand in a degree the venom with which the barren woman is despised, hounded and calumniated.

Sterility becomes a grievous fault and shortcoming, an un-pardonable sin and a loathsome affliction. The woman is avoided, because evidently none of the spirits have deigned to be reborn into the world through her particular agency. She has made a failure of her evident worth in life, becomes a negligible quantity, if not an eye-sore to her husband and folk. She is made the butt of jokes. Such women are "unsexed" and may even appear at the circumcision and puberty ceremonies, where ordinarily women are forbidden attendance under the direst threats. Such women are buried "without benefit of clergy", unceremoniously, out in the open bush in graves so shallow that the hyenas may find them.[17] A barren woman, to primitive man's way of think-ing, is "persona non grata" to the spirits, since they have not favoured her as a vehicle of reappearance. Hence she needs no particular preparation for the other world, in which she has no place.

Among the Baganda of East Africa, the barren woman is sent away because, through sympathetic magic, she prevents her husband's garden from growing.[18] Where there are no children the blame is always laid upon the woman's shoulder, never on that of the man.[19] The name of the barren woman among the Bakongo "is bandied from mouth to mouth in the village song, her life is rendered intolerable by the sneers of her neighbours, and suicide has not infrequently been the result of the treatment meted out to her. . . . She feels degraded in the eyes of all, and however much she may blame her husband, or may try to prove that she is bewitched, yet her shame is bitterly felt and resented". Livingstone adds of the Angola : " In their dances, when anyone may wish to deride another in the accompanying song, a line is intro-duced, ' So and so has no children, and never will have any '. She feels the insult so keenly, that it is not uncommon for her to rush away and commit suicide." In the case of an ordinary quarrel with another woman, this is the keenest insult which may be uttered, as in New Guinea.[20] Ridicule is a keen-bladed social force that cuts out the non-conformist as an object of contempt.

The basis of all durable sexual relations (which we call " marriage ") lies in the complementary economic aptitudes and inclinations of man and woman. Essentially an economic tie, it serves to reinforce a personal inclination between the sexes, or may even supersede or render immaterial such affection.

In the present connection this is exemplified by the fact that the creation of a relatively durable union with the woman is for the sake of the children she may bear and only inci-dentally because of an insistent affection for her. Hence, the marriage tie is revoked in the case of barrenness. A durable bond remains only because of the offspring, and where none appear it is dissolved completely. Thus, among such African tribes as the Masai, the Bassuto and most of the Bantus, sterility is the only unequivocal cause of divorce and the only one not subject to litigation.[21] Among the Wakamba, the woman herself procures another wife to beget for her man children. Among the Kafirs, another method is resorted to, for " if a woman fails to bear children her husband will sometimes exchange wives with another man for a certain period. This is said to be a very effective remedy for sterility ".[22] It is also common for the man to claim the sister of the wife, which is perhaps a survival of older forms of group-marriage.[23] Batchelor remarks that he has known of an Ainu native of Japan who divorced no less than three wives because they bore him no children.[24] Among the Yakuts in the icy wastes of Siberia, the same social phen-omenon is found. The woman has to put up with the presence of other women as an inevitable consequence of her failing in this regard.[25]

E

Nothing short of heroic measures can alleviate the miserable plight of barrenness. The spirits must be interceded with, in order that they may relent in their obdurate spleen. They must be coaxed or placated by the medicine-man who has acquired the technique of dealing directly with the denizens of the imaginary environment. The wives to whom maternity has been denied assemble, " fearful and panting around the dwelling of the astute magician . . . and one sees them, panting and haggard, running from village to village, to execute dances in favour of their patron god ".[26] Among the Bagesu, women so stricken would stand on an ant-hill and call upon the gods to help, promising substantial gifts in return for a child.

In Borneo, such women prepare small houses of rattan or bamboo, fill them with earth and send them down the river to serve as houses for Djata, a spirit-god. In return, the latter blesses them with children. Among the Yukaghir, in Siberia, the shaman descends to the world of the deceased and persuades the soul of a relative to enter the woman's body.[27] With allowances for differences in the details of environmental influences and scene, one can thus often envisage glimpses of the panorama of the history of culture. Men have fallen into parallel if not identical points of view on the larger problems of life, such as sterility, but have embodied the expressions in usages of varied dress. These superficial differences can never erase the foundation-stones of common interest, although such variations have meant the essence and bulwark of the cultural systems of the past by which men have sworn and fought and expired.

The practices may, therefore, be expected to vary, but all run true to an attempt to enlist supernatural aid through various magical performances. In New Zealand, among the Maori, " there was also a household god, an image in the form of an infant, which belonged solely to females ; this

was nursed by women who were barren ; as if it were a baby,
to remove the reproach ; it was made with great care, and
generally as large as a child, adorned with the family jewels,
and the same garments which they usually wear, and was
addressed in the same endearing terms.[28] To choose another
instance, the Nishinam Indians of California take a community
interest in the problem. When a Nishinam wife is childless
her sympathizing female friends sometimes make out of grass
a rude image of a baby, and tie it in a miniature baby-basket,
according to the Indian custom. This is a variety of imitative
magic. When the woman and her husband are not at home,
the tribes-folk carry this grass baby and lay it in their wigwam.
When she returns and finds it, she takes it up, holds it to her
breast, pretends to nurse it, and sings it lullaby-songs. All
this is done as a sort of conjuration, which they hope will
have the effect of causing the barren woman to become fertile.[29]

It may become necessary occasionally to wink at the fact
that a child is born of parents who have not expressed a wish
to undertake a durable sexual relationship in the manner
dictated by the folkways. The fervent desire for offspring
may eclipse the fact of " illegitimacy." Such a taint may be
overlooked. The evidence clearly indicates that many taboos
are relaxed in times of emergency, as in case of famine or other
exceptional circumstances. The old and outworn modes
stand again revealed. The Ugogo husband, in East Africa,
for example, claims all the offspring of his wife as his even if
it is quite evident that she has been faithless.[30] The same fact
has been noted in Savage Island in the Pacific, in Siberia among
the Yakuts, and in British New Guinea.[31] Among the natives
of the Marshall Islands, the marital arrangements may not
be exactly *comme il faut*, yet the children are welcomed
because of the high rate of infant mortality.[32]

An advantage accrues to the individual from life in society.
In the event that ordinary natural means fail in getting

children, one can fall back upon the aid of one's fellow-tribesmen or blood-relations. This is especially the case in the simpler societies in which the individuals, who feel personally a direct solidarity, are a large group. The idea of " meum et teum " is not stringently defined, so that in case of sterility, the relation of parent and child can be artificially created. This is a bond which may become as enduring as that wrought by nature itself. The antidote for sterility is thus found in the elaboration of a social fiction, adoption. The idea of adoption and the clarity of the distinction between the natural mode of securing children and the " sociological " one emerges with greater definiteness as the culture-system develops and marital relations become narrowed down out of the vague original conditions. The relation of father to child is not yet so narrowed down in the simpler societies. The " children " seem to be a stock comprising all the younger people belonging to the group, the bond holding them together, in the eyes of the folk, being the possession of a common blood. The family is thus a larger unit. Where the adopted child comes from a captured tribe or from any " out-group," then it is necessary to assimilate him into the " in-group " by a vivid ceremony, which is a typical societal device. And as the notion of parenthood becomes delimited, then it becomes necessary to recognize adoption as more and more unusual and requiring the seal of the ceremony.

In Africa, in general, adoption is a rare resort because it is easy to remedy the defect in other ways, by acquiring more wives, claiming the wife's sister or divorcing the barren wife, as we have already seen. In Borneo, however, adoption is common, the parents preferring the child of a relative, but perhaps taking even a captive or slave child whose parents are willing to relinquish it. A dumb show is the ceremony to impress upon others the serious intention of " adoption " : " . . . both man and wife observe for some weeks before the ceremony all the prohibitions usually observed during the latter months of pregnancy. . . . The child is pushed forward behind the woman's legs, and if it is a young child, it is put to the breast and encouraged to suck. . . . It is very difficult to obtain admission that a particular child has been adopted . . . and this seems to be due . . . to the completeness of the adoption, the parents coming to regard the child as so entirely their own that it is difficult to express the differ-ence . . .''[33] In this way, the primitive man is convinced that the order of nature has not been disrupted. His fears of treading new and dangerous ways is stilled by such naïve expedients.

The salient motive for adoption in Melanesia seems to arise out of an attempt to bring to an end the ridicule heaped upon the childless individual. It is a restoration of lapsed prestige. Among the Omaha Indians, on the other hand, '' when a war party took a captive, anyone who had lost a child or who was without children, would adopt the captive to fill the vacant place. After the ceremony the person became an Osage in all respects as one born into the tribe . . . .''[34] In the ancient and classical civilizations, adoption was resorted to mainly in order to acquire male heirs to carry on the ancestral worship and family tradition, and to manage the property left behind. These motives are the fruit of a more developed culture. The ceremony of adoption became correspondingly more complex and conventionalized, as in Rome. It took place before witnesses and in extreme solemnity.[35]

From these examples it is clear that children are man's most precious possession in the simpler society. The primitive man's heart is full of this desire and much of his life is engrossed in the attempt to consummate it by the means just passed in review. Where such deep-rooted desires exist, there must also lie unusual worth and value in the actual benefits derived from children. We may dismiss summarily much of the pathos—enlightened though it be—that is apt to encase this topic of the uses of children to-day. The primitive man does not customarily wrap himself up in the child for the child's sake and the child's destiny. The parents' urge is first of all an utilitarian and selfish one. It is only after culture has reached the stage where surplus means, or capital, is created, that the parent may be freed from the desire of realizing present personal material value and enhancement from the child. Only then can the parent afford to allow the child to devote himself unreservedly to the development of his own individuality apart from parental demands. Until then the child's value lies in the contribution he can make to the all-consuming battle for existence. The child is a practical asset in a simple society.

This attitude is well epitomized by the Kafir father who acted thus upon becoming a father : " The father then lifted the baby in the air above his head and kissed it on the thighs, calling out ' My Cattle,' for that was what it represented to his imagination."[36]

In the west of Africa, in Dahomey, it was early observed that the child was essentially capital for an entire family, such that his care would become one of the great pivots of social life. The child, if a son, would help to fish or hunt or paddle the canoe, while a daughter would be sold to a suitor for a considerable material return, usually in the form of cattle.[37]

If the group is poor and economically backward, the help of the children is invaluable, as in the Andaman Islands where the boys especially are wanted to aid in hunting, turtling, etc.[38] Yet, as we have seen, if the condition of the available food supply becomes threatening, some of the children are killed, thrusting upon the shoulders of those remaining an even more arduous life and a critical importance in the life of the folk. This attitude is evinced unexpectedly in the ditties sung while at work in the fields by the Wabemba men in the Congo region of Africa. That the feeling is expressed so frankly is ample proof of the usualness of the idea. One of these refrains runs thus :

"My mother brought me into the world—to cultivate
  She put a hoe into my hand—to cultivate . ."[39]

In case the food-supply is assured and the struggle for a bare existence does not require the help of all hands, then the child becomes of use as a lever by which to raise the level of life of the parents. Well-being is assured and an invidious position in folk-life contemplated in having children. This ambition unmistakably stirred the heart of the Marshall-Island woman who said : " Only wait until next spring, then I shall come with another child. Children are good, because my eldest is already earning money and brings it to me every month. As soon as all the children are grown, then I will become a rich woman."[40] In the Torres Straits Islands, parents find that two or three sons mean luxuries for themselves in the way of " calicoes, coats and trousers, camphor-wood boxes, tobacco and so forth."[41]

In Samoa, strangely enough, the returns from the children are more immediately forthcoming because at the feast celebrating the birth of children, the parents have " the satisfaction of having seen what they consider a great honour—heaps of property collected on the occasion of the birth."[42]

It is significant also that children as economic assets serve to enhance the dignity, respect, prestige, social dimensions and ego of the parents in the developing society where differentiation of classes begins to appear. Degree of elevation in folk-life so often is founded on possession of material means. Like the man who holds much cattle, the man with many children acquires renown and " social prowess." Vanity, in addition to the desire for means, becomes the motive for having children. In Africa, generally, " every head of a family desires to have as many people around him as possible, as his influence and importance are thereby increased. Grown-up sons build their huts close to, or in the near neighbourhood of that of their father."⁴³ Through amassing wealth in this way, in Natal, a father may even become a chief when the sons grow up and settle around him. . . . " Were he to remove to an unoccupied country, he would become the natural independent ruler of his people."⁴⁴ The father's name is glorified among all his people, as in New Zealand where the clan assembled to congratulate the parents and express their gratification at the occurrence of a birth " which meant much to a communistic folk."⁴⁵ In Washington, on the American northwest coast, children were valued as a sop to vanity, as plenitude of children was considered a particular badge of virility.⁴⁶

Not only does the child perform yeoman service in keeping body and soul of parent together, but he is also of inestimable worth in attending to the separation of these elements at death, and in the care of the ghost-spirit of his parents in the imaginary environment. The burial of the body and the after-care of the spirit are tremendously significant duties, so much so that among the Yoruba, " in consequence of this, the epithet *isokun*, ' a mourner,' is often applied to the female child ; a male, on the other hand, being sometimes called *iwale*, ' a digger,' i.e. of a grave. A father might thus say that he had begotten two mourners and a digger, meaning two daughters and a son."⁴⁷ This is corroborated in the case of the Bakongo. It is said that the strong desire they have for children springs from the same motive—sons to bury them properly and daughters to cry for them. A typically human note is added : " They prefer daughters to sons, for there is not only the portion of their marriage money, but they cry longer and better than boys and men."⁴⁸

Man has always tended to project the features of this life into the next, or imaginary world. It has been peopled with beings whose appetites and actions are mere reflections of his own, distorted perhaps in scale by the vagueness of the medium in which they are thought to carry on. The same passions actuate the ghosts but are projected on a vaster scale. Thus, it was thought, that if the children were not there to attend properly to the funeral rites, the poor ghost would be despised by its ghostly-clan-fellows and the other ghosts would completely ignore it—as in the more " earthly " existence.[49] Once duly entered into the spirit-world, the beneficence of offspring was to be further felt, " due to the fact that children are expected to sacrifice to the spirits of their dead parents, and the ghost of one who has left no posterity is therefore in a piteous plight."[50] The advantages of children extend thus beyond the grave as ministrants to their parents. As has been remarked of the Siberian Yukaghir, " The old parents will therefore enjoy in the other world, after their children's death, the same respectful position, as heads of their families, while during their children's lives they will receive offerings from them."[51] There is thus no respite for the child himself under this constant weight of the services to be performed—none until he has attained to the position of the parent himself.

The worth and use of children is further reflected in the casual ambitions of the child himself, who has unknowingly imbibed ideas from the social environment. The Kafir children " dream of the day when they will have many cattle of their own and a number of wives to work for them and bear them many children ; for then they will have many cattle of their own and be men of great importance." The little girl, as among the Akamba, shudders at the thought of the uncertainty of having children, as " this implies something infinitely terrible. . . ."[52] How these ideas enter the child's head may be gleaned from the lullabies sung to the child, such as the following Hottentot " number " :

> " Thou son of a bright-eyed mother ;
> Thou far-seeing,
> Who will soon track the wild ;
> Thou of the strong arm and bone
> Stout-limbed one,
> Surely thou wilt shoot,
> Marauder the Herero ;
> And bring thy mother their fat cattle to eat."[53]

The poetic climax of the last line portrays graphically the basis of the desire for children and the song weaves an ideal of life from which children later derive their springs of action in society.

Light is shed upon the use of children by an examination of primitive usage and belief as to the relative merits of the boy-child and the girl-child. It generally amounts to a weighing of comparative worth in the light of the standards we have just passed in review. In the simplest groups where the division of labour between the sexes is not prominent, it is the child as an additional head, or rather, pair of arms, be it male or female, that is welcomed. Both can help in the work. Such a group is that of the backward Igorot in the Philippine Islands. Of the sexes it has been said that one " is practically as capable as the other at earning a living, and both are needed in the group."[54]

As society develops, a marked division of function appears for the sexes and preferences are established. The distinction of sex in the desire placed upon children is characteristic in greater degree of those stages of societal evolution blocked out by the growing power of the father. Boy and girl assume a distinct value. Children also become the merchandisable and disposable property of the father.[55]

The case for the male-child is clearly stated by the natives of the Slave Coast of West Africa : " A woman, who bears

. . only female children does not enjoy in the eyes of her husband and public opinion generally the same respect as one who has more boys than girls, or at least has boys also. The boy can defend home, and hearth, at the approach of the enemy; he accompanies his father to war. Only the boy can help his father with the laborious field work, and through his aid, the father becomes rich. Sons are a protection for the elders against scandalous tongues of neighbours for he who is surrounded by a large progeny, remains victor. The sons' huts are near that of the father. When the latter has passed off, it is his sons, who upon the ruins of the father's house settle down and continue his name."[56]

Reasons for preferring boys exist also in Tahiti. There the fisheries, temple service, and war were purposes for which it was thought desirable to raise children. As women could not qualify in these duties, female children were frequently not suffered to live.[57] Among the Pima Indians of Arizona, it is succinctly stated: "Male children are preferred because 'they would grow up to fight Apaches.'"[58]

The extreme development of this preference for the male-child was reached in the classical civilizations and among the Hebrews, the Chinese, and other societies of more elaborated cultures founded on male predominance. Among some of the Chinese, for example, women are still beaten for the indiscretion of not bearing a son. The dead-hand of a long-stagnant culture requires sons for proper homage to the ancestral spirits.[59]

Girls become valuable with the gradual onset of the patri-archal structure of society, as they begin to command a bride-price when sold in marriage. Purchase is the characteristic mode of cementing durable sex-relations on this stage. However, old notions of social relationship prove obdurate and remain long after the organization for self-maintenance has become transformed. The inevitable reflection of the changed economic folkways reacts but slowly upon the rest of the social fabric. There is no immediate and perfect adjustment between the various institutions of society at any time unless that group has been long isolated.

Among the Akikuyu of East Africa, a girl-child is preferred because she will fetch thirty goats for her father at marriage—a leading consideration in his eyes. Among the Abipones, in Argentina, in another hemisphere, " mothers spare their female offspring more frequently than the males, because the sons, when grown up, are obliged to purchase a wife, whereas daughters, at an age to be married, may be sold to the bridegroom at any price."[60] The same is reported of the Araucanians of Chile. The poor are especially desirous of having female children, while the boy is considered a debit because he carries off property at his marriage.[61]

On the other hand, traces of the matrilineal system are to be found in the event that the son-in-law comes to inhabit his wife's home. In such an instance, a daughter is preferred also, as among the land Dyaks of Borneo, because not only will she assist in getting food and water for her parents but " moreover, at marriage a son may have to follow his wife whereas a daughter obtains for her parents the benefit of her husband's labour and assistance."[62] The custom is, at times, variable with particular circumstances—a condition typical of transitional stages in societal evolution, so that the man may choose to join his father-in-law or take off his bride to his own home, according to the relative prosperity of the respective family. Where the struggle for existence is difficult, it may therefore prove more advantageous to secure the son-in-law's help rather than the actual bride-price to be secured for the daughter, as among the Point Barrow Eskimo.[63] On the whole, a daughter is prized as a means of realizing a gain to her parents at the marriage-age.

To our way of thinking, the limit of selfishness is instanced in the island of Ponapé, in the Pacific. The parents among these people pocket the proceeds of the daughter's prostitution.[64] While in the Gazelle Peninsula, though the girl is carefully guarded, protected and shielded from harm, it is mainly because of her great value as a worker.[65]

The calloused, selfish regard for children is well expressed in the picturesque phraseology of the Rhodesian blacks, according to well-informed observers, like Smith and Dale. The natives observe that " the *mwana*, or child as he is in regard to his elders, is likened to a bag which can be taken by you to carry things, out of which you can help yourself, and it can say nothing ; also to a *lumano*, a pair of pincers, for the elder uses them to convey things to himself ; also to a soft skin which can be turned this way and that. . . ."[66]

The tenderness and touching intimacy that sorrounds the parent-child relation in historic times is based upon this rude and unadorned primitive desire for children. They are a needful aid in a struggle, not usually for life itself, but that measure of worth and social prominence which is based on the possession of a superior abundance of material goods. Thus the evolution of social prestige is based upon an abundant offspring as a major type of material wealth. Comfort in this life and security in the next are also assured by progeny. These are the deepest roots, probably, of the insistent desire for children in historical times, as well as in the simpler groups here described.

CHAPTER V

THE NAME

ONE of the first definite steps in the socialization of the child is accomplished by means of the name. The child is singled out by this descriptive tag which is imposed upon him at a naming ceremony. For folk-thought this occasion is of extreme gravity in the individual's life. Each group attaches the identification mark in its own way, in a manner determined usually by the mores, which in turn are a sign of the type of social organization the group has attained. The name, and the manner of its bestowal, are initial reactions of the folk to the new addition to their number. The ceremony itself is an expression of the child's " social birth," because thereby lasting initial ties are forged between the individual and his social heritage.

So essential is the name and with so much " place " does it endow the child, that an unnamed child is hardly to be distinguished from the animals of the neighbourhood or even the lifeless trees and stones. Such a miserable child is never counted in the enumeration of a family. For instance, among the Kayan of Borneo, if a child should die before the naming ceremony, the mother " would mourn for it no more deeply than had it been stillborn. This is true even if the child lives to be nearly a year old."[1] Thus, the child lives under an ignominious neglect until he acquires the needed semblance of membership in the folk-life. " It must not be bathed in the river, but in the private apartment of the parents ; it must not be carried down the ladder from the house to the

ground ; even to mention its future name is so ill-omened as
to be prohibitory ; it is known only by the indefinite appella-
tion, *Angat,* if a boy, and *Endun,* if a girl—*Angat* meaning
literally a ' little worm ' ; what *Endun* means, if it have a
separate meaning, I do not know."[2] Thus in Borneo the
lack of a name diminishes the individual's prestige.

Examination of native tongues reveals further illustrations
of the rôle played by the name. These languages have preserved a rich realism, and are not yet overcoated with the
conventionalism and emasculated meanings of the more
developed languages. Significance, and the original import,
peer out usually more directly. Thus, in the Kafir, the verb
" to name " is an extension in meaning of the word *Uku-ta,*
meaning " to pour into anything with a small opening."[3]
Evidently it is thought that by the act of naming, something
is ' poured into " the child which serves to amalgamate him
with the folk and transform him decisively. The name thereafter adheres so closely to the individual that it quickly
becomes an inseparable part of the personality. It has been
an almost universal belief, held even by the widely dispersed
Aryan races, that the name is that intimate part of the man
which is termed " the soul, the breath of life."[4] This is
characteristic of the usual confusion between (what appears
to us) appearance and reality, symbol and actuality which
pervades primitive life and thinking.

The social personality is thus portrayed in the name—
that is, the individual as regarded and distinguished by his
people. The name is at once representative of the uniqueness
of the individual—mainly, his physical uniqueness—and the
type of society in which he dwells. The element recording
the physical individuality becomes overshadowed in importance by the social pressure toward using the name as a record
of social relationships—tradition, family connection, and the
like. As this development takes place, we can trace a cor-

responding evolution of other social forms from the simple matrixes into the deepening, hardening and narrowing categories of tribe, clan and family relationships. The element of conventionalization and standardization thus eclipses the picturesque naming of the simpler societies.

In these less developed groups the social personality is vague and elementary, so that the name remains a temporary designation, subject to chance happenings and changing with them. There are numerous instances in which the purely " human " element dims the traditional social stress and apparently does violence to the ordered evolutionary scheme of development of society as it affects the name of the child. Thus, among the Murray Islanders (in defiance of the folkways of the name), parents often cannot agree on a name for a child, and as each persists in his choice, the child will be called by several names.[5] We must reckon with another phenomenon in this connection, namely, old customs which hang on doggedly in a changed social system. These are important clues to the culture-history of the folk. For example, the Mohave Indians are accustomed to give an unusual ancient name to a child born out of wedlock.[6] Thus from the name given to the child, the sex relation would be recognised as contra-mores, yet as one that had been a more common practice in the past.

The occasion of naming the child becomes a festive ceremony, for a great deal of show is needed to impress the primitive man. In order that an event may be remembered, it is necessary to pound the thing in : so to arrest the senses that the event is indelibly grooved in the mind. Hence, a feast or carousel of some kind is employed to point out that something of social consequence has transpired, in this case the investiture of an individual with a name. The gods or spirits jealous of all earthly doings must also be informed of this " clothing " of the child. Among the Sioux Indians, to take an instance, " the child is held up, turned to all sides of the heavens, in the direction of the course of the sun, and its name is proclaimed."[7]

The person who assumes the office of naming the child becomes closely connected with the child. Among the Thonga of South Africa, " it may be that somebody asks the favour of giving his name to the new-born child ; a friend of the family may do so, but it is often also a traveller who happens to be in the village and to whom the privilege is accorded. He will ' name himself in the child ' . . . This fact will establish a special relation between the person and the child. . . . Once a year he will come and give ' his name ' (viz., the child) some presents."[8] Such a person becomes bound equally with the father in caring for the child.[9] In this manner one may, so to speak, give birth " socially " and create a fictitious parentage. This, however, appears very real to the primitive man because of the intensity of the contact set up in the act of bestowing the name upon a child.

Without a written language memory is short-lived, it is often believed, therefore, that the birth of a child merely marks the reappearance in this life of an ancestor recently dead. These ancestors are believed to be taking another " turn" in the scene of their former activities. The child is the recent dead in a new make-up and with a new lease of life. Only thus can we interpret the custom of the Labrador Eskimo of treating the child with all the deference due an adult, and in asking his will or opinion with " mature respect." They imagine that in the newly-born they have the reappearance of the last person who died in the village, and consequently give him the latter's name.[10] Among the Rhodesian blacks, also, it is believed that the child is an ancestor returned to earth, and so must bear the name he had during his previous sojourn. A significant note is appended by our informant that this name " is not to be lightly used,"[11] but must be treated as befits the worth and dignity of a soul probably old and experienced in the ways of life.

The ingenuity and mental capacity revealed in accounting for one's actions in society often surpass the aptness revealed in these actions themselves. That is, men usually react unintelligently, though forcefully, to the life-problems presented by the environment in order to maintain and propagate life. Yet in the attempt to explain and justify these ways of life, a more amazing subtlety and inventiveness is often revealed. Thus, it is here maintained that the primitive man naturally fell into a crude belief in the reappearance of the " dead " in the form of children. Yet, as social organization progresses, this custom comes to be variously interpreted by the natives themselves until the original, frank basis of the belief is slowly lost altogether. So, in South Africa, among the Ba-thonga, it is said that " the parents like to recall the name of one of the ancestors of old times," for the proferred reason that " it is a nice thing to remember them ".[12]

With due allowance for the dramatic emphasis of the author, the Iroquois version was this : " He who takes the new name, takes up also the duties appertaining to it, and thus he becomes a captain if the deceased was one. This done, they check their tears and cease to weep for the dead, having placed him among the living in this manner."[13]

Gradually it becomes more difficult to discover the identity of the returned individual, and the attempt is made simply to associate them with some one of the deceased, in order that they may carry on the latter's life.

Among the Greenland Eskimo, the child when grown up, was bound to brave the influences which had caused its namesake's death. " If, for instance, the deceased had perished at sea, his successor had only so much greater an inducement for striving to grow a skilful kayaker."[14] Among the Stseelis of British Columbia, the names were again not mere tags but

" were always connected with the family legends and had reference to some true or fancied incident in the life of the ancestors of the family possessing them." Dim antiquity in this case, has erased their individual distinctness so that it is now impossible to get their significance.[15]

The custom of endowing the child with a name formerly employed by another is also explained as an effort to impart to the infant qualities and characteristics possessed by the deceased, which are supposed to cluster about the name. Obviously, the belief in a true reappearance of the absented (or " dead ") individual is not held here. Thus, among the Bakitara of Central Africa, it was well to choose one's ghostly antecedents wisely, for, we are told, " the name was usually that of some ancestor who was noted for his long life and good character, who had had a large family and had been a prosperous man."[16] Practical considerations enter into the naming, as in Brazil where Hans Stade observed in a particular instance that the name of one of four forefathers was given, as the " children who bore those names throve well, and became cunning at catching slaves."[17]

With increasing numbers, longer history, and increased complexity of social organization, the identity of the returned ancestor is not so readily determined. Antiquity erases individual distinction and memory fails so that the secret of the identity of the child can be known only through magical practices, often with the aid of the medicine man. Various methods are employed for this purpose. One method is to float the navel-string in a pot of water and divine by its resting position the identity of the newcomer. This is done in various parts of Africa.[18] Among the Nandi, the ghostly occupant makes himself known, with encouraging aid from the living. The ceremony is performed thus : the paternal grandmother, or near relation of the father, mentions the names of various ancestors or relatives who have died, and the child's assent to a certain name is signified by its sneezing. " In order to make sure that the child will sneeze a little snuff is blown up the nostrils, just before the ceremony."[19]   Among the Maori of New Zealand, who advanced to the stage of possessing a large body of tradition and recorded geneological lists, the custom existed of reciting a long list of ancestral names.   As the child sneezed, the name then being uttered was the one selected.[20]   (Sneezing has by many peoples been believed to be a mode by which spirits make their presence known.)

Among the Malay peoples other variations exist.   On the island of Ambon, the child is put to the mother's breast while the father recites a number of ancestral names ; if the child begins to suck, it has evidently recognized its name and the one then uttered is chosen.   When the Batak child smiles at the mention of a name, that one is apparently preferred, and henceforward used for the babe.   The Dajak goes farther. He offers the child a bundle of sticks on each of which has been inscribed an available name.   The name on the stick grasped by the child becomes attached to him for life.   The spirits of the tribe, like the tribesmen themselves in this instance have become literate.[21]   Among the preliterate Chukchee of Siberia, the custom is somewhat more naïve.   " The mother, while holding the suspended object (divinitary stone or some part of the mother's or child's dress) in her hands, enumerates, one by one, the names of all deceased relatives, saying with each name, ' This and this has come ? '   When the object loses its balance and begins to swing, the name is selected."[22]   In some such way is the spiritual tenant of the infant given an opportunity to announce its presence to the living.

Mistakes may be made, however.   In case the child ails, or does not prosper, something must have gone wrong ; either it is a case of mistaken identity or else the spirit is ill at ease in his new body.   Under such circumstances it is imperative that the name be changed, as among the Bontoc Igorot in the Philippines and other peoples, who invoke more " fitting " ghostly auspices in this way.[23] The manner in which the chosen spirit inhabits its new abode is rarely exactly known. Notions of this sort—whether they may be termed tenets of theology or facts of science, in the minds of the folk, is hard to say—give witness to changing conditions of life. The most primitive belief, as we have seen, is in a corporeal reappearance of the dead. This idea slowly changes into the vague adherence of the ghostly personality about the child, as in the latter instances cited. The vagueness of identity, and manner of inhabiting the child compel the use of magical methods for discovering the spirit that is aggregated to the name.

Among some of the African tribes the ghost or spirit chosen is a protective one, hovering about but no longer dwelling within the child, although exercising a decisive influence over it. In illustration, we are told that the Basabei believe that the ghost-in-the-name will resist any attempt on the part of another ghost to influence the child, " telling the other to wait for another child to be born and take charge of it."[24] This enlightening touch is an indication of the recurrent tendency among most peoples to project into the spiritual world the characteristics of this one.[25]

Not only is the child in many ways a reappearance of, or tie with, persons and spirits of the ancestral past but he has also a definite rapport with the environing conditions surrounding his advent into the world. The place and time of birth, current circumstances and occurrences, things seen and heard at the time, are all memorialized in the child's name as bearing an integral relationship to the event and the child itself. The aspects of the times hold the mysterious act of childbirth in their grasp and are registered in the name as they are thought to be causative agents or influences in the birth of the child. The name may thus become a unique form of chronicle and, in a manner, the child's credentials to his society—as intimate a distinguishing part of him as the colour of his eyes or hair.

African instances are given by Miss Werner : " The father may have been making a canoe . . . and finished it on the day of the child's birth, so he will name it *Ngawala*, ' canoe,' accordingly. I knew a small boy called *Chipululu*, ' the wilderness,' because, as his mother explained, ' he was born at the time of the hunger, when the people had to go into the bush to gather food.   Most names have an obvious meaning— ' Leaves,' ' Affliction,' ' Wind on the Water,' ' It Goes,' ' We Shall See When We Die,' ' I Have Been a Fool,' ' Ends of Grass,' ' The Day of Beer,' are a few specimens."[26]   The name may embody, thus, the caprice of the hour or what appears to us utterly fortuitous or extraneous circumstances. To the native, however, they distinguish the child and are deposited in the name.

In Australia, " one man in the Melbourne district was named *Ber-uke* (kangaroo rat) in consequence of a kangaroo-rat running through the *miam* at birth. . . . *Weing-pain* (fire and water) was so denominated in consequence of the *miam* catching fire, and the fire being put out by water, at the time of his birth." In New Guinea the same effect is produced indirectly as children are called *Magaui* (wallaby) and *Borona* (pig) if there has been a quarrel in the family just before the birth.   A Hawaiian child was given the sobriquet *Renan Nech*, " Laughing Fish," which owed its origin to a nightmare experienced by the father.   In the East Indies often " Thunder " or " Lightning " is the name given to children born during a storm—a novel system of keeping weather records. In Northern Mexico, however, the natives were none too meticulous in choosing the name, as the mother " having walked around the house once, opens her eyes, and the name of the first object she sees is chosen as the name of the child."

Among the Caribs, in the West Indies, it was usual to name the child after something which occurred to the father or mother during the pregnancy.[27]

The child is thus stamped with a mark of uniqueness through the instrumentality of the name derived from the peculiar circumstances of its birth. In the folk-life here under discussion, naming customs have not yet become rigid and conventionalized so that the underlying motives behind the name are discoverable. There is thus a tendency to distinguish the child by including in its name striking or unusual physical characteristics—a custom which runs athwart the general course of social development, for it appears in all stages, even in the most evolved. In such instances it is of less consequence than the more formal method, and remains as the "nickname." Without a load of tradition and other complex social developments the name of the child simply photographs personal traits. Here again it is well to note how smoothly external events and phenomena of nature are amalgamated with the internal personal traits of the individual, as natural phenomena have not yet been classified and objectified.

Thus among South African natives, the name records " some personal characteristic or peculiarity of gait or figure."[28] In this connection amazing results are achieved, as among the Aranda in Australia. A boy came to be called *Tankiya* (" Big Mouth ") and a girl who in her infancy had her head infested with ulcers was denominated with " the euphonious but hardly desirable name, *Katabukaia*, that is, ' Stinking Head.' "[29] Among the Pima Indians, " a man who worked several weeks for the missionary was so well fed that he began to lay on flesh. Ever afterward he was known as ' Preacher's Fat '. One is known as *Ovaa-tuka*, ' Spread Leg ', from his peculiar gait."[30]

Frequently the personal appellation is chosen with a view to transferring through the process of contagion, the desired

or admired qualities of bird, beast or even plant. The name
also furnishes a convenient form of emotional or aesthetic
expression for the parent. Tessmann classifies the names given
to Pangwe children in West Africa, as (1) those indicative of
good qualities which are desired for the child; (2) those
bringing good fortune; (3) those which make known that the
child shall become the terror of his enemies, and (4) those
which connote evil qualities, but thereby influencing the
bearer to strive for better things.[31] All of the emotional
reactions of parenthood can be thus poured into the name.
The Maori feminine names express the poetical genius of the
people, as Plume of the Precious Bird, White Heron, The
Young Lady in Love, The Diamond, etc.[32] In New Guinea,
children carry names of abstract qualities as Hunger, Thirst,
or are named after plants as Yams, Taro, Bananas, or after
animals, as Kangaroo, Pig, Dog, etc.[33] Among the North-
west Amazons, to choose another instance, boys are called by
the names of animals or birds; girls by the names of plants
and flowers, and as our informant notes, these are more comic
and expressive than the Christian names later given them.[34]
Certainly in the Gran Chaco of Argentina and among the
Araucanians this is so, because the girl is often called symbolically *mulla rayun*, " flower of gold "; a boy *nahuel-tripai*,
" the tiger jumped out ", or *cahrinancu*, " young red eagle ",
etc.[35]

Another aspect of the graphic, descriptive name is illustrated
by the names with offensive and disgusting meaning which
are bestowed upon children in order to ward off the unwelcome
attentions of the spirits who bring ill-luck. It is felt by these
people that the spirits are apt to begrudge man the bit of
happiness that may befall him. In Uganda, therefore, it is
considered very unlucky to give a good or well-sounding name
at birth, hence contemptuous and disgusting appellations are
chosen.[36] In Borneo, similarly, parents who have lost several

small children will give to the next child born, when the time comes for naming it, some such name as *Tai* (dung) or *Tai Manok* (bird's dung), or *Jaat* (bad), " in order that it may have the better chance of escaping the unwelcome attentions of the *Toh*."[37] In Hawaii, such names as *Pilau* (stench), *Pupuka* (ugly or worthless), *Kukae* (excrement), etc., are employed.[38]

We pass now to a consideration of the naming folkways as an evidence of the general trend of societal evolution within the domain of the family organization. There is abundant evidence of the typical parent-child relation of the folk through the instrument of the name. Only the broader lines of development can be traced here. The story of society is yet to be pieced in and the threads of culture-development to be extricated and followed through. Still we can discern in the study of the name, in spite of hiatuses of time and disruptions of space and contacts among peoples, a gradual encroachment of the father family, or patrilineal system, over a generally antecedent system of maternal filiation, or the mother family. It is an error to insist that a group can always be pinned down to a particular stage in the evolution of social organization. Yet in a wide comparative study of groups spread over time and locality, we are nevertheless able to glean a comprehensible trend of development which seems to be a common motif in the development of folk and cultural life. Some groups follow perplexing and contradictory ways. Some never attain to the posited stages ; others have overdeveloped certain aspects, and still others have backslid. Yet the evidence accumulated from many seems to point to a gradual encroachment of the paternal system over a long regnant, but somewhat vague, maternal system.[39]

It is exceedingly difficult to find tribes naming children solely after the mother, because the very notion of setting down parental relationships in the name of children only came when the loosely bound matrilineal groups gave place to a more ordered society. Under the matrilineal system children are distinguished only by some designation of physical peculiarity, or what is closer to our notion of the " nickname ". Perhaps the ghostly forbears were ascertained in the manner already described. The child in such a society—which, to a great extent, is a hypothetical group, for few altogether consistent and perfect " matriarchies " have been found—was rather a broad generic term marking out a generation-group, than a connective link with a definite family group.[40] Much of the delimiting and narrowing tendencies in the development of the family have been tied up with the accumulating power of the father. In the mother family the physical and genetic relationships of paternity were but dimly understood and remained in this state until male dominance came in with the cattle-raising stage of culture-history. For these reasons, few instances are discoverable of names related purely through the mother. More often we can catch the lingering survivalistic touches of the matrilineal system along with the emergence of the more strident, definitive male form—often the two in juxtaposition, as they affect the naming of the child.

Among the Masai it is the elder brother of the *mother* that gives the first name to the child. This is considered the chief name. Later the father adds another name.[41] Among the Pangwe in West Africa the name given by the mother is always the most in favour and used in *informal* discourse. This is the " great " name because it is used exclusively in the person's youth. The name given by the father, however, is publicly announced and remains the name to be used exclusively after the puberty rites, which give the child, for the first time, full social recognition and social adulthood.[42] This mode is somewhat emphasized by the well-marked, decisive separation of the sexes among some tribes so that the mother continues to name the female children and the father or paternal relatives the male children.[43] An interesting parallel case is that of the natives of the island of Yap. Here the father has his say as he chooses for his children the names of *his* grand-parents but restricted to his mother's side.[44] The maternal influence thus seems to be fading out.

Somewhat the same situation obtains among the Wabemba on the Congo where the male influence is much stronger and more highly developed. Here, according to sex, the first child receives the name of its *paternal* grandfather or grandmother ; the second, the name of its *paternal* uncle or aunt. The third and fourth receive the corresponding names on the *maternal* side.[45]

The Tlinkits of Alaska provide an informative case. Soon after birth the child is given the name of an ancestor on the mother's side but without any accompanying form, solemnity or festivity. Later, a name derived from its paternal ancestry is conferred in the midst of a great feast and attendant solemnities. " Poor Tlinkits, who have no means of giving a feast, sometimes retain the mother's name through life."[46] This shows clearly the appearance of the paternal system of relationship as a later societal product, accompanied here by a typical societal function of the feast which necessitates the accumulation of economic means, or capital. Commonly, as we shall see, the assumption of the paternal name is deferred until after the manhood rites.[47]

There is a widespread custom by means of which the child does not receive the name of the father, but the converse occurs. It is customary that the parents drop their names and in place thereof take the name of their child, preceded by the words " father of " and " mother of ". Speaking to or about such parents one may use only this name. So names of the parents do not live on, but are lost in those of their children, particularly in that of the first-born. As an example, in Borneo, among the tribes that follow this practice of " teknonymy ", after the naming of the first child, " the parents are always addressed as father and mother of the child ; e.g. if the child's name is *Obong*, the father becomes known as *Tama Obong*, the mother as *Inai Obong* and their original names are forgotten."[48]   This folkway with slight variations has been found among peoples in Africa, Australia, Melanesia, the Malay peninsula, Siberia and in various parts of America.[49]   The custom appears unique and outlandish if we regard it from the vantage point of a society with a highly developed culture.   Still its almost universal occurrence marks it out as an important milestone in the development of culture-forms, and something more than an oddity.

Wilken has interpreted teknonymy as a significant episode in the transition from the matrilineal to the patrilineal system, inasmuch as the father is making a gesture or demonstration to the family and all concerned that the child is *his*— an action which was then necessary in the face of the long regnant system of reckoning descent in the maternal line.   " The man seeks, above all, to devise a means of bringing to light his connection with the child ; he wishes to tell everyone that he is the father of the newly-born babe ; he wishes to proclaim his fatherhood.   And how may that be effected more completely and unequivocally than by dropping his own name and calling himself ' father of the child ' ? "[50]   According to Tylor, this custom must be associated, rather, with the mother family.   His statistical evidence establishes a correlation between teknonymy and two other customs characteristic of maternal filiation.   In this light, the practice is merely a means by which the mother's relatives recognize this particular man as father of the child.[51]   That this custom appears so often among patriarchal peoples where pure male descent obtains, is explained by Steinmetz as a survival form maintained in vigour by the extreme desire and love for children under the later system.   " We must then regard this as a long-preserved vestige of the matriarchy, in the most primitive as well as more regulated forms of which, the man had no other function than that of fertilization of the woman ; his own social duty was completed therein ; he was not then the provider for the family nor the trainer of its children ; the duty marked out for him was only in wakening new life."[52]

This opinion involves an over-emphasis of the regulative powers of the mother-family. To our minds, the most primitive family system is probably a large aggregation of individuals centering loosely about a real or mythical common blood-ancestor. Sex relations were not durable and the allegiance of the man to one woman was extremely short-lived. If, as is to be presumed, the men under such conditions had communal rights to the women, there was certainly no motive for attempting to relate the child to a particular man. Nor is there a need socially to relate the child to a particular woman as its mother, for this relationship is a profoundly unmistakeable biological fact. The attempt to place the father more definitely, illustrated by the custom of teknonymy, must be an evidence of the encroachments of the more highly developed economy and cultural system of the patriarchy. As the maternal system gave way gradually to more definitely ordered social regulations that followed in its wake, there arose a desire and need to bind the child more definitely to his father. The change is imperceptibly accumulative and gradual. Tylor and Wilken differ only as to the point where teknonymy fits into this movement in the history of culture.[53] Tylor attributes the custom to the lingering maternal system because of his preoccupation with survivals as ties to a pre-existing background. Wilken interprets the custom as evidence of the incoming patrilineal system as he is more concerned with metamorphoses of social institutions under the male sway. Wherever we place this bizarre method of naming we inevitably reach the conclusion that it is another evidence of the begin-

nings of the paternal system which unpremeditatedly culminated in the full-blown patriarchy of the nomadic tribes.
As far as the child is concerned, his position is also profoundly
changed during this development as our further study will
show.

It is the significance of the name that alone can explain
why so many widely dispersed groups have struck upon the
same means of expressing this transition into male filiation
and cultural dominance.   The name mirrors the personality,
physical and social, with increasing stress on the latter element.
According as the person changes—in this instance as his social
status changes—the name is also changed.   The man who has
a child born to him becomes in the eyes of his folk a totally
changed being and signifies it in the change in his name, in
the fashion of teknonymy.   If in addition, we recall the great
economic and " spiritual " value of the child in these simpler
societies, we may understand what a vastly different personage
a man with a child can be from the childless man.   The mother
also adopts the child's name, perhaps in imitation of the father.
Here is evidenced what we might call the backwash of the
custom.[54]

In this manner in the naming of the child, one of the most
comprehensive and thoroughgoing transformations in the
history of culture has been recorded.   In many other ways
the child's name reflects the history of societal changes.
During infancy the child may carry the original name
given it or determined by relationship on the maternal side.
With physical or social maturity the influence of the father
may be evidenced by the change in name or in the addition
of another name.   For instance, among the Nandi, after
circumcision, which is a mark of maturity, the name is changed
for the last time, and both men and women are known by what
is equivalent to our surname, *Ar-ap* and *Che-po* (meaning
son of and *daughter of* respectively).   This is prefixed to the

father's second name. In the case of younger sons, however, *Ar-ap* is frequently prefixed to an uncle's name.[55] These probably present a bridge from the older maternal system which is fast becoming archaic among the Nandi. The " name of manhood "[56] is conferred when the child definitely reaches maturity and ordinarily is a clear expression of the paternal system. The name at this important stage in the child's life is more of a family name than a nickname, or a sign of imputed ancestry.

The Maori chief " generally receives three names during his life : the first, immediately after birth, is given by this mother and may be called his child's name, such as *Tangi Kai*, from the child crying for food ; *Poaka*, pig, from its greediness ; *Moe one*, a lively little grub . . . etc. The next one was given at the *tua-tanga*, or naming, being that of some ancestor, and was assumed as he grew up ; the last was taken at the death of his father, which might be called the family name. . . ."[57]

The change in name is always significant of a critical change in one's life, and does not necessarily involve deep foundations in culture-history. Thus, among the American Indians, " personal names were given and changed at the critical epochs of life, such as birth, puberty, the first war expedition, some notable feat, elevation to chieftainship and finally retirement from active life was marked by the adoption of the name of one's son."[58]

The folkways surrounding the naming of the child do not always present a glimpse into a universal and consistent order of societal development. Yet it can be confidently affirmed that a broad line of evolution is discernible as the past rolls on its way and carries along tenaciously in the naming-folkways survivals of older forms. These latter forms inevitably become archaic and ordinarily inexplicable in the face of the pragmatic needs of new conditions of group life. Names are indeed often derived from out of the hoary past,

" having no meaning, having been handed down for centuries ";
but our informant hastens to add that " I have little doubt
that they all originally referred to some person's peculiarities
or some circumstance attending the birth of the child or its
after-life."[59] Ancient names are not ordinarily employed
and while often untranslatable and without apparent sig-
nification to the natives themselves, are used for the child
which arrives in a manner not sanctioned by the mores of
the day.   So a breach of custom may reveal vestiges of the
culture-history.   Among the Mohave Indians, for example, a
child born out of wedlock received some ancient name, not
commonly employed in the tribe.[60]

The name is a means of " pegging " the child—of setting
it off in the life of its folk.   The physical peculiarity of the
child is the most direct evidence of individual difference and
is remembered in the name of peoples on all stages of cultural
development.   Aggregated to this are often fortuitous circumstances surrounding the debut of the child but which seem
integral to the event in folk-thought.   Such denominations
of individual differences drop off in significance and remain as
nicknames. An attempt to tie the child to a maternal, and
later, to a paternal line, is accomplished through the name.
The child that is adequately named is thus formally put into
a niche or is received into his society.   Later changes in the
name are indications of further progress of the child in social
status and prestige.   Because of all this the name is thought
to be closely affiliated to the person, marking him out in the
eyes of his folk and yet developing him completely in the
characteristic ways and mores of his people.

CHAPTER VI

PRELIMINARY ORIENTATIONS OF THE CHILD

THE influence that is exerted by society upon the individual is that of an intangible pervasive medium that inevitably bears upon and shapes one's conduct, ideas and ideals for life. Before the age of discretion and independent query comes, the impact of an established body of ways and mores have laid the entire foundation of the individual's code of right and wrong in his contact with his own and other folk. In the simpler societies pressure towards conformity bears down likewise with an incessant force but it is more consciously evoked and more spectacularly displayed. The individual is rigidly held to abide by the mores of his people. The weight of tradition is, however, not as great and imperatively forbidding as in the more evolved groups with their written languages, established religions and the like. The social forces in the primitive society do not impinge upon the individual from so many directions and as resistlessly as in our times. The social heritage is yet scanty and poor and its survival-value so insignificant that the child does not have much of value to be gained from it. The child's biological equipment of instincts and interests serve as a guide quite as important as the acquired culture-outfit of his folk.

The social milieu of the child in the simpler society does however impinge upon him. The makeshift tools, processes, customs, beliefs and ideals of the folk do not amount to a preponderant heritage, as in the more developed groups, but they do work during the child's life to shape him into conformity. The child is not "schooled" exhaustively nor transformed by a thousand and one suggestive social contacts and influences. There are, rather, very definite occasions upon which the folk impress their ways and psychology upon the youngster. Actual overt acts of a magical, symbolical nature often with a transparent meaning are utilized to bend these twigs into the life of the tree. The struggle for life is so severe that conservatism is a needful impulse for trimming the child's life to the same pattern as his forbears'. This is done by means of ceremonial acts which leave definite impressions and are peculiar to the ways of the people concerned.

The social environment is brought to bear upon the child upon very definite occasions and in a piecemeal fashion. This is not to assert that the child is "accultured" in a rational, purposive manner but to emphasize the episodic and often spectacular nature of these culture-impressions. The primitive man is vividly realistic. His language, which is a reflection of his life and thought processes, has not evolved the expression of subtleties, as in modern educational methods. There are tools for hunting and fishing, which have worked well and these must be brought to the child's attention immediately. Certain qualities of the body and the mind are also to be invoked as soon as possible to aid in the affairs of life. This is not preached to the child at the outset, but a real attempt is made through the ceremonial practices here to be described, to make him skilful with the successful tools and weapons, to inculcate the desirable qualities and characteristics, and to invoke the favourable spirit-auspices of his folk, so that the child whose life has been preserved and whose identity has already been established in the name, will prove a boon and joy to his parents and folk. The form and nature of these preliminary orientations of the child are again representative of the degree of cultural development of the society.

The idea was commonly held that personality inhered in

all parts of the body in an amorphous way. The exuviæ of the person—that is, all the cast off portions of the body such as the nail-parings, hair, blood, faeces, etc.—were thought to contain his essence. Hence, to subject these exuviae to appropriate treatment was tantamount to working the same treatment upon the apparently more organized individual himself. Therefore one heeded the disposition of one's leavings lest they be sntached up by an evil-doer who could wreak havoc.[1] The umbilical cord belonged to this class of objects. It is interesting to note how universally the notion has persisted that an indissoluble part of the child is encased in it. If it was intended to assure the child's fortune in its later pursuits, what better way was there to compass this than to subject the navel-cord to practices suggestive of the child's intended future occupation and station in life ? The placenta, or after-birth, often termed the child's " dress ", or " little brother ", could be manipulated in a similar manner.

In Banks Island, Melanesia, for example, " the child is kept in the house till strong, the idea being that the after-birth, which is part of him, is in the house, and if the child is taken to another village before he is strong he will be sulky and cross away from his *migiria* (or nest) which is a name for the fire-place and the part of the house surrounding it. The after-- birth is regarded as the house of the child before it is born."[2] Among the Semang of Malaya, should the child prove to be a boy, the after-birth is tied in a cloth and suspended upon a tree, where it is left. " If, however, the child happens to be a girl, the after-birth is buried somewhere without further ceremony in the neighbourhood of the house. The reason given for this difference of treatment is that the women are obliged to remain in the house, whereas the men lead an open-air life, and do not remain in one place like the women."[3] Evidences of the sexual division of labour are thus enforced upon the child even before a direct benefit or impression can be said to be gained by him from these manipulations of the umbilicus.

Among the Chukchee, in Siberia, the after-birth is treated exactly as if it were the child itself, for it is placed in a corner of the hut and three small sticks are tied together in imitation of the principal poles of the tent-frame and set over it.   Later, a piece of leather is wrapped around the sticks to represent the tent-covers.[4]

Sometimes the *raison-d'être* of the treatment is more easily discerned, as among the Jakun of the Malay peninsula.   There, " if the child be a boy, the umbilical cord is tied to one of the father's throwing stones, preferably to one with which the father has killed an enemy.   It is then dipped in sea-water, and washed and hung to dry in the smoke.   When dry it is carefully guarded, together with the stone, until the boy is grown up.   At his marriage the stone is made over to him to be carefully kept, since such a stone never misses its mark."[5] It is reported of the Polynesians that the umbilical cord of the male child was severed on a club, to make him valiant in battle, while that of the girl was cut on the board on which the native cloth was beaten out, to make her industrious.[6]   In Ponapé, the cord was wrapped in a mussel and then hung on a tree in the hopes that the child would become dexterous in climbing.[7] In New Caledonia, the priest cut a boy's umbilicus on a particular stone so that the youth might be " stone-hearted " in battle.   " The priest, too, at the moment of operation, had a vessel of water before him dyed black as ink, that the boy, when he grew up, might be courageous to go anywhere to battle on a pitch-dark night, and thus, from his very birth, the little fellow was consecrated to war."[8]   There is thus very clear and definite meaning behind the use to which the umbilicus is put—a rationalism that exhibits no limit to its utilitarian thoroughness, as is further exemplified in the Marshall Islands, where, if a child is a boy, the navel-end is thrown into the sea that he may become an excellent fisherman ; if a girl, it is hidden up in a pandamus tree which has many leaves so that the girl may develop a liking for plaiting these leaves ![9]

This method of preparing the child for its life-work by treating its umbilical cord reaches heights of splendid mimicry, examples of which can be culled from almost all of the races of simpler culture. Among the Thlingit Indians, as soon as the child entered the world, its navel-string was placed in a bag made especially for it, dried inside of this and hung about the child's neck until it was eight days old. " In the case of a boy the cord was placed under a tree on which was an eagle's nest, so that he might be brave when he grew up."[10] Among the Oraibi in Arizona, an arrow shaft or a piece of wood is placed under a boy's umbilical cord, which is then cut ; a girl's is cut on a stirring stick, or a piece of wood representing it. Later the part of the cord which has been cut is tied to the arrow shaft, stick, or a piece of wood and thrust behind some joist of the house, " because the boy will later become a hunter, or have to carry fire-wood, and the girl stir the food in the kettle and grind corn."[11] This may be compared with the Tewa custom of burying the dried-up cord of a girl " deep near the grinding stone so that when she grows up she will not be lazy ; for a boy it is buried in the field ' so he could work '."[12]

The culture-outfit of the group may advance in complexity and efficacy, yet old ways of doing things persist. The use of the child's exuviae as potent instruments for shaping the child's future fortune in the life of his people, still remains in practice. In fact it becomes used for a greater variety of needs and purposes, as is illustrated by the case of the natives of Java. They are accustomed to wrap the placenta in leaves with strips of paper adhering, upon which they describe characters (so that the child may learn to read earlier). In addition a needle is placed in it (that the *ari-ari* or spirits should exercise a good influence on the child), a few weaving tools (that the boy may be able to stretch his hands out well, and if a girl, that she may be able to sew and make fine clothes), etc. The bundle is then placed in a dish to be buried or consigned to the river to be borne away by the current[13]— probably to the distant residence of the tribal spirits.

The needs of life call imperatively for the aid of all who can add a mite of strength. This gives rise to a marked tendency to initiate the child into the circle of folk-life activities as soon as he opens his eyes. The child is raw material and completely open to early impressions which remain indelibly impressed upon him in later years. In a variety of ways the infant is " trimmed to the task " and has his culture, that is, the ways of life and thought of his parents and folk-fellows, fitted on at an extremely early age. Not only are the tools and maintenance-equipment exhibited to him but various medicinal manipulations or suggestive acts are used to doctor him and insure lasting characteristics of fortitude, courage or prowess in the mode usually acceptable to the folk.

In almost every instance it is believed possible to transfer characteristics to the child by suggestion or mere contact. Thus, the child's social characteristics in many forms are " acquired " not through inheritance but through the force of manipulating the immediate environment in order to initiate him into his place in the folk-life. The importance of the first years of life were thus recognized long before modern psychology had come to stress them.

There are various specifics to be used or avoided in order to induce the needed qualities of physique and mind. Among the Bushmen, it is thought that " a little child is wont to be timid ; therefore the little child does not eat jackal's hearts because the jackal is not a little afraid ; for the jackal runs away."[14] Among the Kafir, a meteorite which has been well burned and then ground to fine powder is given to the child for it is believed that this has the power of " strengthening and making firm the base of the skull, of imparting vigour to the child's mind and of making the infant brave and courageous." The child is also passed through a fire of aromatic woods in order to impart to him " valour and eloquence."[15]

There is a beetle in Bechuanaland which will survive for a month after it is suspended on a thread. Therefore mothers who have lost children in infancy suspend one or two of these beetles from the baby's neck or tie them to his hair to prolong his life.[16] The recipe for good sight among the South-east Australians is revealed by the mother who will rub her hand under her arm and then rub her son's eyes[17]—the otherwise inexplicable body fluids there collecting being conceived as possessing potent spiritual qualities.

The Sioux Indian in America was given character in this manner : " Should the infant be a boy, a brave and good-tempered man, chosen beforehand, takes the infant in his arms and breathes into his mouth, thereby communicating his own disposition to the infant who will grow up to be a brave and good-natured man."[18] The utter simplicity of these methods is logically convincing among folk whose greatest generalizations are those of universal animism in nature and the efficacy of contact and sympathetic magic. Among the Bering Strait Eskimo, an incident is related of a shaman putting into the boy-child's mouth a carving of a white whale so " as to feed him on something that would make him a fine hunter. The shaman beat the drum and sang over the boy for half-an-hour to make him stout-hearted and manly."[19] This is again clearly demonstrated by the Hopi Indians. A swift-running insect is placed on the wrist of a male child in order to make him a good runner ; while on the girl's wrist is placed the cocoon of a butterfly in order to strengthen the wrist for grinding corn ![20]

Turning to other cases, we find that the infant directly after birth is at once introduced to the tools and weapons which he is to use in his daily labours. Among the Baganda, " directly after the child is born, if it is a boy, a spear is placed in its hand, if a girl, a knife such as women use for household duties, is put in its hand."[21] The Maori place a small reed or weapon in the boy's hand at birth, the mother assisting the infant to retain it. In the case of the girl, a small hank of phormium fibre was placed in the babe's hand, this was the emblem of weaving.[22] In Madagascar, also, the baby is carried out of doors and if it is a boy, the axe, large knife and spear generally used in the family are taken out, because, as Ellis remarks, " the implements are perhaps used chiefly as emblems of the occupations in which it is expected the infant will engage when it arrives at maturer years. . . ."[23] The natives in New Pomerania in the South Pacific collect a heap of odoriferous shrubs at birth by the side of which are placed all the tools the child will need in its future life—if a boy, a spear, sling and stone, bamboo knife, digging-stick, etc.— if a girl, a raincoat, basket of betel and areka-nuts, a piece of tapu, and a bamboo-knife.[24]

Among the Maya Indians in Yucatan, as soon as the child is six months old, its limbs are " opened " for the first time. In the hands of the female-child are then placed a needle, a spindle and the implements with which they weave their cloth ; if it is a boy, he is given a hatchet, a machete, and other implements to be used later in life.[25]

The forecast of the child's future activities is often symbolically arranged for success and prosperity. This is particularly true in the more developed societies where with added experience doubt may arise with respect to the efficacy and wisdom of merely handing to the child tools and weapons. Yet it is imperative that acquaintance with these objects be assumed as early as possible. Hence, on Leper's Island, in Melanesia, when the infant is ten days old the father goes down to the beach. As he proceeds if it is a boy he scatters along the path little *toy* bows, as a sign that he shall be a strong bowman ; if a girl, he throws down bits of pandanus fibre out of which mats are made, for making mats brings in money, and this is to be her work.[26] Similarly, the Dajak midwife receives as a reward for her service a piece of rattan which signifies long life for the child, a torch, that he may become intelligent and distinguished, rice that he may have many offspring, and a knife that he may be brave.[27]

We find the same thing among such people as the Indians of Northern Mexico, though they are not as richly endowed with symbolism, because of the poorer cultural outfit. The child is gaily accoutred : " If the child was a boy, one of the old men took it in his arms and painted on its breast an axe or some implement of husbandry, on its forehead a feather, and on the shoulders a bow and quiver. . . . If the child proved to be a female, the same ceremony was observed, with the exception that an old woman officiated, and the figure of a flower was traced over the region of the heart, while on the palm of the right hand a spinning-wheel was pictured and on the left a piece of wool, thus indicating the several duties of after life."[28] Among other American Indians a like symbolism was practised. The Kitchi-gami babe had a miniature imitation of a bow and arrow hung over the cradle and carefully worked little moccasins as good omens of prowess in hunting and running.[29] The Tillamook cradle was shaped in the form of a small canoe and the shaman was engaged to perform a dance carrying the child in it. " This was believed to make the child an expert canoe-man and to prevent the capsizing of the canoe."[30]

Attempts to mould or direct the child into winning ways in life often reach picturesque if not dramatic proportions. A naïveté of imagination is revealed, which survives in more developed folk-life, but which is then considered as " poetry ". Among the simpler peoples, however, this is a trend of thought that is an integral part of the mores.   Like cause is thought to produce like effect by the Tlingits, for the woman who wants her baby neat in later life places on her breast the borings that come out of a woodworm's burrow and lets the child suck this substance along with her milk.   Red paint was also placed on the child's nose to make it strong.[31]   In New Hebrides the natives are revealed as incurably optimistic, or mentally agile.   The baby boy has a small bow and arrow placed in its fingers.   " A male relation is the target, and if the tiny arrow hits the mark, the infant will become a great warrior, while if it misses it will become adept in dodging the arrows of the enemy."[32]   The young Alfur of Celebes at twelve months of age undergoes an elaborate ceremonial which has already become conventionalized.   He is dressed like a full-grown man, bears an empty miniature bamboo which he is to fill with wine, a knife to hack a tree, a little ladder to climb it and arms to resist head-hunting savages.   " The child's feet are placed three times on the steps of the ladder and henceforth the child will be expert in obtaining the wine from the sago-plant ! "[33]

Among a few of these tribes a complete exposition of the technique of food-getting and other worldly concerns is presented to the child in some detail as a preparation for his future activities.   We are told of the Wagogo in East Africa, for instance, that in the case of a male child, " the midwife takes a billhook, axe, hoe, adze and a kind of spokeshave, with the child on her back, when she solemnly goes through the form of initiating it into the mysteries of its future life.   ' We clear the forest ', she says, ' in order that we may cultivate ; we sow in order that we may eat and get rice '.   She then sprinkles water on the child saying, ' It rains here on earth '.   She winds up by telling it from whence its ancestors came, and their different totems. If a female, the midwife goes through the process of corn-grinding, and says, ' We grind corn, we are females '. Next she goes through the process of pounding and sifting corn. She then takes a vegetable vessel, and calabashes used in carrying water ; also a piece of firewood which she chops up. She concludes the performance, as in the former case, by telling the babe from whence its ancestors came."[34]

Obviously the infant does not benefit much from the efforts expended upon him in this direction. The child is rarely old enough to grasp the significance of these employments and the performances themselves are in the nature of pantomime or so directed as to secure results by magical means. Nevertheless, these practices portray graphically enough the early onset of the culture as it weaves itself about the child in his tenderest years. The child, as we have seen, is thought to be " old " in so far as spiritual or animating force is concerned, and it is mainly to cajole or bend these spirits into the ways of earthly life that these practices are undertaken. The actual method depends upon the belief in the make-belief of imitative magic as the means to gain this end. Such erroneous beliefs extend into more highly developed societies as can be seen among many peasant populations to-day, there being no immediate pressure to test these methods. We pass now to consider other features of the orientation of the infant to its social milieu—practices whose results are probably more lasting and distinctive.

Most prominent among these is the custom of inflicting body mutilations on the child. The motives are confused and but dimly apprehended by the natives themselves who follow these customs merely because they have been followed in the past. Primarily, by tatooing, sacrification, knocking out of teeth, cutting off of fingers, and the like, attempt is made to conform the child to the tribal idea of what is " fit ", and hence, beautiful.   By the latter term is often intended merely the ideas of normal physical appearance.   But even these notions are deeply-rooted in the culture-complex of the group and as a certain mark of distinction, the group ethos may over-accentuate a particular trait, as elongated ear-lobes, pierced noses, etc.

In these traits we may also unearth traces of human sacrifice which prevailed among these peoples at one time.[35]   Instead of offering up a life, a composition is made by taking a member of the body which is often useless or which can be done without. Ages of such practices habituate the folk to consider the person as " normal ", " fit " and even " handsome ", only when bereft of a finger, tongue-pierced, or scarified.   The more immediate practical significance of the mutilation appears when it is intended thereby to make the limbs more deft for handling tools.   Whatever the dominating reason the child is marked for life with the sign and symbol of his folk and is fit to belong to it and accept its protection and aid in the life-struggle.

In Central Africa, " in earliest childhood there are practised those tatooings and mutilations which are to be both the individual's distinctive tribal marks and, as it were, his ticket of identification.   They are extremely dissimilar and include perforation of the nasal septum, and of the nostrils, of the lips, of the lobe, of the concha, of the edge of the ear, or scarifications in the forehead, the cheeks, the chest, stomach and arms, and depilation of the eyelashes and eyebrows."[36]   As an example, consider the Ila native who carries this coat-of-arms about with him : three slits on the temples and four upper incisor teeth knocked out, sometimes the canine as well.[37]   Among the Herero, the mode prescribes knocking out two lower incisors and cutting the upper ones to the form of a Roman five (V).[38]   On the Congo, tubes sharpen their teeth to points.   When reproached that such teeth looked like a dog's, the quick retort was that those of the white man resembled those of a bat.[39] There is evidently no accounting for tastes ; especially if they are good in the eyes of one's own folk.

In Australia, custom demanded that the person of the child be maimed in some manner. The usual method was piercing the septum of the nose or knocking out of the teeth. This way is beloved of the gods, who are always ready to sanction the practices of the group. On being questioned, the Dieyeri, for example, assign no reason for disfiguring their children other than that, " when they were created the Mooramoora knocked out two front teeth of the upper jaw of the first child, and pleased at the sight, commanded that this should be done to every male and female child for ever after ".[40] In New Zealand, the infant's nose was flattened and the knee-joints rubbed down in order to reduce the inner parts and make them " handsome ". In order to accomplish this, the legs and knees of the child were squeezed for many weeks.[41] In New Pomerania, blacking of the teeth is called for, and on Savage Island the forehead is flattened that it may appear narrower in conformity with tribal standards.[42] In the Society Islands, " the forehead and back of the head of the boys were pressed upwards, so that the upper part of the skull appeared in the shape of a wedge. This, they said, was done to add to the terror of their aspect when they should become warriors."[43]

Distinguishing marks of family and other tribal divisions are conferred upon the infant in a similar manner. Among the Omaha Indians, the hair was cut in a pattern to indicate the gens or band of the parent ; among the Iowa to indicate the particular protecting medicine of the father.[44] Even the more prosaic distinctions of wealth are exhibited in the physical distortions of the child, as among the Indians of British Columbia, for " in the case of the base-born of the tribes the heads of their children were customarily but slightly deformed while the heads of the children born of the wealthy or noble persons . . . were severely and excessively deformed."[45]

There are, on the other hand, more rational mutilations which subserve an immediate utility. Such is the custom among the blacks in Eastern Australia of bending the first joint of the thumb of a girl to enable her to use the fish-line more successfully. Similarly in New Zealand, female infants " had the first joint of their thumbs half-disjointed, or bent considerably outwards, to enable the woman better to hold, scrape, weave and plait flax ".[46]   In other parts of Australia, two joints of the thumb of the left hand are cut off and thrown into the sea, it is said, to insure luck in catching fish. It is thus possible that the custom of bending the finger secured a rationalization of an ancient form of actual sacrifice of the fingers, perhaps, a vestige of human sacrifice.

The child has to undergo severe and more painful mutilations which signify the entrance into maturity, a consideration of which we have therefore postponed until the stage of initiation is reached in our order of development. Circumcision, for example, is a typical initiatory rite which, it may be objected, is practised among many tribes upon children during their earliest years of infancy. It will be found, however, that among such peoples as the African tribes particularly, and some of the Melanesians, that the meaning and purpose of this folkway is a ceremonial celebration of the child's coming of age in the physical and later, social sense. That circumcision is performed in early infancy is often an indication of the custom lapsing, becoming conventionalized, or losing its original import and vigour.[48]

The infant is more formally received into the arena of his life activity and attention thus called to the new arrival by the folk. It must be presented to the ghost-spirits for benediction in order to begin life under their favourable auspices.

The guiding forces that are thought to sway primitive life are resident, as we have seen, in the inanimate as well as in the purely animate realm of animal and human life. The reception of the infant is thus conceived to be undertaken by all the forces of the unseen, imaginary environment—not merely the human society of the folk and the features of the geographical environment, but also by all the ancestral and tribal ghosts who people these objects and who give their force and sanction to all the processes, ways, customs and mores of the society. To bring the arrival of the infant to the notice of the group and the spirits it is necessary to register the event by a public ceremonial typical to the culture of the group. The ceremony is all the more necessary if a written language has not been developed and the means of recording and remembering events are still those of witnessing and being impressed by the events themselves.

Thus, in parts of Western Africa, " the moment a child is born it is proclaimed in the streets so that everyone may know it. A public crier announces the fact, and claims for it a name and place among the living. Someone else, in a distant part of the town, acknowledges the fact, and promises on the part of the people, that the new-born baby shall be received into the community, and have all the rights and immunities pertaining to the rest of the people. The population then assemble in the streets, and the new-born babe is brought out and exposed to public view. A basin of water is provided, and the head man of the town or family sprinkles water upon it . . . Most of the people present follow the example of the head man, and the poor child is pretty thoroughly drenched before the ceremony is ended."[49] Water is commonly one of the most precious of possessions of the group and the use of it may signify group-adherence.

The use of food in common is also of a binding nature. Thus, in Fiji, " on the birth of an infant, its father acknowledges it as legitimate, and otherwise acceptable, by a gift of food ; and his kinsfolk formally signify approval and confirmation of his decision on the part of the clan by similar presentations."[50]   Among the Ba-thonga in South Africa, it is by the tying of a string that the child is officially aggregated to the family as a human being ; before he was a *shilo* (thing), *khuna* (incomplete being).[51]   The Omaha Indians prepare the mundane reception to the infant by cutting a small hole in the first pair of moccasins made for him.   " When the relatives come to see the little one they examine the moccasins, and seeing the hole, they say : ' Why, he (or she) has worn out the moccasins ; he has travelled over the earth ! '   This is an indirect prayer that the child may live long.   The new (whole) moccasins put on the child at the close of the ceremony for introducing it into the tribe constitute an assurance that it is prepared for the journey of life and the journey will be a long one."[52]   Among the neighbouring Osage, the medicine-man recites to the infant the story of Creation and of the animals of the earth.   He then places the tip of his finger on the nipple of the mother, presses that finger on the lips of the child and passes his hand over its body.   Then the infant is allowed to take nourishment and no harm will befall him.[53] On Banks Island in Melanesia, " when the male child goes out for the first time the father and mother go with it and tie leaves together and throw them down on the path so that when the people see them they will know that a male child has been added to the community."[54]

As the spirits and ghosts peopling the environment hold much power for weal or woe, it is highly essential that the infant be put under their benign influence at once.   On Hudson Island, in Polynesia, since there is no time to be lost, the infant while only a few seconds old, and before anything else is done to him, is hurried to the temple " that its first breathing might be in the presence of the gods and his blessings invoked on the *very first* essentials of infantile life."[55]   Ten days after birth the Zuni women bring the child in touch with the spiritual forces in the folk's cult.   Two of the women " sprinkle a line of sacred meal, emblematic of the straight road which the child must follow to win the favour of the gods.   Thus the first object which the child is made to behold at the very dawn of its existence is the sun, the great object of their worship."[56]

These spirits which are later assembled or systematized into a group of nature-gods are, as we have seen above, considered to be the real parents of the child or the ultimate causes of its being.   Hence, it is fitting, as among the Huichol in Mexico, that the infant child should be presented first to the Mother of the Gods and then to the " grandfather Fire, Father Sun and the Goddess of Corn,"[57] the deities that control the destinies of the folk and its children.   Somewhat similarly among the Basutos in South Africa, it is only after the child has been shown the full moon and it has been observed that he has fixed his eye upon it, that the infant is allowed to make his appearance among men.[58]   Among the Baholoholo to the north, after the umbilical cord has fallen, the father takes the child, raises it towards the right, then towards the left and towards the mountains where the great chiefs are buried, so that the spirit might be favourably disposed to the newly-born.[59]   The Maori have developed a prayer of blessing and invocation which the priest recites over the infant : " On high let crashing thunder roar . . . Here am I, a proper child, a male child of Io the Parentless, of the origin, of the acme of godlike power, of the powers of the heavens, and of Papa the parentless . . . Let godlike power and mentality rest on the child ; a descendant of thy godlike powers, O Rangi ! "[60]

Notions of propriety and legitimacy as to the forbears of the child—its parentage and spiritual origins—are included in this latter instance as a definite mark of a developed culture

H

with a written language and recorded traditions. These advances are thenceforward to be enjoyed by the child as its superior social heritage. At this point it is of interest to note that the differences in cutural development of the folk are brought to bear upon the child during its earliest years, among other ways, in the manner of accommodating it advantageously to the tribal spirits or gods.

The various orientations of the child which have been described are eloquent in portraying the early influences brought to bear by the group to prepare the child's life in the ways of the folk and to ordain it with favourable chances in the struggle for self-maintenance. In few instances, however, do we have reason to believe that these customs of treating the exuvial remains of the child, of inflicting body-mutilations upon it, of symbolically giving it tools and weapons and of introducing it to the spirits and the folk, have any apparent utility for the child in its later life. There are, however, more efficacious ways of providing for the child, such as setting apart for it some bit of property, as a head of cattle or fruit tree, and permitting the present or future returns from these to accrue solely to the child. This considerate folkway is in the nature of creating a material endowment. The existence of ideas of private property are presupposed in order to provide for such usages. Social phenomena are hardly ever isolated and simply motivated. There is often an entanglement or merging of interests. For example, the planting of a tree for the child may also imply a use of imitative magic in that the growth and prosperity of the child may be thought to be consequent on that of the tree.[61]

The case is clear with the Banyonkole of East Africa. At the end of four months, among these cattle people, the father takes the boy-child and choosing two cows, brings them before the house and places the child on the back of each in turn. These two animals are dedicated to the boy's use and belong to him.[62] Among the Ama-Xosa, the father takes some hairs from the tail of one of the cattle and the mother ties it in a mysterious way around the child's neck. The cow is thereafter set apart particularly for that child's use. All this is done amidst great feasting.[63] Among the Bori, a special goat or ewe is set apart for the child. " It shares the milk of the animal with her young, but no other human being may partake of it, and if there is any surplus milk it is not sold."[64] The Koryak, in Siberia, give to each newly-born child, irrespective of sex, one reindeer-heifer or more with a special mark on the ear. Under favourable conditions a whole herd may be formed by yearly increases of the herd of these heifers before the child is ready to marry.[65]

With the domestication of animals, ideas of personal property became distinct, for the animals provided valuable economic means, and meant immeasurable benefits in the life-struggle. These instances of child-property reflect this condition. There is a stimulus to endow the child with cattle as its own in order to provide a valuable source of food-supply in the future. The means undertaken to establish the priority of the child to these bits of income-yielding property serve to illustrate the root-meanings of property, as something attached or assimilated to the person. Thus, among the Xosa an exuvial part of the cow, a hair, is attached to the child, thus setting up an intimate tie. Among the Bori, the milk of the child's ewe is destined solely for the child's consumption, and may not be used by others under any circumstance. " Property " is that which has been appropriated and made fast to one's self.[66]

Trees are often planted at the birth of the child, and remain his first bit of property, as in Central Celebes.[67] In the Solomon Islands, a coco-nut palm is planted for the child which is tended solely by it in later years The child alone

can sell its surplus produce.[68]   In Hawaii, these trees are
often handy reminders : " After burying the afterbirth, a
tree was in old days planted over the spot and on no account
was it to be cut down as long as the child lived.   Mrs. Pakin
knew a woman on Hawaii who had a row of trees of uneven
height in her garden to which she could point one after the
other and say, ' Why yes, that one is Irene, that Agnes and
that Elijah '."[69]

Children's property is held in high respect, and cannot be
taken or used by others.   Among the Omaha Indians, children
were given ponies and colts and " a parent did not assume
the right to give away one of them without the child's consent ".   It is well-nigh impossible to purchase children's
property from the parents among the Brazilian and Guiana
Indians no matter how glittering and tempting the objects
offered in payment.[70]   This was graphically illustrated in the
experience related by King with respect to the Fuegians he
encountered.   " It appeared that they allowed their children
to possess property and consult their little whims with regard
to its disposal."   A mother refused to part with a certain dog.
" At last my offers became so considerable, that she called a
boy out of the thick jungle . . . who was the owner of the
dog.   The goods were shown to him, but the little urchin
would not consent . . ."[71]

Such property may grow in value and prove a profitable
endowment.   In most instances the issue of the cattle also
belong to the child but may be kept by others until his marriage day when he is further set up in life.   Among some of
the Melanesian tribes a fowl is given the child to start in life,
and as the fowls multiply, he changes some of them for a
young sow and so gradually the property increases considerably.[72]

We have examined outstanding episodes in the earliest
years of the child in which the culture of the folk is woven

about him in a more or less consciously experienced desire to initiate and prepare him successfully for the life-struggle. Symbols of future place and activities, particularly in food-gathering are thrust before the child and the sign of the tribe is placed upon him. The child is adjusted to the spiritual forces which determine the fortunes and misfortunes of his future career. Thus orientated, accepted, admonished and equipped, the child grows into his social milieu with greater awareness as he increases in years. We now turn to consider the manner of this further socialization of the child.

CHAPTER VII

INFANCY AND CHILDHOOD

THE human infant left to his own resources would almost instantly succumb. His original outfit of instincts and interests and his entire bodily organism, is the end-result of a long series of adjustments to life-conditions. This is, however, woefully inadequate, and cannot unaided, enable the child to appreciate the nature and purposes of societal life. In the eons of organic evolution, the cultural or societal mode of existence of life occupies but an infinitesimal fraction of time. We cannot but believe, therefore, that each child when newly-born is a highly-developed organic being, wholly unfit and unprepared for the folk-life. Culture cannot be transmitted directly through the germ-plasm except perhaps in a most subtle, indirect way, as the capacities for acquiring and assuming it in the child may be inheritable. The physical equipment of the human infant lacks the protective devices, as well as the aggressive features, of other animals. Left to himself the human infant is the most helpless of all animal young. He is bare, tender and weak. It is in the social heritage that this severe handicap is overcome.

The whole system of tools, folkways, institutions and mores are the adjustments made by the folk to accommodate themselves to their life-conditions. In lieu of claws, nails, fur, or feelers, the society is able to furnish the child with tools, clothing and weapons of every description which are superior adjustments to the material needs of life. In every instance they represent materialized forms of mental adjustments, or ideas. Culture or civilization is a complex of such adjusted forms and processes with which the child is endowed and his natural physical ineptness is overcome. The period of infancy, in a social sense, is thus the period during which the child experiences a form of recapitulation of past adjustments to life-conditions. They are re-learned afresh by each generation. The period of infancy is one of dependence upon others for sustenance and support until the child has been fitted with his cultural heritage. The possibility of supporting the individual, incapable of self-support, during infancy, is in itself a societal achievement. It is made possible only through the pursuit of a developed system of the industrial arts—the domestitation of animals and plants, the use of artificial foods and the ability to draw upon an accumulated surplus of means or capital during the non-earning, unproductive years of the infant. In turn, this period of the life of the child has meant further progress in culture-achievement, for it has enabled the young to profit by the past and often leads to improvement and refinement of the ways and beliefs of the folk. Infancy is essentially the period of social apprenticeship.

As society develops, this period is proportionately prolonged. The simplest and least evolved of societies, (that are the subject of our study), have relatively the shortest periods in which the child is totally dependent upon its parents and folk. It will be seen that the closer we approach to the origins of society and its forms, the closer does the condition of the young resemble that of ordinary animal young. The child's innate tendencies which are resident in a complex of automatic adjustments suffice to guide the way toward self-maintenance. But as the societal phenomena such as tools, instruments and processes of hunting, fishing and tillage, develop, there arises a slowly lengthening period devoted solely to the acquisition of these culture-aids. At the same time social forces arise such as the pressure toward conformity, ideas of welfare and the otherwise inexplicable in life which permeate the child's stock of ideas and manner of thought more gradually and imperceptibly. It is our present purpose to pay some attention to the early years of the child's life in these simpler societies, which may best be characterized as the period of infancy in the social sense. It will be necessary to go beyond these years in order to compare them with the condition of the children of more developed societies, in which practically all the years of physical adolescence and youth may be included in the conception of social infancy.[1]

"Infancy" is therefore an extremely short period in the simpler societies, and during these years the child is regarded as an utter nonenity, a thing of little importance in the folk-life. It is much like an animal and perhaps fondly cherished by its parents only as an attractive toy. An individual's worth, importance, distinction—in short, his "character"—exfoliates only in a web of social relationships, in his capacity as a huntsman, worker, or heir, as a provider in the struggle for existence and well-being, or as the symbol of the unity and dignity of the folk. Without such acquired status the infant is disregarded as an object beneath notice. As we have seen,[2] the name is a tag or label attached by the group through the immediate parents as a form of recognition. Children during the infantile period remain nameless, as among American Indians, carrying merely general appellations as "child", "baby", or "boy" until they are old enough and important enough to exhibit and claim an individuality. Then they are named.[3]

We have the testimony of a Winnebago Indian who did not doubt for a moment that the early years of his life were identical with any subconscious condition occurring during his more mature years. In Australia, similarly, a West Kimberley native claimed that until the boys were subincised (a typical ceremony of recognition or "reception" of the

child), " they were all the same dog (or other animal)".[5] To
all purposes, the " infant " is in an utterly futile condition.

In the more advanced groups, as in Sarawak, children
attain the age of seven or eight years without having received
a name, being known until then merely as *endun*, little girl,
or *anggat*, little boy.   In Borneo, during this nameless period
of its first years, the boy is spoken of as *Ukat* and the girl,
Dwing, " both of which seem to be best translated as Thingumybob ; among the Sea Dyaks *Vlat* (the little grub) is
the name commonly used ".[6] The more developed culture-
complex evidently lengthened the " infantile " condition
considerably.   Should the infant die, during these years, it
is of course soon forgotten and no remembrance of it kept
at all.[7]

The infant is believed to be a fresh arrival from an imaginary
world of the spirits and hence his ways are peculiarly inexplicable.   He comes directly from the ancestral haunts
into the parents' and folks' ken mysteriously and often un-
awaited.   Hence he takes on menacing and dangerous qualities from this contact.   His ways are in addition all his own,
and anything inexplicable is feared and must be discreetly
handled.   Infancy is thus a period of danger approximating
sickness.   For this reason in the early years the child is continually being treated, protected or cleansed of the coating
of the ghostly world.   This condition persists until the infant
emerges in the plain and understandable character as a social
unit conformable and comparable to the rest of " men ",
that is, in his social character as an auxiliary bread-winner,
worker, cult-fellow or heir.

For example, the Yakuts in Siberia " think that a child
who does not yet understand human language understands
the talk of the fire, the singing of birds, the language of beasts,
lifeless objects and spirits, *but that he loses this gift when he
acquires human speech.* " This superstition ", it is added,

" may be due to the habit of children to stay about the fire,
the warmest and pleasantest place in the house, and also the
most interesting, where a child stands staring at the flames
with his big black eyes and listening to the hissing and snap-
ping of the fire ".[8] The infant is considered peculiarly able
to see and understand cryptically and is dealt with as are all
" unclean " new beings.

Ceremonially, these " shady " connections are wiped out,
as among the Akamba in East Africa : " On the fourth day,
the father usually hangs round the child's neck a necklace,
ipa, consisting of one of the fine iron chains made by the
Akamba . . . As soon as the *ipa* is hung round the child's
neck, the child becomes a real human being ; before that it
had been looked upon as a being in more or less intimate
connection with the spirit-world, from which it has come
and is called *kiim* (cf. *iimu*, ' a deceased relation, spirit ') ".[9]
Iron is a particularly potent " medicine ", prophylactic against
spirits.

During the days of infancy, traces of ghostly influences
abide, even after the infant has been made to cast off the hold
of the spirits. The ideas and notions concerning this imaginary environment of the strange and otherwise inexplicable,
are peculiarly ill-assorted and often inconsistent as they can
be rarely verified or disproved by actual experience. Certain
it is, however, that the child during the early years remains
liable to the depredations of the spirits, and there arises a
host of prophylactic measures employed to surround the
infant with a safety zone. It is very common in Africa to pass
the child through smoke or fire.[10] Similarly in New Pomerania,
Melanesia, the medicine-man, after holding his hands on smoke,
rubs the child's eyes, ears, eyebrows, nose and mouth with
ashes, " so that thereby he is protected against evil spirits
and evil magic ".[11] In addition to being smoked, the Kafir
infant is scarified on both sides of the head near the temples

and on a spot at the base of the neck, considered popularly as vital lurking places of the spirits. Into these the medicine-man rubs medicine, " and it is thought that the child is now fortified against most of the risks of life ". In addition, long strips of skin are wound around the infant's neck as a further charm against evil.[12] On the coast of Guinea, when a child is seven days old (seven, strangely, being considered a portentous number), the infant is considered out of the danger zone. Yet to appease the evil spirits, " they strew all the ways with dressed victuals ".[13]

The troubles and ailments that afflict the child during these years of infancy are also attributed to the spirits whose influence still lingers. Infancy is thus considered a transition period in which the folk-life combats the imaginary environment for the control of the child's life. This may be said to apply to the entire course of the individual's life as all misfortune, accident and chance are traced to the same authorship. But the infant is more completely soaked in this element, as we have seen. Among the Buryat in Siberia, if the child is slightly unwell, or his teeth trouble him, or he has a slight fever, the shaman is at once called to pacify him. " Sometimes he will spend three whole days carrying the child in his bosom."[14] Things that are unaccountable and strange imply some fearsome contact with the malignancy of these spirits, and must be warily guarded against for the infant's sake. Among the Malays, " if a stranger steps into a house where there are children the father takes off the child's skin ornament and gives it to the stranger, who, after holding it for a time in his hands, returns it. In this fashion, the child is protected against the evil influence which the glances of a stranger may produce ".[15] This is like the widespread fear of the " evil eye " held by peoples more advanced in culture throughout the world.[16] The purpose of all these practices, we are told by skilled investigators, " seems to establish and maintain about the child a certain atmosphere (or, as they say, a certain odour), in which alone it can thrive ".[17]

The growth and development of the child from the perilous state of infancy is anxiously and carefully traced. During the first years, the age of the child is not reckoned in a conventional astronomical calendar, but by the more obvious and closer events in physical growth. This is a more natural system of age-measurement as the culture of these societies does not include a body of generalized mathematical knowledge. The primitive man is struck, therefore, only by the outward evidences of physical growth and maturation and these he uses as counters of the child's age. The positions successively assumed by the child is taken as a measure of his age among the Atjehers in Sumatra. Thus the child's age is denoted by these milestones : " Lying on its back ", " rolling on its side ", " bending double ", " sitting ", " creeping ", " standing ", and " running ".[18] Among the Akikuyu of East Africa, " the age of the child is always explained by holding out the hand to show his height." Mothers plant trees on the birth of their children, but appear as a rule to lose count of the ages of the trees and therefore of their children also.[19] The age of the child among the Bakitara is also calculated, not by the years, " but by its size and natural episodes of its life, such as the cutting of its first teeth, and later, if the child was a girl, the growth of the breasts ".[20] The Hopi Indians in America kept a record of these episodes of the child's age by thumb-nail scratches on the wall.[21]

The physical growth of living organisms is an exceedingly gradual, expansive process recognizable only by imperceptible changes and transformation. These subtler differences are ordinarily unknown to the primitive man. Growth to him is not an easy unfolding. Life is rather made up of a series of well-marked episodes or turning-points that are explosive in nature. Each change is a climactic one or is made so by ceremonial observances. Each distinctive physical episode is accompanied by rites to indicate the individual's separation from one state of existence and entrance into another. It may be even supposed that these life-events are considered tantamount in folk-thought to a death followed by a resurrection.[22] The broadening accumulation of experience and later scentific, that is, purposeful, investigation has slowly built up the conception of the gradual, subtle nature of organic growth. It is typical of social life, however, that the individual's place in it be marked by definite, impressive occasions. These conditions are such as to make a lasting impression upon the members of the group. For that reason feasting or noise-making is essential as producing a convincing impression upon the senses of the partakers or beholders. In the same way, the record of the infant's growth is celebrated by ceremony.

In Samoa, each episode is marked by a feast. "When the child became strong and able to sit there was a feast", for the "sitting of the child." Another followed "for the creeping of the child". There followed a feast to commemorate the standing of the child. But the greatest was the fifth when the child could walk. Then there was singing and night-dances.[23] Among the South African Bantu a ceremonial observance was made on the first creeping of the child, and later, the first answering to his name.[24] The Fijians punctuate the stages of growth by food-offerings to the gods. This is done on the occasion of the first bathing of the child and on the event of his first turning over without help.[25]

The episodical nature of the social growth of the individual is more clearly evidenced as soon as the child attains to the years in which it begins to acquire its culture-heritage. As these years are reached the child is invested with status and place. These occasions are determined by the mores of the people. Thus, after the child has attained to the ability to move about unaided, its further marks in " age " are those singled out by the folk-thought as significant. As is to be supposed, these more characteristically societal growth-marks are often coincident with evidences of physical development and change, but it is not long before a divergence can be marked and physical changes become symbols of attainment of social, rather than physical " age ".

We are, for instance, informed that among some of the Australian natives, " the terms which we translate *young man* are in fact designations conferred on the males at from sixteen to twenty years of age, after having gone through certain ceremonies more or less painful. Hence the appella-tion, strictly speaking, results from having submitted to ceremonies, and not from age . . ."[26] In Victoria there are five stages of mutilation marking the child's growth in " age ". The first is *Moodlawillpa*—boring the septum of the nose—an operation which is performed when the boys and girls are from five to ten years of age ; the second is *Chirrinchirrie*—the extraction of the teeth—which is done when the children are between the ages of eight to twelve years ; the third is *Kurawellie Wonkanna*, (circumcision), which is performed when the hair makes its appearance on the face ; the fourth is *Willyaroo* (to procure a good harvest, supply of snakes . . .) when the young man is scarred. He is cut on the neck and shoulders with a sharp-edged stone so that ridges may be formed. And finally *Koolpie*. As soon as the hair on the face is sufficiently grown to admit of the ends of the beard being tied, the ceremony of *Koolpie* is solemnized.[27]

The events selected as marks of age are indicative of a growth in social maturity of the child as he spasmodically takes on the culture of his people. The progress of the Borneo child is marked by successive offerings of pigs—and its first wearing of a real sword, and assumption of clothing.[28]

Between the period of infancy and the acquisition of degrees of social worth or " age " as here described, there is a short interregnum in which the child is left free to his own devices. During these years the child is immune from the restrictions and tabus that serve to regulate the societal life of the adults. This period intervenes in Borneo between the second naming and puberty. The children are permitted, for instance, to eat deer, gray monkeys, snakes and a certain variety of bird ordinarily tabu to the tribe. At religious festivals, also, no restrictions are laid upon them. They are not forced to pull out the eye-brows and eye-lashes as do the older tribes-fellows.[29] To all appearances their life is totally free. Among the New Guinea pygmies, " at the age of five or six years the boy frees himself from . . . trammels, goes out when he wishes, does what he chooses and merely returns to the family hut for his due allowance of sago and fish, or occasionally to refresh himself at the maternal breast ".[30]

The Indian children, after leaving the cradle, Charlevoix declares, are " under no sort of confinement, and as soon as they are able to crawl about . . . are suffered to go stark naked wherever they have a mind, through woods, water, mire and snow . . ."[31] Of the Araucanian child it is declared that at the age of eight years he is " lord of space and time ", no less.[32] This unconstrained liberty is apt to prove a distressing burden to be borne by the child.

Left to himself, he must attend to his own wants unaided. This has provoked the comment of investigators who have necessarily contrasted this condition with the extreme precautionary care and tender solicitude of societies well advanced in material culture. Thus, Johnston describes them as " lank, lean little shrimps at this stage ", who " receive a large share of cuffs and kicks, and not over much food ".[33] Speaking of these Central African children, Cureau adds : " More than once I have witnessed the pitiful sight of a mere baby cooking his solitary dinner in an old jam tin over a wretched fire ".[34]   And Hahn is moved to remark of the Bushman baby : " How such a poor worm can survive, how it withstands without any covering or washing all the ravages of the weather, and soon learns to chew tobacco—is almost incomprehensible—but the child muddles through and grows up ".[35]

At a very early age the child is put into the harness.   In the simplest tribes he is forced to struggle for his own self-main-tenance, as the material culture of tools and weapons does not provide for more for the idle.   Life is a struggle against great odds and it takes all of an individual's efforts to dig or grub nourishment from a sterile environment.   The child must therefore carry on for himself.   This is the base condition from which development has proceeded.   In these simpler societies, food-getting is a communal effort of the family or tribe in which the children also join early to add to the yield of the entire group, and thus help to support themselves. Nevertheless, even under these primitive conditions the en-listment of the child's aid is dictated not simply by the struggle for existence of the folk, but by a desire to maintain a certain level, or standard of material welfare.   The child thus supple-ments and extends the parent's exertions with primitive tools and weapons in order to provide uninterruptedly the usual " standard " of life, however feeble and crude this may be. Intimately interwoven with this is a growing stress toward working out a superior yield and greater munificence of food, clothing and shelter with this early aid of the children.

As an example, MacCauley says that " just as soon as the Seminole baby has gained sufficient strength to toddle he learns that the more he can do for himself and the more he can contribute to the general domestic welfare the better he will get along in life.   No small amount of the labour in a Seminole household is done by children, even as young as

four years of age.   They can stir the soup while it is boiling ;
they can aid in kneading the dough for bread ; they can wash
the ' Koouti ' root, and even pound it ; they can watch and
replenish the fire ;   they contribute in this and many other
small ways to the necessary work of the home."[36]

The boys are apt to be inducted into the men's work at an
early age, and the girls take up the women's tasks.   This
division of labour according to sex is the only specialization
or division of labour of any consequence in the simpler culture-
groups.[37]   In Borneo, " the task of hulling rice falls exclusively to the women and girls ;   they begin it when they
are so small that they can barely lift the pestle, and once
started in proficiency, the task becomes an element of their
life, and their winnowing-baskets are hung as symbols of
industry on their graves."   The boy has his work, as " he
accompanies the men in their excursions on the river and
in the jungle, and is taught to make himself useful on these
occasions and also on the padi farm, where he helps in scaring
pests and in other jobs ".[38]   Likewise among the Yukaghir in
Siberia, " from the age of eight to ten years the children begin
to help in the household—the girls in sewing and the preparation of food, the boys in fishing and bird-hunting around the
house ".[39]   In Central Africa, " children enter early upon the
duties of life.   Little girls soon begin to assist their mothers
in preparing food and in garden work.   The little boys mind
the goats or fowls or scare away the baboons from the crops,
and when they are seven or eight years old commence to
follow their fathers on short journeys."[40]

The child's lot is not an enviable one.   Childhood is grim
and earnest among these folk of the simpler culture.   The
Masai boy works exceedingly hard, " and in addition to his
regular tasks of tending the cattle, milking the goats, cleaning
the cooking utensils and fetching the water, much else is
imposed on him.   He is the universal scapegoat and everyone

is entitled to chastise him."[41]   Among the Mossi, the boys
are sent out before the sun rises and the dew has dried, " to
gather the fresh ants and other small animal-life the young of
which are greatly prized."   The girl carries pots on her head
when she is just beginning to walk, and as she grows the pots
increase in size and weight.[42]   Similarly, quite tiny girls
among the Kikuyu, " may be seen trotting along by their
elders carrying their own proportionate burdens.   A girl of
about thirteen came into the camp one day at eleven o'clock,
bearing a load of bananas weighing thirty pounds which she had
carried some fourteen miles since daybreak."[43]   The Chukchee
children also toil exceedingly, as " a young girl will work for
a whole day on skins, then watch the herd all night long, and
in the morning return home and busy herself till evening,
without any visible strain upon her strength . . .   It was
strange to see these young children wandering in the bush
without any protection or shelter . . . "[44]   " It is quite
usual ", we are told of the Yucatan Mayas, " to see a little
Indian girl of three trot daily to the woods with her parents
to help cultivate the fields ; very often her excursions extend
to neighbouring villages and she seems to make those trips
of four and even six leagues with the greatest ease, on foot ;
and after she has reached five or six years, she even carries
her little bundle on her back."[45]

We can therefore appreciate the amusing portrait of the
infant inhabitant of New Guinea drawn by the famous traveller and ethnographer, Miklucho-Maclay.   He describes a
small boy of about four years of age who makes himself a
small fire with most earnest mien, fetches wood, washes the
dishes clean, and helps his father skin fruit.   Then he suddenly
runs to his preoccupied mother and despite her work, finishes
an interrupted meal.[46]

A common employment for these young children is the
toting about of the still younger children on their backs.   The

latter are often but few years their junior. Thus, among the
Hopi Indians, "it is a common sight to see children only
six or seven years of age carrying babies one or two years
old."[47]

The child is thus thrust into the business of life at an early
age. The ability to take a hand in the incessant struggle for
existence and the usual degree of well-being comes very early,
as the arts of life have not yet been greatly developed. The
infant is hardly weaned, therefore, before he takes on his
proportionate burdens without the necessity of an extended
course of instruction. Childhood that has its carefree, joyous
associations is the product of a more complex and developed
culture. Such a period in these simpler societies is extremely
foreshortened. A maturity and sophisticated worldliness is
developed in the child, rather, while the mother's milk is
barely dry on his lips. Thrown on his own resources at an
early period the child discovers reality almost before he is
even permitted to play.

The Ainu of Japan, a people extremely undeveloped in
culture, consider the child who has reached one and a half
years of age and is unable to provide for himself as "of no
good as an Ainu".[48] It has been remarked also that the
African child at 6 or 7 years of age is already mature and
knows almost all there is to be known. He never possesses
the slightest characteristics of naiveté or childishness, as we
have come to know these traits.[49] The "childish" trait is the
note of the unlearned, so that where there is little to be learned
there is little room for the appearance of naiveté, which is
thus simply a relative term.

In New Guinea, accordingly, the child is mature at six
years of age. We learn that "it is curious to notice the very
old look that many of the boys and girls have, especially
the latter ; it requires a glance at the bosom to discover
whether they are young or not."[50] In the Solomon Islands,

bright-looking lads of eight or nine years of age stand smoking
their pipes gravely ; far-removed in Chile, the Araucanian lad
is early addicted to drunkenness to the evident pride and
satisfaction of his father. In West Africa, boys of eight or
nine already put into practice the suggestions included in the
" immoral " songs of their seniors.[51]

To indicate the completeness of this early maturity, allusion
may be made to the accounts given of the youngsters that
leave the elders and parents to shift for themselves. On the
Niger River, Desplagnes reports to have seen children of
six to eight years leave their parent's home, build themselves
huts, hunt and fish independently, and even practise a crude
form of cult. Among the Orang Kubu of Sumatra, boys
and girls may sever the connection with their parents, run off
into the bush, live their own lives and often contract permanent alliances among themselves.[52] Practically, a new
society is formed. The children can do this as they have
willy-nilly acquired in the few years of their childhood all
that is necessary for an independent existence with the material
equipment and ways of the folk-life.

Observers have frequently noted the extreme precocity
of mental development among the children of these primitive
peoples. The faculties seem to ripen prematurely as compared with those of the children of historical and literate
peoples. This is probably caused by the exigencies of the
life that surrounds the primitive child. The bareness and
meagreness of the culture, as we have seen, forces the youngster to bestir himself immediately for self-support. Self-
reliance, rather than reliance upon the social heritage and
accumulated surplus means, sharpens the senses and pro-
vokes the mental faculties. There is also evident a marked
tendency to learn and grasp things that are newly presented.
The capacity to learn seems to be more highly accentuated
than in the modern child. The potentialities for mental

improvement and advancement, we are told, are as great as those of the modern child. Thus, " in New Zealand it has been found that Maori children, when they can be induced to work, are quite equal to their white schoolfellows. Fijian boys educated in Sydney have been proved to be equal to the average ; Tongan boys who have never left their island write shorthand and solve problems in higher mathematics. Of the Bantu youth, it has been said also that " in mission schools children of early age are found to keep pace with those of white parents. In some respects, indeed they are the higher of the two . . ." The Australian children " learn reading, writing and arithmetic more easily than white children ".[53] It does not appear, therefore, than an essentially different type of mentality is necessary to comprehend a developed culture with its language, ways, customs and societal processes. A body of culture is a veneer which must be acquired anew and must be transmitted artificially to each new generation.

The perspicacity of the primitive child comes to a dead halt, however, about puberty. On this a unanimity of opinion also exists. The declaration is made of the Africans that " after the native reaches the age of twelve or fifteen his faculties, which are at first fairly quick, grow blunted and dull, his understanding becomes sluggish, he withdraws into himself, the childishness of his primitive nature crystallizes, and henceforth he will never exceed the height to which the swift progress of his early days has carried him ".[54] Torday believes therefore that " the highest period of the intellectual life of the negro is between the ages of ten and twelve . . ."[55] Likewise, the nimbleness of intellect so often remarked in the young Audaman Islander does not appear to be long maintained.[56]

Many reasons have been assigned to explain this " mental ossification " and decay of the native child at puberty. The physical exhaustion consequent upon excessive lubricity is offered by Maugham as an explanation of this lethargy of mind.   Torday contends that " the highest period of intellectual life of the negro is between the ages of ten and twelve ; after that age he falls into a slough of sensuality and his powers fall off . . ."   In addition to sexual excess, is often mentioned continual intoxication.[57]   In speaking of the Baholoholo of Central Africa, Schmidt offers a summary of the problem : " Undoubtedly extracted from his milieu, he would become an intellectual machine of the first order, a factor of great progress.   Unfortunately, abuse of the pipe, intoxicating drinks, sexual indulgence and the fear of sorcerers rapidly stifle all his nascent talents.   At twenty years he is nothing but an ignorant savage whose promise has been forever destroyed . . ."[58]   All this excessive over-indulgence is apparently, therefore, an aspect of the culture of the folk so that it is well to say that the falling-off in mental development is caused by the limited powers and extent of the folkways and the mores of the group.

The development of the individual is bound up securely with the give-and-take of his social contacts.   The child of any culture, however well elaborated this may be, is born an utter stranger to these ways, customs, institutions and beliefs of the folk.   There is no reason to suppose that a more marked disposition toward the approved conduct in life is the endowment of the modern child than it is of the child of the simpler society.   Children of all races start on a practical plane of equality, biologically.   Culture, like clothing itself, must be fastened upon the child making for an early conformity. Social pressure inevitably tends slowly to attach to the child those marks as in the system of naming, mutilations, reception to the folk and its attendant spirits, which make him typical and recognizable as a member of the tribe.   In this way the cohesion of the folk is reaffirmed by conferring upon its new arrivals the various insignia of membership in it.

Until the child has assumed these preliminary marks and forms of group-fellowship, he is hardly considered human. Without the benefit of the ways and mores of his people, he is an " infant ". Infancy, in the social sense, is the period in which the child waits upon his society to be slowly drawn within its portals. During these years each child relearns afresh the technique of the ways of self-maintenance and grasps unwittingly the system of sentiments which make for the preservation of the coherence of folk-lore. These years are fewer in the societies of simpler culture as there is less to be learned. As society progresses, infancy is prolonged and the process of socialization becomes necessarily more systematized, more tortuous and more specialized. At the same time a larger and larger part of the efforts of the group —a larger number of persons and a more extensive material equipment—is reserved for this process.

We have mentioned also the observable stages by which the child attains worth and a semblance of maturity in the cultural sense. Growth is punctured by definitive ceremonial observances as the child first assumes clothing, takes up hunting, begins to speak intelligibly, and the like. Without a written language, notice of these significant steps can be brought to consciousness and retained in the memory of the tribesfellows by the most direct methods of bombarding and striking the senses through feasts, bodily-disfiguration and ceremonies. It is not long, however, before the child is independently bestirring himself by the side of the physically adult, he is socially mature, and has acquired the culture of the group ; for the child in its development generally recapitulates the culture-history of its folk. In the more developed societies, by virtue of cultural aids alone, for example an elaborate language-apparatus, this recapitulation may be appreciably telescoped and many steps of culture-history omitted. Where this is not extensive, however, as among the peoples here considered, it is not long before the infantile dependency is dropped, a carefree childhood left behind and the child has become the man. At the same time, the mental development follows the same path. The repressive weight of a harsh struggle for food and shelter with the aid of a thin culture-stratum confines the individual early to a stagnated monotony of interests and activity.

To enable a society to maintain its continuity it is necessary above all that the body of ways and sentiments tested by experience should be transmitted unimpaired to its individual members. In each individual there must be built up in some way, a way characteristic of the folk and its culture-history, a body of motives and sentiments and a definite mental attitude. In the study of the " education " of the child which we are now to examine more closely, the intention is to trace the various ways in which the basis of social cohesion is developed in the individual, and the continuity of the characteristic folk-life promoted by inculcating the child with this social heritage.

CHAPTER VIII

PRIMITIVE EDUCATION: (1) IMITATION AND SUGGESTION

THE primary need of man is to adjust himself to the geographical environment which is the source of material sustenance and hence the point of departure for all human activity. With the growth of the group there arises pressure to adjust the contacts of men appropriately to the density of population, in the light of the efficiency of the arts of food-getting. The folkways are the devices and processes slowly elaborated to fill these two pressing needs, which early become interwoven. Each tool, weapon, process of hunting or fishing, article of dress, type of hut or shelter is thus a tentative, gradually elaborated and adjusted to man's needs. There arises also a body of beliefs which give sanction and support to these ways and deem them right, good, and even moral. Attitudes of mind and hardened ways of thought accompany these mores and " institutionalize " them about certain definite interests. Thus, polygamy may easily arise as a competent arrangement of the relations of the sexes in the light of the relative numbers of the sexes and the productivity of the arts. Beliefs as to the validity and righteousness of this arrangement constitute a group of mores which after long habituation and custom crystallize this comparatively durable relation of the sexes into an institution.

The folkways are the objectified ideas of individuals. They represent the struggles of the individual to procure sustenance for himself with the aid of the natural forces surrounding him, and the attempt to create a condition of peace with his tribesfellows in order to pursue the struggle more effectively. These unit ways of life are amalgamated and conjoined, however, by purely social forces, to constitute a variegated web or mosaic which is the culture of the folk. The mores bring consistency and unity and construct institutions of these folkways and evolve ethos or folk-feeling. Then it is impossible to distinguish the individual contributions to the culture and the whole web persists in as concrete and undeniable a form as the natural environment itself. Essentially, the culture exists only in the complex of the individual's behaviour if it is the culture of a living people. The less tangible, immaterial forces residing in social contacts, however, aid in welding the mass of folkways into an incorporated whole.

The child is in this respect heir to a culture which has been wrought by the efforts of countless individuals that have preceded him, fused into a type of organic consistency. This is as real an inheritance as the aspects and elements of the geographical environment itself. It is necessary for the child to acquaint himself with this heritage. To accomplish this there is no need to recapitulate the trials and struggles of the evolution of the folk's culture-history *in toto*. The set-backs and failures are omitted, and the child is granted the net results of this long history of trial and error in the effort of his forbears to accommodate their lives to the environment of nature and of other men. Each generation is indeed a stranger to its culture, but this crystallization of the culture-history of the folk handed down soon elevates it into a social setting from which to start the life-activity of a new day.

Much of this heritage sinks into the child unwitnessed and unobserved. The folk-ways provide an immediate environment for the child which infiltrates during the years of his greatest plasticity. The tools and weapons, dress, speech, and the more tangible elements of the material culture are brought to the child through the agency of his own senses and inborn appetitive interests. A major part of the child's education into its social milieu in the simpler society consists in this unpremeditated absorption of the life-activities of the folk through mere suggestion and imitation.

There is little in the material equipment of these peoples which the child cannot acquire through imitation. He needs only to heed the testimony of his senses, to drink in all that is to be seen and heard, to be casually transformed into the typical Bushman, or Fuegian, or Veddah. The tools are simple and the processes of food-getting direct. As the hunting and agriculture stages are reached, however, tools become developed and costly, training becomes needful and imitation does not alone suffice. Otherwise, most of the definitive units of the culture are apprehended in a haphazard, uncontrolled manner, and one can no more visualize this aspect of the socialization of the child than one can catch the growth of a plant. In both instances portions of the given environment are transmuted into the individual life unconsciously. The actual process of the transformation can only be conjectured or divined after the child has been already "affected" with its folk-heritage. The results, however, are apparent to the most superficial observer. The Bushman child undoubtedly differs from the Sioux child, without our being able always to trace the process of this marked differentiation.

There are few traces of an ordered, purposeful "education" among the people of simpler culture. We are told that among the Australian blacks, the Malays, the Polynesians, and Melanesians there is rarely a form of systematic instruction; almost everything is learned from the copy-book of nature.[1] Among the lowly Ainu aborigines of Japan, we are told, "children were never troubled by schools or schoolmaster. The mountains, the rivers and the sea were their schoolhouses; necessity was their instructor; inclination and the

weather were the only forces which made them work ".²
Nothing caused the California Indians less trouble and care
than the education of their children, " which ceases as soon
as they are capable of making a living for themselves—that
is, to catch mice and kill snakes. If the young Californians
have once acquired sufficient skill and strength to follow
these pursuits, it is all the same to them whether they have
parents or not. Nothing is done by them in the way of ad-
monition or instruction . . ."³ Likewise in South America,
in the Orinoco region, there is no education of the children
by their parents because they have nothing to teach them ;
the young grow as their parents did before them, like the
young kids jumping and springing about in the mountains.⁴
The children receive little enlightenment from the parents
when they are occasionally prompted to question the life
they find about them. For instance, the Kaffir children
" grow very puzzled when they see the moon in the daytime
and run to ask their parents why it is visible. The only
reply they receive is that the moon is in the sky because it
is its duty to be there. This explanation is final and
satisfying . . .", for they all say in resigned fashion, " What
is the use of puzzling about such things ? The trees will grow
as well without my troubling about the way they grow."⁵
Or again, " if the children say to their parents, ' How is it
that you say the spirits eat the meat ? We notice that there is
always as much left after the spirits have eaten it as there was
before, yet you say the spirits eat the meat '. The old men
then tell them to hold their tongues ; they laugh and say,
' O, the spirits drink the blood, or drink the odour ; this is
all they care for '. Or else they will say, ' The spirits licked
the meat '."⁶ We are here confronted with the significant
fact that the child receives no more directed instruction in
the more intangible beliefs or mores of the folk. These have
become implicitly ingrained into the thought of the old but

are still highly strange, if not unbelievable, to the children.

In the main, the children are left to imbibe their education unguided and unguarded. Little attempt is actually made in the first years to improve the child's nature by precept enforced by discipline. He is left to secure his own experience, much as the chick learns to scratch and get its food unaided.[7] Thus, in Central Africa, " it has been remarked that what knowledge they have seems to come to these African children instinctively—for no one ever sees them taught, or chastised for not knowing ! "[8] The Mangbetu child learns to solve all the physical problems of life only through chance conversation with his comrades or elders. On the Gold Coast, " no sooner are the senses of the child awakened to the realities of life, than it becomes initiated into all the practical concerns . . . and as these are confined to the necessities, habits and customs of a very simple and primitive mode of life, its education is readily and almost intuitively acquired."[9] In Australia, New Zealand and Tasmania, the native child also learned *ex usu*. In Sumatra and Borneo, nature is again the teacher ; in Polynesia generally, the boy or girl soon learned in its first years those practices which served it well in daily life, and as their sum was not imposing, they soon reached the required degree of capability.[10] Among the Indians of Brazil, to choose another instance, the children were rarely guided or corrected. There was no thought of doing so, because it was not a matter of great import to the group in the early years how the child grew up.[11]

Nevertheless the child learns at an amazing rate to distinguish the features of his natural environment, an open book, which he reads sympathetically and fluently. Just as there is little evidence of early schooling and utter freedom to roam and delve, to the same degree is the child able to acquaint himself with the details of the tribal life. In unrestrained intercourse with environment, family and play-fellows, the child absorbs an understanding of the ways of nature and the folk at an age when the child of the developed cultures is just beginning to peer into the treasures of the accumulated stock of knowledge and experience. The stress is to be laid upon the informal "learning" rather than "teaching" in the simpler cultures. It is instructive even to our more tutored and didactically-harassed minds to realize the great effectiveness of this absorbing type of education.

In Madagascar, for example, the child's observations in the open fields supply a large fund of information in natural history. He learns the specific names and habits of the various species of plants and animals in the neighbourhood.[12] The African youth " study each animal in the herd, its appearance, habits and footmarks until they know their beasts as well as they know each other . . ." " Most lads of 14 or 15 knew the names of the innumerable fish in the rivers and creeks, their habits and the best mode of catching them. They also knew the names and habitat of most bush animals, either by experience or repute ; the names of the birds, insects, trees, plants, etc., were all well known to them and easily distinguishable."[13] The Eskimo children also " acquire an extended knowledge of the country by early accompanying their parents on hunting trips, and as they have to rely on memory alone, they must observe and carefully mark the surroundings from all views afforded."[14] In Ecuador, the Canelo youngster soon learns to understand the language of field and stream : " He also learns to fish and follow game ; and soon becomes an adept in woodcraft, recognizing at a glance the slightest trace of a track of a man or animal, the nature of the thicket before him and the trees above him . . . Besides this, he acquires the knowledge . . . of locality and direction, so difficult to understand, but which undoubtedly is acquired by almost unconscious observation . . ."[15]

The child learns in this rather undeliberate way the lore of field, forest and stream. This knowledge is highly desirable because it is to the nature of these precincts that his life is to be adjusted. This nature-lore is primarily an aid toward food-getting. The folk-ways of self-maintenance—that is of hunting and fishing, of cattle-herding, of tillage, etc.—where not extensively developed, are also often acquired merely by following the ways of the elders. For example, the boys in the Loango coast very early learn to fish and make palm wine unaided.[16] In California, "an Achomaivi mother seldom teaches her daughters any of the arts of barbaric housekeeping before their marriage. They learn them by imitation and experiment after they grow old enough to perceive the necessity thereof."[17] Among the Cheyenne Indians, "from earliest babyhood infants were familiar with horses and their motions and children two and three years of age often rode in front of or behind their mothers, clinging to them or to the horse's mane. They thus gained confidence, learned balance and became riders, just as they learned to walk—by practice."[18] Likewise the Patagonian youth was wont to climb upon old or quiet horses' backs at a very early age, and to swing the *bolas* used in hunting.[19] Explanations are considered superfluous for the Carib boy of Guiana in the making of plaitwork, bows and arrows. The Maya girl of Yucatan learns to cook, grind corn and shape the tortillas and other native dishes through observation of the mother.[20] The little Vedda girl soon learns to dig yams and the boys learn to hunt when about ten years old.

So thoroughly does the child grasp the folk-ways of self-maintenance in this manner that it becomes deeply ingrained and fosters an early conservatism. Thus, of certain East African children we are informed that they are very soon skilful at the bow and arrow. But when presented with fish-hooks, "they would, to please me, use them at the end of a reed pole, but no sooner was my back turned than they would resume their old practice of getting a fish by shooting it in the water or by using weirs."[22] The child has indeed early adopted its adjustments to the problems of food-getting, and these ways will persist for life.

The ways of man with man are also gleaned early and carelessly. Among the Boloki, on the Congo, the boy accompanies the father on trading journeys, and learns how to trade. While his father was bartering he would listen eagerly, and thus learn to praise his own goods, and disparage in depreciatory terms the articles which he desired to purchase, so as to lower their prices.[23] As the village-life is usually open, boys and girls also soon know about sexual intercourse, pregnancy, childbirth and all the functions of the body. Among the Papuans of New Guinea, there being no privacy, " they become inordinately precocious ; their elders, invariably speaking of a spade as a spade, familiarized the minds of the children, with topics perhaps edifying, but certainly not helpful to sexual purity."[24]

Other sentiments no less precocious are picked up naturally. Nevertheless these attitudes in a child strike an observer, trained more or less rigorously in a different code, as surprisingly outlandish and at times abhorrent. For example, an informant was astonished at the equanimity with which the children of Sarawak played about in the midst of a collection of smoked heads. " Wherever I asked if the sight of them was not sad, the answer I received was invariably ' No ! ' . . . On the contrary, they would be glad to see more of these spectres hanging up above their heads."[25] The daily exposure to this sight, schooled the sentiments of these children in a nonchalance toward smoked heads. Besides, as in Samoa, the heads of the vanquished as well as the headless bodies, " were afterwards given to the children for further insult, who were accustomed to drag them about the settlements in triumph, and then to spear, stone or mutilate them still further as they might choose."[26]   As this appeared quite usual to the child, he would learn his occupation early, and thenceforward the practice would have excited little comment or notice.   This is a folkway, and for this reason alone, it insensibly becomes " good " in the mind of the child and an integral part of his behaviour.

The traditions and mores that are of a more intangible and impalpable nature are learned to some degree in a similar way, that is, by listening to the discussions of the elders and thus slowly but inevitably learning the rudiments of tribal history.   The boy is not taught the cult of his people ; he watches his father, and as he grows does as he has seen him do.[27]   He listens at night to stories and tales told by the elders about the fire.   In this way he learns to know the hereditary enemies of the tribe and conceives a hatred for them that soon becomes instinctive and unreasoning.[28]   The children " hear the old warriors boasting of their war exploits and it may be said that the principle of war is instilled in them from the cradle . . . "[29]   Mingling in tribal and family councils, the children become " prematurely " familiar with public affairs and tribal law, also.[30]   Even the language is acquired in the same manner without benefit of teaching.   " It is a continual surprise ", we are told with regard to the Papuans, " how soon tiny children speak this difficult language correctly.   They make no grammatical errors in talking, in spite of a verb completely and most intricately conjugated.   A child never hears his language spoken incorrectly by his elders, and like these elders, is blissfully unconscious of the existence of such a thing as grammar ! "[31]

The dances and songs are also learned (as in the Gilbert Islands), by mere observation.   The little fellows will often be found essaying a step by standing behind a participant in a dance and trying to ape his movements.[32]   In fact, a whole body of esoteric knowledge is painlessly and heedlessly learned, for the children " watch the dances too and learn the songs ; they share the wailing over the dead, and listen to the incantations for the sick and the magic songs that hush the winds and stay the fury of the tempests. They learn to reverence their totems, to beat their lips and hoot when the new moon first appears, and not to point at a rainbow lest one of their arms should be cut off while they sleep."[33]   Thus is the precious folk-wisdom won.

The child is flooded with an array of beliefs and attitudes, conventionalized and objectified by the social forces of approval and conformity.   All this gradually hardens and sets the behaviour of the young into the usual channels of folk-thought and gives the child a character which persists for life. That this occurs in a most unpremeditated manner is well substantiated by Kidd, apropos of the Kafirs.   He believes that the child, for example, " hears a grown-up say that if a person should happen to eat two mice caught together in one trap he will have twins ; instinctively the child believes what a man says, for the child places unbounded faith in older people. If the child should know the case of a person (which corroborated this belief) . . . the belief would become immensely strengthened.   The cases where the theory broke down would be forgotten ; the cases where it came true would be remembered, and a certain air of probability which seemed to be inherent in the idea would become intensified."[34]

The head-snatching proclivities of the Samoans mentioned above have probably been bred in the child in a somewhat similar unwitting manner. The domineering attitude of the Polynesian toward the weak, particularly the women, arises in the very young almost imperceptibly.[35]   Thus, a definite " character " is produced in the child, a character which resolves itself into peculiarities of behaviour that are an indefinable heritage of its folk, breathed in as unconsciously as the air. These characteristics are plainly evident only to the outsider whose life has been passed in a different setting of ways and mores, of which even he becomes conscious only by contrast with the variant ways and attitudes in the lives of these other folk.

Some initiative on the part of the child is presumably necessary that it may become thus metamorphised slowly into a frame of mind acceptable to the group-life. The technical apparatus of food-getting, the dress, speech, ways of greeting, and the lesser minutiæ of folk-intercourse will come to the child only if he displays a receptive interest for these things. A large portion of the social heritage accrues to him as we have seen, " unconsciously " in the sense that there is little of an organized directive force instituted by the folk. Nevertheless little can be " learned " or even taught unless the natural interests of the child are evoked, or unless these can be focussed on the material to be administered to it. Likewise, among these more primitive folk the child learns by dint of its interests being voluntarily enlisted into imitation and mimicry of the folk-life about it. Particularly is this the case as the child reaches an early, independent maturity. The road is left open for a self-education. The child essays to hunt, fish, or fabricate simple tools in response to the impulse of play, which is a channelizing of his energies into the activity about him. We shall now inquire in some detail into this mimicry play-acting that is a prelude to the true life-duties of the individual. It is probably because of the efficacy of this method that an organized, definitive educational system is rarely to be observed among these people.[36]

The years of life in which the child toys with his culture are also the years in which he is least encumbered with prejudices imposed by the habitual, so that little choice is exercised in imitating the elders' ways. The entire culture that has a palpable expression is copied in this world of play. Even

the stranger's ways and tools are imitated because the child's
curiosity has not been sated and his interests deadened to
innovation.   He is like a sponge that sops up the social environment, all in all.   There is an amazing amount of mimicry
to be observed among these folk of simpler culture, because
the child's hands are not yet occupied in holding books or
spelling out words, his eyes see more because less is hidden, he
hears more because there is less whispering on the part of the
elders, and above all his mind is not yet distorted or intimi-
dated by the tabus of the later training and discipline that is
to befall him.   There is an immediacy and trustworthiness
about this form of play-education which modern educational
" methods " are seeking in vain to recapture.

It is of profit to examine illustrations of the imitative play-
life.   For instance, the African child imitates his elder's entire
outfit of weapons.   The saber is made of a sharpened piece
of a plant stem with a crude wooden hilt, the blade of palm-
leaves bent together.   Short lances are made of sharp, pointed
bits of wood.   In every detail the weapons are exact counter-
parts of the usual metal ones.[37]   In North Queensland,
Australia, " in those districts where shields are employed by
the adults, these may be imitated on a small scale, and often
with similar ornamentation, out of convenient pieces of bark,
etc."   At four or five years of age, the boy has a miniature
spear, " with which the little fellow fights his compeers, and
annoys his mother and the dogs."[38]   Among the Veddas of
Ceylon, the smaller boys possess bows and arrows and the
" bigger boys " of five years old have quite neat specimens
of bows.[39]   The Papuan boy of eight to twelve years has his
toy fish spear about two-thirds the size of the ordinary one.
In Borneo and in the Gilbert Islands, the boys construct their
own houses and toy canoes which are deployed in the lagoons
much after the manner of the real canoes.[40]   Among the
Chukchee of Siberia, " the children have various toys, most of

them small imitations of objects of every-day life, such as little boats, sledges, wooden or ivory dogs and reindeer with the proper harness, snowshoes, bows and arrows."[41]   The Eskimo children have their own clever model snow shovels of walrus ivory, deer lances of reindeer antlers, drums and boys' bows.[42]

The natural imitative skill of the primitive child knows no bounds. The Omaha children " made many of their playthings out of clay, and some of the boys and girls were very clever in modelling dishes, pipes, dolls, tents, etc.   The writer once came across a miniature clay coffin with a bit of glass set in, beneath which was a clay baby.   Some child had seen the funeral of a white person and had devised a new plaything."[43]   From this it is apparent that the child undiscriminately copies the features of its society faithfully, and were these Indian children to be exposed consistently to the advanced culture of the whites, this also would probably soon be painlessly and voluntarily absorbed.   As a matter of fact because this imitative instinct is so undisguised and free, it is most often the child that appreciates the soonest the superior qualities of the weapons of the " civilized " man, and uses them in miniature.   The adults are too hopelessly steeped in the old and habitual ways.

The Brazilian Indian children have their own model musical instruments in addition to the bows and arrows of a smaller size, both made of plant stems.[44]   The Indian boy of the Amazon region also has a shorter form of blowpipe made of reeds.[45]

The most amazing extent, however, to which this realism extends may be glimpsed from the report of Frič and Radin with respect to the dolls of the Bororó Indians.   These " are made of palm-leaf folded together a few times with detailed characteristics of the sexes . . . one even has an imitation of the monkey-tooth breast ornament, made of small pieces

of light wood and cotton . . . Sometimes they have a belt
of black cloth to signify the menstruation period . . . In
one example a covering of down is meant to signify that the
doll has just been born . . . ! "[46]

There is a note of earnestness and grimness about such
unabashed mimicry which connotes the fact that play of this
sort is hardly distinguishable from the actual work to which
we have already seen the child is directed at an early age.
This is prominently true with the peoples of very limited
culture or sterile environment or a degraded condition which
is evidenced by decreasing population. For example, the
miniature spear made of wood is used by the young Australian
for digging out small roots and the larvae of insects in addition to use in play and frolic.[47]   Likewise, in Brazil, the toys
are hardly different from the true tool. When canoeing,
the young Guato boy sits between his father, who stands in
front with his long oar, and his mother, who sits to the rear
steering. Meanwhile he uses his small imitation oar to ply
industriously in proportion to his strength.[48]   Again we are
struck by the imperceptible nature by which the child is
aggregated to its life-habitudes.

The elements of make-believe predominate in this mirror
of folk life constructed by the young. As such, there exists
a note of spontaneity and chance which often gives rise to
surprising touches of originality. Slight variations and even
improvements may arise as contributions of the child to its
material culture. We are informed of a Congo tribe, that
" there is nothing more extraordinary than to see a young
Muloloholo not only imitate all that his elders make—nets,
mats, swords, paddles, spades—but to bring to them no'able
improvements ; he constructs for example, to catch rats,
innumerable varieties of traps, evolves bizarre musical instruments, blow-guns and pistols of extreme ingenuity ;
baskets of new and artistic forms."[49]   There is a promise

held out in this type of " education " which can hardly be equalled by any of the pedagogical methods later devised and elaborated with more purposefulness. The freedom to play into familiarity with the culture instruments sets free the nascent abilities of the child, with whatever creative instincts may lie innate. At any rate, the excitation of interest is not deadened by the conscious attempt on the part of the child to learn the rigid artificial forms and methods of learning imposed on him which often abort his inherent inclinations.

Imitation leads the child into all recesses and aspects of the life about him. The entire round of folk-activities is mirrored. All the various habitudes of the folk whether in the domain of self-maintenance, sex relations or the simple expressions of vanity, stir the eager sensibilities of the child to reproduce them. Having once been copied, they unconsciously become ways of life. Thus among the For people of Central Africa, the children, instead of making mud pies, were accustomed to making miniature villages, copies of mountains, rough models of men and animals of clay with which they would be employed for hours together, day after day.[50] The Nandi children are also fond of building huts in the sand and collecting snails, pebbles and berries which they say are cattle, goats, and sheep.[51]

This flair for acute observation of things often became vexing to the stranger, as we are informed by Weeks, who relates that " Congo boys (and in a minor degree the girls also) were never wearied of watching us at work, following us about to see what we would do next and asking about our tools, etc. They would stand about our table while we were at our meals, and pass critical remarks on our manner of eating, slyly imitating the action of our jaws as we masticated our food or mimic our gestures as we conversed with one another."[52] The poses struck by their own elders are naturally also imitated:

the Papuan children, for example, like to be seen walking about with the men, to copy their swaggering walk and to sit smoking idly while the women work,[53] exactly as their fathers do.

This mimetic bent carries the child over into play which is carried on purposefully, as an end in itself. The labour and work of the adult becomes the material out of which are constructed the play and games of the child. In this aspect of play, lies its supreme educative value. The primitive child's school is its playground, and, as we shall attempt to demonstrate, his playground is everywhere; his games embrace the total outfit of customs, attitudes and mores of his folk. Left to themselves, the children make sport of life until they are initiated into the serious business of life. For this, their play serves as an adequate preparation and schooling. The following cases are intended to show this close correspondence between the work of the adult and the play of the child.

The children of the Cross River natives in West Africa busy themselves on the sand making imitation yam-fields, scooping up hillocks of sand, and then going from one to another pretending to plant a yam in each.[54] In South Africa, they build little houses where they dwell during the day. Girls break down soft stones between harder ones, after the fashion that women grind flour; the boys go about with miniature bows and arrows, playing at war and "stealing slaves."[55] In South America similarly, "the Indian child learns to live through play. When the mother fetches water in a jug with her little baby in her arms, the latter also carries a smaller but exactly similar jug. If the mother fills her water jug, the little tot does likewise. The little girl grows and the jug grows. She soon accompanies her mother on foot and carries, like her, her own jug on her head. If the mother spins, so does her child also on her own toy-spindle. This, while the boy plays with his trap in the village. He catches leaves and bits of clay with it."[56] The Cheyenne girl, likewise, imitated her parent in all things : " Even when only three or four years of age, she might be seen marching proudly along, bowed forward under the apparent weight of a backload of slender twigs, which she carried in exact imitation of her mother, who staggered under a heavy burden of stout sticks."[57]

The entire round of the daily life is played at. The Warega children first construct an entire model village of houses 40 to 50 centimetres in height, build small fires before them, catch fish and roast them. Suddenly one calls out : " It is night ! " and immediately they make a pretence of sleeping. Later one imitates the crowing of a cock. They all now awake and commence the day's work. The day usually ends with a combat or the burning of the village.[58] It is of value to ponder over this summary ending of the game as to whether it is inherent in the nature of man to pull down all his efforts at constructive living, or whether this destructive practice is still part of the faithful portraiture on the part of the children of the mores of the folk. At least the social sentiments are inculcated in this way and the needful uniformity induced as it is observed that the children in this play attempt to outdo each other. The inefficient are ridiculed unmercifuly.[59]

Among the Mailu-speaking peoples of New Guinea, temporary shelters are built by the girls of old cocoanut leaves, and under each " cooking " is practised with miniature clay pots. Then there is the " baby game ". " The baby (represented by a stone) was new born ; it was taken down to the sea-beach and washed, held over the fire to dry, put to the ' mother's ' breast and laid down on a leaf to sleep. I have seen them playing weddings, funerals and widows. As widows these little mites arrange their skirts so that they will trail on the ground at their feet. A favourite game is to copy the thief who steals the produce from someone else's garden. The thief gets no mercy. . . . Everything connected with community life is imitated and played at, from the game of running amok through pot-and-basket-making to the big ceremonial spirit feast, when small crabs, standing for pigs, are killed, put over the fire ' to burn the hair off ! ' and then cut up and distributed in proper fashion. . . ."[60]

All that is subtly characteristic in social relations is rather adventitiously reproduced by way of play, particularly with respect to family life.   For instance, the Pangwe girls pursue the boys (while playing " married life ") in the midst of a great tumult, scolding and upbraiding them for their laziness and waywardness.   Meanwhile the child, a doll, is dragged about but very carefully tended.[61]   The game of the Australian children is to the same effect.   The youngsters " will build an impromptu hut and sit contentedly in its shade ; suddenly a boy rushes forward to steal the gin (woman) over whose possession he and the husband now make-believe to have a fight."[63]   The sophistication wrought in the modern youth by the cinema is thus manifestly outdone in the play-acting of the youngster himself in the society of simpler culture !

The entire array of social distinctions are aped.   These features of the folk-like which are often highly artificial invade the consciousness of the child in this voluntary manner and so serve to set the attitude and school his behaviour.   Among the Kafir children, the little chief begins to assume his position very early in life.   He is given a small white shield, and in play no one would dare hit the boy with the white shield as it was considered a " very bad thing " to do.[64]   Similarly, in the Tonga Islands of Polynesia, this social division was early imposed, as the playmates of the king's son of 6 or 7 years of age were limited to the sons of inferior chiefs who accompanied the boy on excursions and imitated in every respect the habits of their parents.[65]   The distinction between the conduct of the sexes was faithfully observed, and the boy would not deign to play with a girl-doll until it was raised in status by becoming apparently a wife by purchase with clay cattle.[66]

In fact, among some of these people, the children form their own miniature folk-life or society, as in Liberia. This includes children of six to eleven years of age and is formed originally for collective work in busy seasons. Yet, we are told, " it is wonderful to witness the stormy debates of this little society and amusing to see them punishing each other for real or alleged offences by putting pepper in the eyes, beating ", all this ostensibly done in unsuspecting imitation of the elders.[67]

The language is among the constituents of culture now imbibed by the child through its own efforts and inculcated into him by a system of training. The child attains a lingo of his own and would develop speech of one sort or another but he is given as part of his social heritage a developed means of communication in the folk-life. This is one of the most influential and important products of societal evolution, without which indeed the process would be gravely hindered. It is instructive to study the manner in which the child learns the tribal tongue. The development of his speech parallels closely the probable evolution of the folk-language. Between the savage and the modern child, for example, there is a point of resemblance in the evident feeling for the pure sound of the word and less for its meaning. There is also an exactness of pronunciation which is indicative of the primitive onomato-poetic tendency.[68] The words for father and mother, for example, among the first vocables uttered by the child, betoken respectively the most immediate source of sustenance and a relatively more remote provider. The first few articu-lations of this nature show a surprising similarity throughout the dispersed primitive peoples and also the " baby-talk " of the modern cultures. Thus, to choose an example, in the Suahali of East Africa, " *Mama*, for ' mother ' and *titi* for a

'nipple' reminds us of the use of these words in English ;
ku lala, 'to go to sleep', and *ku kwenda tata*, 'to toddle',
also agree with English usage."[69]

These first utterances reflect in a wholly impressionistic
manner not merely the pleasurable sources of food but also
come to be attached to many things as though they had been
shaken in a bag and pulled out at random to express the notion
that came first, doll or uncle, nurse or grandmother.[70]   Thus
these self-same syllables come to mean different things as the
child is born into different culture.   In the Suaheli, the primitive sounds have different meanings and are suggestive of
differences in custom.   " Thus *dada* means ' a sister ' which
is an indication of the importance of the elder girl in the
nursery.   *Bibi* for ' grandmother ' reminds us that, owing
to early marriages and to women sharing in the hard labours
of the field, grandparents play a more active part in the care of
children. . . ."[71]   It is from the mother that the child
assimilates unknowingly most of his speech, however.   The
influence of the women in fixing the language is thus not to be
overlooked.[72]   In general, the child acquires its language
untaught, " lisping his words and confusing the grammatical
distinctions at first ; but with the precocity incident to a wild,
free life, he usually acquires correct expression at an earlier
age than the average white child."[73]

One of the chief requisites that the mores, as adjustments
to life in society, perform is, as already observed, an accommodation to the unseen forces that sway the destiny of the folk.
This is ascribed to the ghosts or spirits of an imaginary environment.   There arises a complicated technique of dealing
with these forces in order to escape their evil workings, to
placate them or to manœuvre their potent aid for one's prosperity.   These cult practices are also imitated by the children
in the spirit of play.   Among the Pangwe, thus, the children
perform an imitation ancestor-worship, at which they dance

and supplicate an improvised bark-vessel for prosperity, good food, success in the hunt for lizards and perhaps also obedience on the part of their make-believe wives.[74] The Igorot in the Philippines possess a child's game, called *fug-fug-to*, which is an imitation of the ceremonial of the men after each annual rice harvest.[75] Accordingly, some intimation can be drawn of the manner in which much of the child's religious behaviour is drawn into the make-up of the mature individual.

The primitive man has at times recognized the educative value of play and so has encouraged games for his children as a preparation for the latter's independence. The Tschi natives of West Africa have a proverb to the effect that "no one teaches the smith's son his trade ; when he is ready to work God shows him how ", and the explanation of this obtained from the natives indicates a clear realization of the efficacy of imitation : "God has implanted in children the faculty of observing and imitating, and when the son does what he has seen his father do so often, it is as if he knew it himself. It is indeed, God who teaches him ! "[76] Some of the American Indians also utilized play for the purpose of instilling the more intangible parts of the culture, as the cult.

Thus, dolls were made for the little Indian girls during the spring ceremonies. These were so adorned that the child would unconsciously become familiar with the complicated and symbolic masks, ornaments and garments worn during tribal and religious ceremonies by copying these figurines which were representatives of mythical personages.[77] In New Guinea, likewise, the parents encourage the children to play with toy nets, fish spears and toy canoes as a most fit preparation for the life of sailors and fishermen.[78]

Where conditions of life are usually desperate or where the population is thinning out rapidly, this sort of play is hardly to be separated from the work to which the child is early assigned. Among the Veddas of Ceylon, for example, the

game of "honey-getting" from the combs of the rock-bee
is encouraged on the part of the elders in recognition of the
fact that it is the swiftest method of initiation of the child
into the necessary state of self-provision.   The emergence of
play in the stricter sense is possible only as life-conditions are
not too exacting.   Such a condition permits of a preliminary
period, however brief, in which, as illustrated, the child is
enabled to devote his energies and attach his spontaneous
interests to playing with aspects of his cultural heritage.
This very toying will serve as a partial training in the mode of
self-provision for life.

The folkways and mores also retain, as play, occupations
and devices that formerly were conspicuous parts of the culture
of the people.   Though the serious practice has long been
superseded by superior methods or fitter adjustments to life-
conditions, the mimicry that lies in the games may be con-
served.   In this manner, the game of the child survives as a
token of the cultural past.   Among these primitive folk the
culture is transmitted as a whole usually without benefit of
system or selection so that traces of the antiquated and outworn may often persist.[79]   However, these survivals lack
vigour and completeness and atrophy as the living compulsion
for their use is slowly obliterated and each generation receives
a more tattered, fore-shortened trace of the ancient usage.
Thus, among many of the American Indians, although bows
and arrows had been discarded for guns long since, the boys
still used blunt-pointed arrows for killing small game.[80]   In the
Patagonian regions of South America, the children still play
with the *boleadora*, or sling, which is an evident survival from
the days when these tribes, the Chorotis and Ashluslays, used
them as weapons on the pampas or plains, for which alone they
are suited.[81]   In Java, likewise, many of the games played by
the children show unmistakable signs of antiquity, pages out
of the culture-history of the folk.[82]   Many of the games played

by children of to-day in the nursery were at one time in their expanded forms the serious occupations of former culture-epochs.

The springs of cultural continuity in the simpler societies rest upon the untrammeled focussing of the child's energies and instincts upon the ways of the elders. Imitation is the most spontaneous reaction of the child to the suggestions which the societal heritage thrusts upon him in mutltifarious ways. As soon as this mimicry is to a certain degree formularized and practised more or less consciously by the children as an end in itself, it becomes play and creates " games ", which, by their rules and methods, also imitate in a way the more serious concerns of the individual's life in the group. Play cannot be definitely isolated to a particular period in the individual's life. Play and work often alternate among these people even throughout the more mature years. Yet, with extended culture-development, the play-period becomes restricted to the childhood years, into the nursery, where are deposited the remains of outworn occupations and behaviour no longer of consequence to the life of the day. In the primitive culture, however, play is the most adequate introduction to life, and imitation the indispensable medium by which that culture is made continuous, preserved, and may become the basis of further accumulation and increase.

The things to be learned, however, soon become diverse, complicated and remote so that imitation cannot be relied upon to adapt the child satisfactorily to his acquired social heritage. The natural interests of the child, which are acquisitive, appetitive and curious, cannot necessarily comprehend the more abstract and evolved aspects of culture such as the body of religious beliefs, folklore, language and traditions. Some method of training must be instituted gradually to bring the child into line. The " curriculum " is hardly to the child's taste, hence there must also arise, an enforcing or disciplining system to force this later, heavier, artificial and typically societal mass of the folkways and mores upon the child. Always bearing in mind the original use and power of the purely imitative faculties as the ground-work of education of the child, we now turn to examine the elements of the more formal pedagogy of the simpler societies.

CHAPTER IX

PRIMITIVE EDUCATION: (2) TRAINING OF THE CHILD

IT is not to be supposed that the child's education is wholly unreflective, or casually imitative in primitive culture. There are, indeed, insistent motives which direct the purposive attentions of the elders of the group to the children in order to prepare them for their active participation in the folk-life. For one thing, the early economic maturity of the child commands in its wake an early social adult-hood or independence. The elders are soon made aware of the impending rise of a younger generation ready to supplant them, so that the training, though consciously administered, is not a systematic or regularized schooling. By this primitive type of training it is proposed to fit the child definitely into its folk-life by a repressive, dominating subjection. The elders attempt to substitute a psychological rule to compensate for their waning physical prowess. This aim is dimly apprehended, but the social force working towards this conformity becomes definitely marked as the primitive child approaches maturity. The voluntary infiltration and adaptation of the folk-culture to the child which we have already observed confers upon him an economic maturity which soon tends to dispute the social preponderance of the elders. Therefore, some attempt, fitful and sporadic though it may be, is instituted to train the child— that is, to transmit purposefully the folkways and the mores so that the child shall be invested with the proper emotional disposition to accompany his economic maturity.

A need for training the child is also felt as the advancing

culture evolves ways too elaborate or remote from the natural interests of the child. The social heritage of this type can be transmitted in the main, only through a definite inculcation on the part of the elders. The child cannot simply idle into an acquaintance with the language, folklore, cult and prosperity-ways of the folk. These cultivated flowers are wholly artificial to the child with his unrepressed physical urges. The path labouriously worked out by centuries of folk-experience is ever strange to the child and hence he must be jostled or cajoled gradually into position. Otherwise the culture would certainly perish, for in the society devoid of an established system of writing, the outfit of folk-heritage can live nowhere but in the mind and behaviour of the younger generation.

The impulse towards imparting the fruits of the social life is heightened considerably as soon as a folk comes into contact with other peoples. An appreciation and realization of the outstanding characteristics of the folkways is then rendered live. The desire to equip the child with the usual body of ways and precepts arises on the part of the elders to preserve this folk-uniqueness. Also, this training serves to discipline the child for the avowed purpose of preserving his heritage against assault and destruction by other folk. The ethnocentric force of exaltation and laudation of one's ways leads probably to an emphatic desire to produce an early conformity in the child. It would be sufficient, then, to allow the child to play into his social environment, and often little thought is given to an expressive training in this direction until contact with other folk produces a sudden realization of the necessity of bulwarking the precious heritage by straitening the minds and whipping the bodies of the young into a respectful and efficient conformity.

The primitive curriculum, if such it may be called, includes two general groups, vocational and moral, in content. The training of the child for hunting, fishing and the like is rarely consciously adopted on the part of the parents and the folk. As we have seen much of this is voluntarily and gradually acquired by the child himself. It is not long, however, before even these ways of self-maintenance become elaborated to the degree that some actual instruction is needed for the handling of the weapons and tools. To achieve an earlier independence for the child and an efficiency in the employment of tools some type of training is obviously necessary. Along with this social compulsion which is itself an outgrowth of cultural evolution, it is always useful, however, to recall the characteristic " human " note. This is the evident desire of the parent to mould the child after his own model—a desire which cuts across all types of societies—but which aids to accentuate the drive toward equipping the child in conformity with the folkways.

The Australian father takes advantage of every opportunity to instruct his son upon the short excursions which they take together. " For instance, if they arrive at a place concerning which they have any tradition, it is told if the child is old enough to understand it. Or he shows him how to procure this or that animal, or other articles of food in the easiest way." Small arms are also prepared for the son, and the father demonstrates their use. The result is that the father becomes proud of his apt pupil, his chief delight being to see his boy " balance himself with his feet astride and throw his spear at his sister's back, to observe him tomahawk the sleeping dogs, maltreat birds . . . and insects . . . bite his mother, hear him lisp foul words . . ." etc.[1] It is the natural, universal pride of the father in the deportment of the offspring that provides the informal grounds for the child's training. And it is also well to observe that the training is definitely based upon, and interwoven with, the imitative function of play just passed in review.[2]

Harsh conditions of life are instrumental in forcing the parent to instruct the child instead of waiting upon the latter's own capacities to develop through imitative play. The Australian child is generally trained to follow the tracks of animals, and to recognize by the faintest indications the near presence of birds and reptiles. The girls are instructed in the art of weaving cord and making baskets. Above all, they are obliged to be observant of small things which in their mode of life have a true significance and value. Among the Ainu of Japan, it was necessary to teach the boys to fish and hunt ; to make bows, arrows and traps ; to set spring-boys in the trail of animals ; to decoy deer, and to judge the weather by the skies.[4] The Bushman father shows his child at a very early age the sources of his food and the methods of securing it.[5] The boys thereupon practice archery and throwing the knobkerrie at small game so that they are the sooner independent in striking out for themselves—which is imperative in a rather sterile environment and a dwindling population.

An elementary if rude form of training is necessary as the arts of life advance beyond their most rudimentary stages. Such things as trading, tanning of hides, pottery, etc., require some form of instruction. There is a need to hurry on the child to acquire these and other more elaborated methods necessary to food-getting and self-support. The elders are not content to rely upon the child's own unguided efforts in these fields. The Congo boy learns canoeing, to be sure, with the aid of a toy-paddle which the father gives him. Yet he is taught how to back-water, to steer and to move his oar in unison with others. Nor was this all, for there were over fifty words and phrases dealing with canoeing which he had to learn by means of the instruction of his elders. Other parts of the child's " curriculum " included a training in, " not the movements of the clock's hands, but the crowing of the cocks, the notes of the *nkuku-npembe* (name of the bird), and the movements of the sun ".[6] Among the Mattaol of California, also, the squaws taught the boundaries of the tribes to their children in sing-song chants. Over and over, again and again, they rehearse all these boulders, conspicuous trees, springs, etc. So faithful is this instruction that later when the children are taken the rounds they generally recognize the objects from their mother's descriptions.[7] Such knowledge would not be ordinarily apparent to the child. It is needful to impart it as tribes come into contact with each other. This was markedly the case among the American Indians who came in constant contact with each other.[8] In other primitive cultures, contacts were not so prominent, due to the limiting features of the environments, impenetrable jungles, water wastes, mountains and the like.

The Bakongo father teaches his boy to set traps for farm rats, wild animals and birds, and he also teaches him to buy and sell on the markets, to trade, and what is certainly foreign to him, to sew his own clothes and to be able to sew his wife's (or wives') clothes as well.[9] The Maya Indians in Yucatan teach their young how to extract salt, and fish.[10] In the Tonga Islands, the ornamental accomplishments of the girls must be acquired through a training supervised by the women. Such occupations include the plaiting of fanciful devices in flowers, etc.[11] The Apache girl was taught by her grandmother, among other things, to make baskets with yucca leaves. The first lessons began at the age of six. The boys were taught to count.[12] A Blackfoot mother had a deal of trouble in initiating her daughter into the mysteries of tanning of hides and their conversion into clothing and shelter, the making of lodges and travois, and in the knowledge of herbs and wild vegetables used for eating and healing.[13] The Warrau in Guiana, even have their music-teacher who teaches the young to play on a sort of oboe—a sufficiently esoteric accomplishment to require instruction.[14]

A definite compulsion towards a training of the child is offered by the menace, or the avowed practice of war by the tribe. Organization, discipline and a regularized training are here necessary to produce the required regimentation of body and mind. It is again, the contact, in this case, a war-like one, of groups which necessitates a purposive training of the young child in defence of the tribe and its mores. Among the Mandan Indians, sham-fights and sham-scalpings were a material part of the boys' education. Experienced warriors led bands of boys between the ages of seven and fifteen out on the prairie at sunrise. Naked, attired only with bows and harmless grass arrows, wooden knives and imitation scalps of grass tufts, the boys were led through the manœuvres of Indian warfare—feints, retreats, attacks followed by a general fight.[15] The Apache boy was taught by his father and grandmother to count, to run, to jump into cold water, to race, and all necessary to constitute him a strong, fearless warrior.[16] Eastman recalls his training for war. His teacher used to emit sudden war-whoops over his sleeping form. Thereupon it was necessary to " leap up with perfect presence of mind, always ready to grasp a weapon of some sort and to give a shrill whoop in reply."[17]   In Borneo, likewise, the boys are initiated by " striking a blow at a freshly taken head, or if need be, at an old one . . . The boy besides watching these martial displays, is instructed in the arts of striking, parrying and shielding by older men, who strike at him with a stick but arrest the blow before it goes home."[18]   Military training, above all, will not permit of the haphazard irregu-larity of the voluntary method of learning by means of imita-tion and play.   The elders are definitely forced into a training of the young by the perils and hopes involved in strife with other folk with their different ways of life.

Some of the rules of social intercourse are also described to the children, particularly in case these have become unusually adorned with ceremony and symbolism as to have become incomprehensible. This posits an older culture, perhaps, which has evolved an elaborated, traditional ceremonial. For example, in the D'Entrecasteaux Islands, the elders early initiate the boys into the " deeper mysteries of sex. The men will go away for a few days to fish or purchase betel-nuts or merely to visit round amongst their friends ; and the youths go with them. At night-time round the fire they teach the lads the proper roots and leaves to rub and mix with tobacco or betel-nut, and the magic chants that must be sung over them, so that when they share them with their sweethearts they may win their love forever."[19] In this atmosphere, a practical skill is developed along with an attendant form of ceremonial magic to win success in affairs of the heart. This type of procedure could hardly be learned in any other way than by demonstrative instruction.

A more complete demonstration and instruction in the mores awaits the initiation ceremonies. In a restricted, degenerating culture, however, or in the observable remnants of it, one may discern a definite, early training in the characteristic mores. Thus, in Easter Island, the girls were taught the rules of conduct in sex-intercourse as early as their fifth year by the old women.[20] Perhaps the initiation-ceremony had in this instance degenerated and broken asunder and the knowledge of the mores purveyed in this way piecemeal. Or the necessity of arranging the sexual contacts had become more insistent with a declining population in order to increase its numbers as fast as possible. Even among the Ainu this is quite apparent, but in addition it may have been the pressure of foreign contacts that forced the development. The offerings and prayers to be used on different occasions were taught to the children very early in life.[21]

Occasionally, in their leisure time the fathers would drop hints as to the meaning and nature of the more general aspects of the folkways and mores. This was, however, spasmodic and irregular in its nature unless some such compulsion as already outlined existed to force this " moral " training to the fore. Otherwise, leisure time was extremely limited or employed for more inconsequential pursuits. It is natural to expect, however, that now and then the consciousness of the folk-life or the selfish pride in offspring would incite the fathers to lecture their children. In this respect at least, culture-history reveals merely the content of these remonstrances. For example, Howitt reports that the old men among the natives of South-East Australia were wont to instruct the young in the ways of the tribe, " impressing on them modesty of behaviour and propriety of conduct, as they understood it, and pointing out to them the heinousness of incest."[22]   The Pima Indian father also lectured his daughter occasionally : " Stay at home with your mother . . . Watch and help her handle the cooking pots, the mortar and the metate . . . Keep the fire alive and have wood ever ready . . . See that the drinking olla is never empty. If you do these things well, you will not goad about after you are married, and leave your hearth vacant . . . for it is the office of the man to kindle the fire but the part of the woman to keep it burning."[23]

The tribal education is characteristically flamboyant, spectacular and impressively ceremonial as in the initiation ceremonies. The parents, however, do contribute toward " socializing " the child by training its general frame of mind or by arousing and accentuating attributes which develop efficiency in folk-life. The attitudes and personal habits of the folk often run counter to the animal spirits and natural interests of the child. It is all the more incumbent upon the elders to inculcate types of conduct that are the fruit of the folkways and like them, represent accommodations and adjustments to the environment. These personal habits are the identification marks of the society. At least, the popular impressions of them as commonly held revolve about these grossly distinctive traits. The amorous, flowery Polynesian, the vicious, blood-thirsty "man of Borneo", the superstitious-ridden African negro are popular pictures of what is most outlandish among these people. The qualities of mind and body that render these bold characterizations partially representative are stressed in the training of the child.

Life in the primitive society is a grim, stern affair. The physical condition of the child must be maintained at its highest pitch of efficiency to cope with the periodical privations, exposure and want that makes inroads in the life of the folk of simple culture. The body must be inured and hardened to the rigours and exertions of life. Certain physical traits must first of all be actively encouraged as part of the child's preparation for an independent place in society. Crantz was able, for example, to distinguish ten different exercises used by the Greenland Eskimoes to prepare the children.[24] The custom of the Stseelis of British Columbia was to force the children to bathe in the river every morning and night the whole year round. They would first whip their naked bodies with small branches which were placed in the flames of the house-fire for a few minutes. "Whipped daily and with such an instrument he would become an active and energetic man, and be able to acquire much wealth." Later, the boy's bodies were lanced and cut with knives, "to let the bad blood out". Long rods were forced down their throats. They would often lie out at night and expose their bodies to the elements till they became so hardy that they could scarcely feel the cold at all.[25] Among neighbouring tribes, the youth was compelled to lie all night on the margin of a stream or lake and keep his hands in the water. "When the salmon-run was over, and scores of putrifying bodies lay rotting on the shore, they would thrust the hands and arms, to the elbow, into the rotting fish and let them thus remain for the greater part of the night."[26]

It would appear from these facts that this process of hardening and weathering is extant among the peoples of a colder climate. This would seem to give a particle of substantiation to the theory of man's origin in a warmer climate. A severe, often cruel, exercise, is necessary to inure the younger generation to the severities of the colder climes. If the infant in the Aleutian isles so much as cried, even in winter, he was carried to the seashore and held naked in the water until he became quiet. This made him hardy and insensible to cold.[27] Among the nearby Tlinkets the men poured cold water steadily over the children's naked bodies until they could stand it no longer and were dragged off; in addition they cut their hands and chest with sharp stones until the blood came.[28] The Koryak of Siberia put their boys through a rigourous training, " to accustom them to withstand privations, cold and fatigue ", as do the Ainu of Yezo island.[29] It was also impressed upon some of the other American Indians that bitter cold and terrible fatigue was to be their lot. " They were compelled to walk with the men for miles through heavy snow-drifts in the face of a biting wind."[30]

Those individuals who were unable to stand up under this vigorous, rough treatment were considered misfits, and incapable of a complete and independent status in the ranks of the folk. Such children were later consigned to a life-long position of servitude and shame. Those who survived, however, fitted into the social pattern without discomfort. The methods by which this hardening policy was enforced was determined usually by the nature of the environment. Among the Kafirs, the boys are forced to lie on the ground without mats in order that they might be hardened. Many die under this discipline. The girls are also inured to bear privation and fatigue, for under the guidance of an old hag, clad only in a dress made of ropes and bits of reeds, girls carry large pots of water. They often bear scars from bits of burning charcoal having been applied to the forearm to test their power of bearing pain.[31] At intervals the boys are deprived of food and beaten with saplings over the arms and thighs to render them indifferent to toil, privation and pain. " That a good many die in the training is a minor detail."[32]

Cleanliness is a desirable quality for the peoples living in tropical climates. In the Malay peninsula, the children have a bathing song, calculated to impress upon them the habits of cleanliness that are also folkways. It is translated thus :

> Bathe people little, bathe-go.
> Let be cool, do — not be hot.
> Let be clean body your. .
> Such is the custom to — bathe people little
> Do not go back upon what is promised
> The — customs that are written within the book.[33]

Gymnastic exercises on the part of the young girl serve other purposes among the Papuans also, as was learned by Miuklucho-Maclay, the famous traveller. Once the witness of a young girl who was evidently weary and tired but busy at her exercises, he inquired its meaning. He learned that the girl was undergoing the arduous gymnastics in preparation for her coming marital duties.[34]

Not only the body but the emotional disposition of the child must be channelized into the folk-mould, his interests directed and attached to aims supplied also by the folk through its culture. Thus the sentiments are schooled to fit the exigencies of group-life. There are built up manners and modes that constitute " character ", which is the stamp of the folk. This mental make-up and emotional disposition must be actively induced in the main, because left to himself the child would hardly cultivate and appreciate the worth of many of these qualities. Again, the exact nature that this assumes is relevant to the conditions of life of the folk developed by its environment, density of population and traditions.   In this connection we discern the accumulating transforming power of society that twists and turns the innate forces of the individual into the accepted forms ; that creates the larger conditioned reflexes of the personality by throwing up a complete cultural environment and forcing the individual to conform to it.

Foremost among the desirable qualities for the young girl is that of industry and economy.   In British Columbia, the young girl is shut up in a small house by herself at a distance from her family for a whole year.   She is kept constantly employed ; " the idea is that by this means she acquires habits of industry and diligence, reserve and modesty. . ."[35] These girls were also employed " in plucking the needles from a fir branch one at a time, or in plucking yarn. . . . In order to make sure that the girl drank but little she was supplied with only a shell of water at a meal, and frequently this has a hole pierced through it for the purpose of letting the water leak away.   Nor must she put even this small receptacle to her mouth, but must suck the water up through a small tube or hollow bone."[36]   In California, among the Cahuilla, the girl is taught from early childhood to use very little salt in her food so that she might become accustomed to the lack of it by the age of twelve to fourteen years.[37]   These are examples of the straits in which the child must be set as a training for the usual want and serious struggle for food that was to be the besetting problem of adulthood.

It is also deemed essential in many instances to instil an uncompromising ferocity in the child, a savagery which becomes a part of the culture.   Man's original nature is not inclined toward depredations of unfeeling cruelty upon other human beings, but it is rather consciously evoked by means of subtle threats and early habituation.   The purpose is, however, clearly to give the child an essential quality that has survival value for him. A vivid description of the impressions of a native Borneo child at his exercise is given by Furness : " My father, a very great warrior, and known and feared by the people of many, many rivers, wanted his sons to be as brave and fearless as he was himself. So one day he dragged out into the jungle old Ballo Lahing . . . and tied her fast to a tree by rattans on her wrists and ankles. She was a slave-woman . . . very old and weak and very thin and couldn't do any work because she was nearly blind. My father . . . told us . . . we must not be afraid to see blood, nor to hear screams . . . . I couldn't bear the thought of hurting her . . . so I flatly refused to take a spear with me. But my father said I must ; there was no harm in it ; *that it was right* and I must take one ; he pulled me by the arm, and I had to follow. Then I was afraid she might see me, so I sneaked around behind the tree and just pricked her with the point of the iron. . . . I pricked her a little harder the next time to hear what she would say, but she only kept on shrieking. . . Then one of the other boys, smaller even than I, ran his spear through her thigh, like this, and the old people laughed and said *that it was good* . . . and that after that, I never thought whether it was Ballo Lohing or not, I just watched the blood. . . . Then my father praised us all loudly, and me in particular, and said we had been good boys, and had done well. How could I feel at all sorry then for the old thing ? I thought only that I had obeyed my father and that I was a great warrior and could wear horn-bills' feathers and tiger-cat's teeth. That's the way to become a Man. . . . My father was *right*."[38] We have a clear demonstration here of the action of social forces in encouraging and developing a quality of mind repugnant to the original nature of the child. Ridicule, vanity, fear of shame and force contribute to mould the character praiseworthy to the folk, and hence make the " Man " in all his " moral " attributes.

In the Moluccas, somewhat similarly, the children are given decapitated bodies to batter with their parangs, as training in the art of snatching heads. This amusement is called " reddening the parang."[39]   In Fiji, " one of the first lessons taught the infant is to strike its own mother, a neglect of which would beget a fear lest the child should grow up to be a coward."   At Somosomo, our informants witnessed a native mother inciting her children to kick and tread upon the dead bodies of enemies.   On another occasion a man's dress had been stripped from one of the attacking party and placed before the child to excite a " revengeful disposition ".[40]   The devious but insistent ways of breeding these forbidding traits are further illustrated by the Apache Indians : " From earliest infancy they are instructed to regard every other race as natural enemies.   Their suspicions and savage distrust are cultivated before they ever come into contact with other people.   An Apache child of three years will run and yell with fear and hate from a white man.   Apache women hush their children by naming an American (sic)."[41]

Other qualities and sentiments are held up for conscious emulation and adoption by the child, qualities which will allow it to be assimilated more swiftly and easily into the folk, and which have proved to be the most adequate adaptations to the life of his people.   These attitudes, manners and even the slighter rules of etiquette and bearing are the results of social evolution through a rough process of trial and error and the resultant selection of those more adequate ways.[42]   The Andaman child is reproved for being impudent and forward and is taught to be generous and self-denying, essential personal qualities where food must be shared and a close solidarity is imperative.[43]   Among the Ainu it is the dependence of the child upon the elders that is impressed upon him.   He is taught to honour and wait upon the men, always to wait to be spoken to before addressing them, always to get out of their way when they come along a path, to cover his mouth with his hand when meeting them and to uncover the head in their presence.[44] The paternal hand is beginning to impose its domineering rule in this instance. Among the American Indians, etiquette was strictly driven into the minds of the young. Direct address was to be studiously avoided. " A term of relationship or some title of courtesy was commonly used instead of the personal name. . . . We were taught generosity to the poor and reverence for the ' Great Mystery '."[45]

Intermittently the parents or elders attempt to convey aspects of the mores through advice and counsel, drawn from their experience in life. The Pima father was accustomed to take the lad into his arms at daybreak and relate some of the mysteries of the great Sun God. " As he grew too big to be held in arms, he had to sit up very straight and pay strict attention while his father lectured to him on the proper conduct of a Pima warrior and citizen ; or, in other words, soldier and gentleman. If he was not fully awake and paid indifferent heed to what was told him the father's stiffened middle finger would suddenly strike the side of his nose, bringing his face around until he looked straight into his father's eyes."[46] Among the Cheyenne Indians, the mother repeated her advice to the daughter. She said : " Daughter, when you grow up to be a young woman, if you see anyone whom you like, you must not be foolish and run off with him. You must marry decently. If you do so, you will become a good woman and will be a help to your brothers and to your cousins." This was repeated over and over.[47] In the light of culture-history, the mention of cousins as a close relative probably alludes to a more ancient classificatory system of relationship, in which cousin and brother had the same denomination. Among the Sauks and Foxes, the chief or principal man went through the village exhorting the young in a very loud voice on their proper conduct and behaviour.[48]

With respect to the American Indians, much evidence is on hand as to definite, consecutive teaching of the young. Other folk of simpler culture, i.e. those without a written language, reserve this systematic education until the initiation ceremonies, at the puberty of the child. This ceremony is merely a climax to the long undefined groups of educative influences of the American Indian. This is probably because the American Indian culture was prematurely forced into a self-consciousness. This development was caused by the frequent, easy contacts of tribes not arrested by forbidding geographical limitations and in fact encouraged by the necessity of roaming far and wide over plain and prairie. In addition, the menace of extinction was dimly felt at contact with the culture of the whites, which caused a shrinking inward in defence of their own indigenous ways. This development also may have destroyed much of the efficacy and popularity of the initiation ceremonies.[49]

A common method of transmitting the culture-traits with a view also toward developing the appropriate emotional attitudes and sentiments is through the folklore. Through the capture of the child's attention under suitable circumstances, myths, legends and tales are constantly recited and under a pleasing guise of fable, instructive lessons conveyed and ideas stimulated painlessly in the child's mind—ideas that will later revert to it in the actual conduct of life. The tribal wisdom is also stored up in this manner and through oral repetition, communicated to the child. Where a written language is unknown, recitation is the only method of preserving and continuing the glories and incidents of the past. The primitive science and philosophy, as well as the folk-history, are thus preserved in tales. Often a rhythm is added to form a song which enables the children to retain its contents

more easily, as among the Dajaks of Borneo.[50] Among the
Boloki on the Congo, for instance, there was no historical
literature as such, because not a single member of the tribe
could write ; nevertheless through oral communication
the origins of the tribe, its migrations, etc., were communicated
from father to son.[51]

In the case of the Maoris of New Zealand we are struck by
the wealth and charm of the traditionary lore. In this
instance, the people migrated from an original home so that
the ordinary connections with the past have been uprooted.
Hence the body of traditions has been preserved more intensely
and faithfully to compensate for the loss of the original
environment where the child could have acquired and felt
sympathy for the legends of his own accord. Many of the
expressions have thus become archaic as no longer reflecting
the living facts of folk-life. New circumstances can subdue
terms and expressions. Yet this lore is faithfully transmitted
in the form of nursery jingles and ditties, and longer historical
rhythmical recitals, to relieve " the ennui of wet days and wet
nights ".[52] The preservative action of these hoary tales is
truly remarkable as they carry on from generation to generation. Of the West Africans it is said that the phrase and words
are often " archaisms handed down from ancestors and
believed to possess an efficacy, though their actual meaning
is forgotten."[53] Among the Indians on the Amazon, " these
tribal lays are so old that the words are obsolete and no longer
understood by the singers ; but what is of importance is the
rhythm. . . ."[54] In the D'Entrecasteaux Islands, likewise,
the stories of bygone days are sung by the old people, men and
women to whom they have become quite unintelligible, as
the actual conditions of life have altered with the years. But
the stories persist little changed.[55]

This type of " intellectual education " is often mere chance-
work on the part of the children who absorb the ideas of the

M

grown-ups as to the gods, creation, sacrifice, sorcery, etc.,
through the report of their eyes and ears. The informal
nature of this training is also stressed by the fact that it is
about the mother that much of it is gleaned. Among the
Bushmen the folktales were largely learned from the mother.[56]
The informal, rather lax method of training is typical of the
primitive organization of society built about the mother.
The child's training in the province of the mores depended in
large part on the memory of the women alone, who were the
only archives of the tribe, as among the Hottentots.[57] The
increasing complexity and definite organization of the folk,
introduced by a superior material culture and the beginnings
of the paternal rule, developed a more definite means of imparting the lore. The old men become depositories of the legends
or " ancient word ". As this body of lore constitutes the last
authority of the ways and customs of the folk, attempts were
consciously made to preserve it unimpaired and hence it was
entrusted to the care of carefully selected youths, as among
the Natchez Indians.[58] Among the Pima Indians, the
" tribal historian " relates to these boys for four nights " the
narrative of how the world was made and peopled ; whence
the Pimas came and how they struggled with demons, mon-
sters, and savage enemies. These tales are not usually told
in the presence of the women, and consequently they know
only imperfect fragments of them."[59] In the Hawaiian
Islands, blind men were the bards in whose memory were
preserved all the songs of old.[60] These societies have developed
a folk-consciousness earlier because of their own peculiar
historical contacts.

The intention of the tales is a didactic and moral one. Each
tale contains a point of native law or manners or aspect of the
cult. Each story when extracted from its allegorical overlay
points a moral or inculcates an aspect of the mores.[61] These
tales are all, however, typical culture-products of unknown

origin, sewn together by countless individual variations, accretions, but swept on by the propulsive action of the massive social forces making for their unhindered preservation. Among the Hova of Madagascar, this body of traditionary lore was termed "heritage of the ear". In addition, there were fables, proverbs and adages which were the "text-books" of the children.[62] In Borneo, likewise, "the growth of the children in wisdom and morality is aided by hearing from the lips of the elders wise saws and ancient maxims that embody the experience of their forefathers."[63] In the Solomon Islands and in Fiji, around the cracking embers of the fire, the young natives drink in the tales of yore as told them by the elders. These stories are then as permanent and unalterable as if they had been set in type.[64] An engrossing picture is drawn by Pritchard of the remarkable results achieved by this form of teaching in making the traditions hallowed and preserved by the young: ". . . Well do I remember that hoary-headed, toothless, half-blind, wrinkle-faced old man . . . surrounded by his sons and grandsons and great grandsons, as, in the dusk of the evening we all lay on his mats, watching the moon rising slowly over the bread-fruit trees that encircled his hut and listening to the legends of the olden times. Eighty years before, he had heard the same legends. Thus their ancient lore was handed down from generation to generation."[65]

These stories have, or have had at one time, a definite moral to point. Some trait is encouraged or some action discouraged as anti-social and bringing with it dire misfortune if practised. There is an enormous repertoire of these tales among all folk. They all carry a miraculous note with considerable allegory and personification, clothed in the language and thought-construction peculiar to the folk. To choose one people, the Ainu, we discover tales whose purpose it is to encourage diligence, reverence for the aged and to discourage idleness and

greediness.[66] In the same way fables and narratives are at
hand referring to " inquisitiveness, rudeness, idleness, vanity,
jealousy, disobedience, cowardice, selfishness, infidelity and
perseverance. The good is praised and rewarded, the bad
action promptly and severly punished, so that these instructive
tales attempt to show a logical connection between morality
and happiness."[67]   In the Kafir tales, the girls who break the
native customs are always brought to some horrible end.[68]
The lasting effect of this teaching of the abstract, moral
(i.e. social or folk) values is not to be gainsaid. " Though
wise words might be forgotten, the story will remain in the
memory with guiding or deterrent power."[69]   The children
are certainly deeply impressed by the narrations. Among the
Eskimo, for example, when evening comes, " they set themselves to story-telling ; adventure follows adventure, the past
comes to life again, and the young people are spurred on to
action."   They sit listening in deep absorption—their staring
eyes and countenances showing their wondering interest.[70]
The moral pointed is faithfully preserved. We are told that
on occasions, " sons and daughters will repeat these stories
to their parents if they think they are not being properly
treated according to native ideas."[71] The lessons are thus
wisely learned and the stories burned into the children's hearts
indelibly. As a net result (as of the Dakota boy), " he learns
to sing the love songs and war songs of the generations gone
by (thus about two central societal interests). There is no
new path for him to tread, but he follows in the old ways."[72]

For the recalcitrant, disobedient or wayward youth upon
whom all these subtle influences have little effect, there are
other effective media, no less powerful, to secure his conformity. Physical punishment among the tribes of simpler
culture is very rare—that is, punishment directed towards
the end of leading the child into the correct path. There is a
good deal of violence which is provoked by personal anger

of a petty sort but there is little actual discipline with a purposive didactic aim. The rod is not employed usually because the child comprehends early the value of obedience. If the child is incorrigibly wayward there are other corrective methods of more lasting effect which are employed. The use of physical punishment as a corrective is characteristic of societies more advanced in culture which have a desire to curb the young. Due to the imperceptible, accumulative effects of the influences and training we have just seen, the children obey instinctively. Obedience to constituted authority hardly needs to be taught, as among the Kafir, for the children notice how everyone in the kraal is ordinarily obedient to the older men. As a result, the small boy delights to say, " I am father's little dog."[73] Corporal punishment is taken very lightly as the children are already hardened to the blows and buffets of a life in the open, and a few more will make but little impression upon them. Beside, the primitive man sets great store by an unbroken, free spirit of the child as a necessary quality for this type of life. Blows and cudgellings are therefore generally frowned upon. The American Indians, for example, rejoiced over the wild unrestrained conduct of their children and it was the intention of their training to induce a fearless spirit. This often went so far that the women teased their more backward children into striking them in fits of anger.[74] In British Guiana, it was believed that a dog, not a child, was to be punished. Among the Patagonians, the obstreperous child was applauded and looked upon as a coming great man. It was believed that punishment weakened and enfeebled them.[75]

From this it was easy to deduce dire consequences from a castigation of the child. The Marshall Islanders believed that the sun would cloud and great storms come were they to strike a son on the head.[76] In a wandering, hunting society fearlessness was quite essential for preservation of life. Societal selection actively worked toward the elimination of the weakling and dependent.[77] The admonitions and periodical counsel of the parents were easily appreciated by the children as they were tested up and verified in practice. Harsher methods of correction awaited more complex culture.

Yet there was a decided need felt to keep the buoyant spirits of the youth in check even in the most primitive groups. The imposition of a generalized or mental sway of the elders was requisite to produce a thorough-going conformity and sub-ordination. This discipline was accomplished in a decisive, spectacular manner at the initiation ceremonies. Before this event, however, superstitious fear was regularly employed to train compliance on occasions of recalcitrance. Among the Australian blacks, from early infancy, the child is trained in the belief " that departure from the customs of the tribe is inevitably followed by one at least of many evils, such as becoming early gray, opthalmia, skin eruptions or sickness ; but above all, that it exposes the offender to danger from sorcery."[78] These occult powers were controlled only by the elders who had thus a mighty force at their command with which to overawe the young. In Borneo, also, the children were disciplined largely by frequent warnings of supernatural dangers which would attend their actions—dangers of which they remained acutely conscious throughout life.[79]

The fear of the malignantly potent depredations of ghosts was used to give sanction to the accepted ways of the parents and to subdue the disobedient child. The forms that these punishments are to take also proceed directly from the folk-ways. Among the Caddo, these assaults of the ghosts are peculiar but very real. The fathers thus admonish the children : " If, in this world, you want everything you see and always try to get things that you do not need, just because someone else has them, you will stop under a tree to gather persimmons. Then you will wander to the next tree and the next, until you lose your way and forget that you are on a journey. Then you will become a raccoon and live for ever among the trees." Or, if too much time is wasted in standing about idle during life, " you will become a tree ". If too dilatory upon the earth, " you will reach the river after the banks have spread and you will be too late to jump across, but will fall into the water and become a fish." Dogs must not be mistreated, because on this journey after death, the abused dog goes to his people and complains. The chief of the dogs then waits. " When you come he tells you to look for fleas on his head and when you find one he tells you to bite it. When you bite it, you become a dog. Then he takes you to where the dog stays, and there they mistreat you as you mistreated them on earth." But an antidote is kindly provided by the people : " For this reason we place a bead on the little finger of the dead person, so that he may bite it instead of the flea and so fool the dog and escape him." And for the forgetful person who leaves tasks incomplete, the fate is this : " You will work until you are nothing but skin and bone. Then you will die but you will soon come to life only to work yourself to death again. Then you will come to life again, and so on. There is no end. . . ."[80] This reflects in its naïveté the informality or unconscious nature by which the folkways persist. These absurd destinies of the refractory or lazy child are half believed by the elders themselves, who have drawn these concepts from their knowledge of nature and life. Yet they pass them on unequivocally to impress the young in the manner of these fabled threats. It is also interesting to point out the tendency toward " projectivism ", e.g. of equipping and elaborating the next world as a projected picture of the life encountered in this one, the only world, after all, that men know.[81]

Some of these threatened visitations may, however, contain a bit of cynicism and purposeful invention on the part of the elders. Among the sedentary agricultural peoples and the

herdsmen, the mildness and unbridled freedom of the child
of less developed culture-stages can no longer be countenanced.
There arises slowly a great survival-value in cultivating the
more ordered, obedient disposition. The child does not,
however, come into the world appreciative of or adapted to
this sedentary life. He is equipped with the unbridled, eager
interests that are his biological inheritance. The more
elaborated and complex the culture, the more purposive must
become the training of the will because the original nature of
the child remains. Besides, the economic interests of the
parents and elders render an avowed discipline the more necessary. As property in cattle, capital and human beings increases, stealing, rape and the like expressions of "spirit"
can no longer be brooked. The forms of brow-beating and
intimidation are more consciously used.

An element of invention is therefore used in some of the
superstitions threats dangled over the heads of the young.
The little Yaos boys were told, for instance, that if they recited
riddles at mid-day, horns would grow on their foreheads.
"This might be intended as a precaution against their attention being absorbed by this pastime when they might be
herding", we are told.[82]   Among the Bambara, certain trees
must not be cut or tampered with, without incurring the dis-
pleasure of the ancestral ghosts.[83]   There are more immediate
means of discipline which always appear perfectly natural
in all cultures. The Kikuyu elders, for example, were accustomed to curb the excesses of the young men by somewhat the
same way that a modern college disciplinary committee would
adopt. They went "to the place where they danced and
placed there a cooking pot and a stick of *mugeri ;* no dance
could then be held there until the young men had returned
from a raid."[84]   A great variety of unfortunate results of
wrongful actions were conjured up by the Omaha sires for their
sons. If a lad should help himself to that which came in a

kettle from another family, the old men would say : " If you eat what is brought home in the kettle, your arrows will twist when you shoot." When a young man tried to drink broth in the kettle, the old men would then say : " A young man must not drink the broth, his ankles will rattle and his joints become loose ", etc. The girls were admonished in a similar way.[85]

Stealing of food and injury to property are offences that call for severe chastisement. Among the Budwean, food is not so plentiful that stealing may be overlooked. The grown-up child who steals is thus often killed by them.[86] The head-strong boy is often punished by being compelled to carry at arm's length a piece of timber in which biting-ants have their nests.[87] Among the Ba-thonga, the recalcitrant boy is punished by having sticks introduced between his fingers. A strong man, taking both ends of the sticks in his hands, presses them together and lifts the boy, squeezing and half crushing his fingers.[88] A very common mode of punishment is the rubbing of pepper into the eyes or lips and then exposing the child to the ridicule of all passers-by. " His screams and yells under this operation are savage beyond description."[89] Through such devices the child begins to feel the force of a greater external power. The rod and the switch are thus express emblems, if not integral parts, of the development of the folk life.

As long as the training and castigation lies in the hands of the immediate family group, the nature of the punishment is capricious and slight. The injury, in a physical sense, is insignificant and flecting. It is the moral effect rather of disapproval, anger or disgust on the part of one's nearest of kin that is supposed to work the required results. This reproof is merely in the form of scolding or viciously personal rudeness or ridicule. Thus, among the Chukchee, if a father is angry with a lazy and bad son he asks to be killed and charges that very son with the execution of his request.[90]   Among the Crow Indians, throwing a little water in the face was an extreme shame to the child which he felt very keenly.   Pouring water down the nose was, however, the punishment for persistently misbehaved children.   Blacking of the face and immersion in a river were also used by American Indians.[91]   The general character of this type of chastisement is well typified by the following treatment of an offending son.   He was bound to a post by his father, who then " felt him all over with his hands, first on the right, and then on the left side, till at length he found the heart.   Then he stopped, felt it, and said : ' Aha, stay there ! it beats ! So, then thou hast a heart !' . . . Then he felt about the head till he found the ears. ' Aha, stay there ! I thought you had, perhaps, no ears. But I see that I was mistaken.   Hence thou hast no excuse.' "[92]   The abysmal shame of this child can be well imagined.   In these instances it appears that the infraction by the child was also a " moral " one, i.e. a disobedient, recalcitrant wilfulness.

But when definite injury is done to a material good of some importance, the gravity of the misdemeanour must be engraved into the child, often in a literal fashion.   If the Pima girl, for example, should stumble and break an olla, or pot, when going for water, her elders would take some of the broken pieces and scratch her naked arm.[93]

A wonder-working method of discipline is the imposition of a curse upon the disobedient child.   By this means the father calls down all the horrible visitations which ghosts alone can effect.   The elders, privy to the correct ways of manipulating the spirits, are able to invoke their aid.   Sickness, bad luck, accident, blindness, sterility, all may follow in the wake of this punishment of the child.   It is invoked, however, only on the most serious occasions, as for instance, in the case of the son who has abused his father's trust and allowed the cattle herd to diminish or has sold them unknown to the parent. Or the daughter may have been duly married and the father received the bride price, but has then run away and the father has been compelled to return the property received for her. These are not trifles; they are calamities of the first order, involving the loss of hard-earned property. Hence the father will place a curse (particularly in the case of the African negroes), on the son to the effect that he shall never grow rich nor have wives. The daughter will be cursed to perpetual barrenness.[94]

The form that the curse takes grows out of the cult-practices of the folk. So, among the Ila-speaking peoples, nakedness is an agency for working evil. The mother may thus curse her wayward son by deliberately exposing herself in this fashion before him.[95] In Uganda, the mode prescribes that the father simply strike the son with his fur mantle to steep the latter under the shadow of such a curse.[96]

As long as the child is under this malediction, he is a miserable, forlorn creature, ostracized from his people. To remove this stain a present must be given to the father in the form of a large fish, monkey or goat or other edible of value, and forgiveness is usually forthcoming. The father, if he accepts the peace-offering, proceeds to spit into the child's hand to signify that the words of the curse are returned to him. Or else he chews a bitter herb and spits this into his hand denoting that he is thus relieving the bitterness of his heart toward the child.[97] For more hidden reasons the Bakongo father blows off three small heaps of dust from the child's knee to remove the calumny he had imposed. Now the child may become rich again and have children (another form of wealth).[98]

Things become really serious in the regulation and training of the child as soon as he begins to meddle with property. The true cases of punishment begin to appear as soon as the child offends against persons outside of his family circle. Then folk-relations are disturbed and hence such actions on

the part of the child become " crime " and violations of the
" law ", that is, of those customs which have become consciously held by the folk for the preservation of the peace.
So, in Borneo, physical punishments of the child are almost
unknown.   The most that is done by the parent is to tweak
his ear and ask whether he is deaf.   But if the child offends
persons outside of his family, he may be haled before his chief
and fined.[99]   The fine is often paid by the father, who now
has an economic motive for more actively bringing the child
into line.   Among the Ewe tribes in West Africa, the parents
are not much concerned with the boy's stealing their own pro-
visions but to pilfer from an outsider merits severe punishment by the father.[100]   Among the Baya, a child offending
in this manner is brought before the elders' council and placed
in quarantine from the entire village.[101]

The primitive state or ruling body thus deals out a form of
justice which is more formal and objective than is the domestic
variety which preceded it.   As an example, we are told of an
Indian council at which an impudent young fellow kept
interfering.   The celebrated old warrior who was speaking
became incensed, drew his tomahawk and split the young
man's skull, and then " continued his harangue as if nothing
had happened."[102]

We have now seen the child as he approaches social maturity.
His education is basically self-acquired but it is touched up
sporadically by means of training by family and elders to
induce the desirable physical and mental attributes that make
for efficiency.   As puberty and physical maturity approach,
all this experience in socialization is topped by a tremendous
climax in which the child becomes the socially mature individual, an independent, thoroughly outfitted folk-fellow
or tribesman.   This occurs in the initiation ceremonies to
which we now turn our attention.

CHAPTER X

PRIMITIVE EDUCATION : (3) THE INITIATION

THE behaviour of the child during the first few years of life springs from deep-set biological impulses that are more of a reflex than of a reflective nature. This is true as well of the individual of a highly elaborated, complex culture as it is of the person of the simpler societies here under consideration. The social heritage is an external and hence "artificial" creation to which every child is a complete stranger during infancy. The first attachments to this cultural milieu are forged unseen and undisturbed, as the child's organic impulses and interests become conditioned to the various folkways of the environment. The child falls into a type of behaviour that is characteristically that of his parents and his folk.

This fixing of habits through conditioned reflexes normally proceeds unobserved in the simpler cultures, except as it is definitely punctured at intervals by ceremonies. The major external steps accentuating the socialization of the child, such as the acquisition of a name, reception into the group, the introduction to the ancestral and guardian spirits, the assumption of clothing and the like are given some sort of public recognition. The ceremony accords open acknowledgment and record of the passage of the child into an ascending status that binds him more and more closely to the folk. Yet the bulk of " technical " culture, that is, the ways of food-getting, making of tools, clothing, shelter and manipulation of the dreaded spirit-environment is assimilated gradually on the power of the child's own natural impulses. The " moral " culture or mores, which are the doctrines or ways of thought and bodies of sentiments supporting the folkways, are, however, but vaguely and incompletely absorbed in this manner. These must be more consciously imposed by the group. The ceremonies mentioned which open the portals of the folk-life to the child serve with increasing force to effect this end, that is, the creation of the social mind, or personality.

As the culture-traits amass in number and develop in complexity this need for a purposive formation of the behaviour and sentiments is made more compelling. The arts of life that make for self-maintenance in themselves advance to such a stage with the domestication of animals and settled agriculture that much of the technique of food-getting must be inculcated in some way. The enhanced value of this material culture reverberates throughout the social structure. A greater network of social contacts are set up, the relationships between the sexes become more durable and more rigidly defined, as the material interests involved, such as the ownership and control of valuable tools and property, make their influence felt. We have discussed the arduous, and, at times, vindictive training of the child as a means of adapting the physical constitution and faculties to the rigours of uncongenial environments. More impressive perhaps are the efforts to school an appreciation of the less tangible values inherent in the mores. A body of sentiments and dispositions are to be encouraged as further adjustment of the child's original nature to a complex social life. As culture evolves, this training becomes more insistent and artificially imposed by the necessary aid of disciplinary measures.

Group-consciousness evolves in the degree that the personal interests of a section or class of the society are affected. It is very often in the first contacts with other folk that this is aroused and a resultant motive toward group-solidarity produced. It is not yet established that all historical cultures have developed in a single path through a parallel, undeviating series of stages, nor is it definitely known that a single original culture was diffused, leaving traces in the existing dispersed tribal cultures. It is, however, evident that social cohesion and solidarity in all cases was instigated by the contacts of primitive groups, whatever their several points of origin. In such societies, the tendency toward an adequate training of the child was also stimulated. Migrations or thinning numbers in the group also serve to awaken an earlier group-consciousness that is enforced upon the young. The threat of extinction, of absorption by others, or the strangeness of a new environment may cause a movement of the elders to clutch their ways and traditions more closely and impel the earlier development of an educational system to bequeath to the young, who alone can preserve a living testimony of this precious heritage. The origins of purposive training and objective control of the young spring out of the growing feeling of exclusive interests on the part of the entire society or a particular class or age-group within it. The value and worth of the ways develop in the folk moral attitudes to subserve these impulses.

As already described, social infancy is a foreshortened period in primitive life. Social adulthood is not attained without a very definite, climactic experience. As the evidences of physical maturity appear at puberty, there is a sudden attempt to clamp the youth down into position as an active member of the tribe. In matters of sex-relations, for example, little seems to matter until puberty, and then there is a sudden imposition of tabus and other societal rules and safeguards as to their conduct. All the motives which compel the training and ordered, purposeful education reach a definite climax at this period. The primitive child is then subjected to an impressive, well-organized group of ceremonies of initiation into manhood and womanhood which, though often harrowing, are significant enough. There is a definite cleavage with

" childish " ways. The social personality, that is, the individual equipped, and trained with, the requisite qualities of body and mind that make for successful participation in the folk-life is completed. These rites endow the individual with a status and merit that is an abrupt, decisive change from the dilatory, insignificant life led as a child. At the same time, the cohesion of the group is promoted by stamping out a conformity upon the individual in an indelible and unforgettable manner. The initiation ceremonies are thus the culmination of the conscious desires of a class or group to immerse the child into the content and spirit of the culture and to fetch him out typical, acquiescent, obedient—a mature " man ", with all that the term connotes.

At puberty certain changes in the physical and emotional make-up of the child attract the attention of the folk. The approaching sexual maturity implies also a critical transition in the social position of the youth as during and after this period he has acquired potentialities of creating new social relationships which may be disturbing to the existing order of things. At the same time, sexual relationships in folk-thought are immersed in a general confused glamour and dread as they are not understood and as they are immediately provocative of such fundamental emotional stress. The initiation ceremonies in many instances were thus originally ceremonial observances of this profound physical change in the individual and preparation for the admission into the status of a person enjoying the recognized sex-rights and duties of the tribe. Thus, we are informed that among some of the Australian tribes, " the proper time is when the whiskers are beginning to show themselves, and when the old men observe that the boys are paying more attention to women of the tribe than is considered decent or proper."[1] Necessarily, the youth must be definitely installed as a full-fledged member of the tribe with a sympathy for and comprehension of the mores ;

or else embarrassing and entangling relationships with the other sex will be created, with no feeling for the responsibilities and duties that should accompany them.

In many instances the initiation ceremonies do not correspond with the puberty of the child. This is because the initiation, although serving originally to mark the physical change in the person soon became the symbol of introduction into the social life of the tribe and as such no longer depended altogether upon physical maturity. Originally, social maturity was not to be easily differentiated because in the simplest societies the child simply flowered into the social scene unaided and very early in life. As culture developed the stock of tried adaptations to life-conditions become more remote and there is much to be definitely learned. As a climax and epitome of its education, the initiation serves, therefore, as a sort of social puberty which does not always converge with the physical puberty-period.[2] To be sure, the ceremonies take place about this age, as most social phenomena centre about certain primordial and undeniable organic needs. Inevitably the development of social forms and the rolling up of the social heritage carries with it a further sundering of the folkways from their original motivations in the physical changes of the individual. Social needs often lose sight of the original basis of these forms and ceremonies, and so the initiation ceremony may lose its " once practical character as a primitive effort to assist nature " and serve as " a mere badge or evidence of incorporation into the tribal community."[3]

Considerations of a cultural nature often determine the age for initiation. Among the Masai, the boys are circumcised and initiated when they are deemed strong enough for military service, which is the most important function performed by the men.[4] In Borneo, the rite qualifying a boy for his place in society is the second occasion on which he strikes at heads taken in battle. The age at which this can be done depends upon the occurrence of an opportunity of head-snatching which commonly occurs between the eighth and fifteenth year. There are, in fact, houses where big lads are still considered " children " because no heads have been taken for years.   On the other hand, some of the boys are so small that the father holds the parang and guides the little hands in making the stroke.[5]   In the Transvaal among the Sotho, also, the time set for the initiation-school depends upon the arrival at puberty of a son of the chief, as all the group attending the session are thereafter subjects of the boy.[6]   No records of age are kept among the Basabei of Central Africa and the decision to subject the boys to the ordeal of initiation hinged upon their appear ance.   There is thus no special age, but significantly enough, the parents will send their children as soon as they are believed to have reached a proper mental maturity, as among the Fuegians.[7]   The Zuñi child likewise goes through a prolonged series of initiations which he is too young to understand, but the final or fatal vows are not taken until he has reached the age when " his heart has become wise."[8]

In the New Hebrides, there are very practical reasons which determine the age of initiation.   It is a matter of payment, of giving pigs.   An infant and a grown-up are equally admitted at the same time.[9]   An instance is recorded in New Guinea of a father whose pigs " were dying fast of some unknown and incurable disease, and though his sons were over-young he determined to stretch a point, so gave a feast at which the initial processes of the entering-in would take place."[10]   There are other cogent reasons for hastening the event which bespeak the underlying purpose, as in Nyasaland.   There, " at the present time, there is a tendency for the rite to be performed at an earlier and earlier age so that the youths may benefit by the instruction given at *unyago* before they come under mission influence and lose the ties of tribal custom."[11]   For these reasons, then, the process may be speeded up so that infants may have undergone the rites who have to be carried in the arms of their parents. Yet the social drive becomes so insistent in such cases as to deprive the custom certainly of all rationality and effect as far as the child's impressions are concerned.[12]

On the other hand, the costs may be so great as to prevent boys from entering the ceremonies. Therefore it is not unusual to see men of twenty-five to thirty years and even aged men and women side by side with callow youths and infants.[13] The effect of the initiation ceremony is illustrated in the instance of the old patriarch of the Biduelli in Australia, cited by Howitt. This sire at one of these initiations was driven crouching among the women and children. The reason was self-evident—he had never been made a man, and therefore " was no more than a mere boy."[14] In particular instances, in Fiji, initiation may be postponed as a punishment for misconduct and the miscreant's life (in society) remains for years that of a child, that is, incomplete and despised.[15]

The divorce of social maturity from the original inciting cause at physical puberty shows a curious involution in that the cultural incident later takes precedence over the biological causation. This illustrates the force of the mores in determining the entire outlook of the individual, and in a sense overshadowing the internal events of the individual as an organism. Thus, among the Kaonde girls, the *chisiungu*, or initiation ceremony does not take place at puberty, but before it. In fact, it is considered very dangerous to leave it until menstruation. At Nanzela, among the Ila peoples it is believed that if the girls do not go through with these ceremonies, they will never menstruate.[16]

Intimately associated with the initiation ceremonies and often its predominating constituent, but not universally the prevalent one, is the rite of circumcision. It is not to be doubted that originally this was considered a fit preparation

for the sexual life and hence related to the physical development of the child.   With cultural evolution a derived significance often became attached to this custom and aggregated it
to the general initiation ceremonies.   It had become symbolical of the entrance of the youth into social maturity and
hence did not necessarily coincide with physical maturity.
Originally the rite was used as a survival or composition for
child—and human—sacrifice to the gods, in the developed
cults.   The growing value of the child militated against the
taking of his life and reduced the practice to mere blood letting
or a sacrifice of an unessential part of the body.[17]   Much of the
original background and motives have fallen away and circumcision remains as a device to mark the youth's entrance
into the full social existence.   The circumcised child, like the
scarred and tatooed child, carries visible signs of adherence
to the folk-life which are rationalized as having curative and
protective qualities.[18]

The uncircumcised Kafir is regarded throughout his entire
life as a boy, is ridiculed and despised by the women and is
even considered " dead " in the social sense, as he can take no
part in the councils.[19]   Such a person cannot hold property
nor be a soldier.   A woman would never think of marrying the
wretch.[20]   The age at which circumcision is effected is immaterial : " As soon as a boy is circumcised he becomes a man,
even if he is no more than eight years old ; as such he is a
warrior and has to go to war."[21]   The ceremony devoid of its
original physical import depends on other material require-
ments, as among the Masai.   They merely wait until the boy
is strong enough to carry a spear and shield.[22]   Among the
Akamba, also, " children of four to five years may be circumcised together with almost full-grown boys, whose circumcision is delayed by special circumstances, such as the poverty
of the father."[23]   Even married men participate on occasions,
as in New Guinea.[24]   Again it is observed that the social

expression grows out of a definite biological impulse in the individual's life but is soon conventionalized. The belief often still prevails among those peoples practising circumcision that it helps procreation and in the cases where it is omitted such dire consequences as barrenness and infertility are certain to result.[25] Among others this motive has entirely disappeared and the custom is the mark merely of membership in a folk-culture, as among the Jews and Arabs of to-day.

The initiation ceremonies thus mark the passage of the youth from social childhood into social maturity. The underlying process of this socialization is fundamentally gradual and accumulative. But to primitive man, all such decisive changes are definitely abrupt and episodic. He publicly recognizes this important change, and its impression on the youth himself is life-long. The ceremonies are intended to cut off the youth from his negligible past as if he had died and then to resurrect him into an entirely new existence as an adult. An exceptional environment is created to make the youth conscious of this important transition in his life-condition. During the ceremonies, he feels himself cut off from the old life which is to be forgotten and placed in an isolated position outside the ordinary life of his fellows so that he may be able the better to examine and learn the new ways. Thenceforward the childhood that has been left behind is unmentionable as something incomplete. Often the awakening from it is an entire removal from the past, as the boy seems for a while not to understand human speech and acts as though he were just born. During the initiation period itself, which is thus a " marginal " or exceptional state, the ordinary tabus and regulations of society are forgotten—licence often prevails, theft and acts of violence remain unpunished. Archaic practices are also indulged in, indicative of the temporary lapse from the ordinary ways of the folk.[26]

For example, among the Nandi of East Africa, the boys and girls are given purges and have their heads shaved as an indication of the removal of ties with their childhood and the forthcoming acquisition of a totally new personality.[27] It is further believed by some that the youths undergoing the rites " decompose and decay until but one bone of each novice is left in charge of the doctor "[28]—the only basis upon which, presumably, the new individual retains a connection with his past life as a child.   In Dutch New Guinea, when the boys enter the men's houses for their course of instruction, they are supposed to go blind and see nothing.   Only later are they able to see the various objects presented there as symbolical of the new state.[29]   Among the Indians of Virginia also, the youths passing through the " *huskinaw* " or " *huskanay* " were given emetics, " whereby remembrance of the past was supposed to be obliterated and the mind left free for the reception of new impressions."   In the words of Lafitau, " these poor unfortunates drank so much of the waters of Lethe that they lost the remembrance of everything, of their parents, their friends, their own past and even their own tongue."[30]   Often this severance or death is symbolized by the casting off of the old clothing, as is practised by the girls in Rhodesia on the approach of the initiatory ceremonies.   These clothes are thrown on the roofs of the parents' huts signifying the removal of child ties.[31]

Once removed from the ignominious state of childhood, the tremendous import of the approaching state of social maturity is further emphasized by allowing the youths all varieties of licence and excess. This creates an exceptional or " marginal " condition for the initiate as far as his part in the folk-life is concerned.   Theft, larceny, etc., on the part of the boys goes unpunished, although, to be sure, if grain or animals are stolen, the parents indemnify the victims.[32] Among the Kafir, " they may rob the gardens as much as they like ;

in some tribes they may even kill the cattle with impunity" during this period.[33] The conversation is also of a "very dubious nature . . . and is directly intended to show that no feelings of shame exist under these circumstances though in daily life considerable modesty is shown in connection with such matters."[34] Promiscuous sexual intercourse is allowed at this time among the Papuans.[35] Among the Xosas of South Africa, the initiates during the period of seclusion may not even speak of objects by their common names, but are taught alternate ones by the old men. Thus *umfozi* (woman) becomes *se 'guardi*. If the wrong word is used, the initiate is "spanked" with flat hands on his arms as a gentle reminder.[36] All these measures heighten the impression of a lull or transition from the child life to the existence as a full-fledged independent folk-fellow. The past fades out and the mind left receptive for the new.

Upon emerging from the initiation rites, therefore, a new life is believed to commence. The past he pretends at least to forget and a new name is in some cases imposed, indicative of the changed person.[37] "At first he effects to recognize no one, and to be unable even to masticate his food, which office friends must perform for him. When he comes to life again, he begins to eat and drink as before, but his understanding is gone and the fetish man must teach him and direct him in every motion, like the smallest child."[38] It is a sort of rebirth. A new head-dress is given as a symbol of the new existence, as the hair has been totally removed before entrance into the ceremonies. Often a thorough bathing of the body is also essential to remove all stains of the old.[39] The lad is often spirited from the family, who lose all sight of him for a long period and then are forced to repurchase the boy because he has been reborn and is now an entirely new individual, as in the Kiwai Islands.[40] The newly-circumcised are exhorted to "open their eyes" at the conclusion of the ceremonies and then slowly one after the other opens his eyes as though awakened from a deep slumber.[41]

The assumption of the complete social personality requires a separation also from the company of the women. As a child, much time had been spent with the mother and sisters and the decisive break with the past includes also a separation from this female society. The initiation ceremonies likewise are usually token of the growing male dominance in society. Very often they are conducted solely by the men and access is prohibited to the women on pains of death. The boys are definitely segregated from the women because the intention is to subject and rule them by terroristic methods. The sexual division is rigidly enforced. An essential purpose of the Australian initiation rites is to effect this severance of the boy from the mother and attach him thereafter to the men.[42] The women take an active part at the outset of the ceremonies by conducting the children to the scene of the rites and caring for their wants. Then " a screen of boughs is erected between each group of mothers and their sons. One or more of the headmen now go along the groups of novices and throw a rug over the head of each boy. . . . All the women are covered with rugs, bushes or grass. . . ." The boys are then taken secretly from the women. They are often seized suddenly at night, while the younger children who remain behind are marked with " a few spots or stripes of paint, the women being led to believe that the evil spirit did this when he was taking the novices out of the ring."[43]

In the Andaman Islands, the women weep over the boys as a requirement of custom. This is interpreted as a symbol of the gradual withdrawal of the initiate from the bonds that held him to the female relatives. " On the other hand the important thing for the initiate himself is to feel that the bonds that united him as a child to the women who cared for him are now severed or modified ; he must no longer depend on

them but must learn to depend on himself. . . ."[44] The
boy's connection with the mother as her child is severed and he
now belongs only to the men and their society. The women
lose all power over their children and even fail to recognize
them, as in Australia : " Having his hair cut off and being
painted white sometimes so alters his appearance that his
mother cannot readily recognize him."[45]

Thus the slate is wiped clean of traces of the old, futile life.
But this is done only that the selected culture-traits and
characteristics of the folk may be drawn all the more vivid
and compelling in the minds of the adolescent child. The
social personality is to be completed by a strenuous inculcation
of those sentiments and that type of behaviour which best
promotes the folk-life and preserves its cohesion and continuity. Coming at a time, as we have seen, when the emotions and dispositions are aroused and in ferment, these
ceremonies serve to effect the final socialization of the child.
Requiring the presence of most of the adult members of the
tribe, these rites " serve also as the chief vehicle for the trans-
mission of the customs and ways of the community life from
one generation to another."[46] The initiation placed the child
into his niche in the folk-life and impressed upon him his
duties and obligations to his folk-fellows and his restrictions
as an individual. Thenceforward he was to do not as he liked,
but as was fitting in the light of the mores, as the head of a
family, as an active contributor to the food-supply, as a
participant in the cult and as a servant and worshipper of the
ancestral spirits. Comprehensively, the ceremony was " to
impress upon the youths a sense of responsibility as men, to
implant in them by means of impressive ceremonies the feeling
of obedience to the old men, and to the tribal moral code of
which they are the depositaries, and to insure that, before the
youth is permitted to take his place in the community, join
in the councils, and marry, he shall be possessed of those

qualifications which shall enable him to act for the common welfare, and not only to support himself and a wife and family, but also to contribute a fair share of the general stock, to which his relatives are entitled in common with himself."[47] In substance, the youth becomes endowed with a social value possessed by an adult alone.[48]

The overwhelming importance of this juncture in the individual life for the perpetuation of folk experience is realized by the tribespeople. The Yahgans of Tierra del Fuego, for example, do not doubt but that their hoary cult stands or falls with this institution of initiation. " And how the eyes of the ancient natives light ", we are told, " when talk is had of the old Tschiec-house " (the scene at the initiation).[49] Howitt describes a young Australian boy who had withstood all the privations of nearly thirty hours of torture and " was now scarcely able to contain himself as he stood and admired his costume. His face was radiant as he looked down first on one side and then on the other."[50]

There is everywhere evident pride on the part of the children, hope and expectancy on the part of the elders. The culmination of folk-glory is reached at this assumption of social responsibility. The folk-ethos glows and sparkles : " It is the hour of their new rebirth, it is the hour at which is established between them and the heads of the tribe the link of a new generation . . . the chief of the tribe and his wife consecrate (the novices) by means of rites of superlative realism, simulating the act of generation. . . ." There arise " triumphant cries, shouts of parents bursting with pride of children, cries of the young men who seem to embrace their comrades in exultation, cries in short of the entire people proud of their race. . . ."[51]

Initiation also signalizes the adoption of the youth by the ancestral and guardian spirits of the tribe. All that vague engulfing imaginary environment wherein dwell the swooping, ubiquitous forces that control the destiny of the folk and that wreak all the mischance and ill-fortune are introduced to the youth. Among the Fijians, the initiation served to admit the novices to man's estate and bring them " into communion with the ancestral spirits who controlled the destinies of their descendants." By these sacraments, " the Ancestors had deigned to receive them as members of the Nanga."[52] In New Guinea, also, the initiates were introduced individually to the tribal deity who would promise them protection in return for continuous loyalty to their tribe.[53] Among the American Indians, generally, a particular guardian spirit was convoked and discovered by each child at this period who was to control and defend his mature existence.[54] Among the Zuni, the medicine-man or Kok-ko transfers some of the supernatural, ghostly power by blowing upon a wand and extending it toward the mouth of the child, " who draws from it each time the sacred breath which passes from the mouth of the Kok-ko over the plumes."[55] The cosmic forces at whose mercy and whim primitive man must depend must be rendered sympathetic and known to the child, now become " man ".

Much more significant, immediately, in the nature of the initiation is the body of rights and duties assumed by the youth. By these ceremonies he becomes warrior, hunter, elector, dancer, smoker and all the other folk-attributes that cling to the independent mature man or woman. These rights are acquired not without the assumption of grave, serious duties, because these offices are the vital bonds constituting a cohesion and solidarity with the folk. The most serious concern is naturally that of food. The whole series of abstentions, fasts and ceremonies that strike the observer as hopelessly odd and grotesque, are intended, in the words of a most acute interpreter of the Andaman Islanders, " to develop in the mind of every new member of the society that sense of

the social value of foods . . . which may be briefly described
as being a realization that food is a possession of the society,
that not only the power to obtain food, but also the power to
use it without danger is something that the individual owes to
society, and that the bestowal upon him of this power is something that involves the acceptance on his part of corresponding
obligations."[56]   To indicate this dependence, therefore, the
boy must be ceremoniously fed by some friend or relative
who has already passed through the initiatory rites.   The
older man thus passes on the " right to eat " to the
initiate.[57]

So fundamental is the right to partake of food that it alone
may constitute the badge of citizenship.   In the D'Entrecasteaux Islands, at the puberty rites, one of the elders delivers
a speech admitting the boy to the fold formally, " by declaring
that henceforth as long as he lives amongst his kin he shall
never want for food."[58]   This is of remarkable significance as
one of the prime purposes of the association of men is in order
to secure sustenance and support more effectively for the
individual.   This is demonstrated at this most conspicuous
binding together of the individual and the group, at the initiation ceremonies.

Another of the outward manifestations of social maturity
is the assumption of the customary dress or clothing.   This
privilege is granted for the first time at these ceremonies of
induction into the full rights of the society.   Among the
Fijians, the boy as a youth " was quite nude, and therefore
of no consequence in the clan ".   At the ceremony of initiation,
however, he is first clothed with the *masi*, or native cloth, which
bestows upon him all the dignity and value of a full membership in the clan.[59]   The granting of the loin-cloth to the youth
works the same effect among the Monumbo-Papuans.[60]   The
very designation of the initiation ceremonies, *Bora*, among the
Kamilaroi of Australia is derived from the word *Bor*, or *Bur*,

meaning girdle, as it is on this occasion that the youth has conferred upon him the belt of manhood. This belt is of great potency as it has the power of injecting sickness in an enemy by being thrown at him.[61] In South Australia, the perineal band is conferred upon the boy very formally by his maternal uncle. Among other neighbouring tribes, the boy assumes not only this " belt of manhood " but the full male dress for the first time---the kilt, armlets, forehead band, nose-peg and necklace.[62] In Bolivia, among the Chiriguans, the father arouses the boy's ardour by holding up the lip-ornament, or *tembeta*, which is the distinguishing emblem of the tribe, as a reward for undergoing the trials of the initiation.[63] Clothing is a typical constituent of culture, and its design and make-up is an outstanding external sign of full adult incorporation into the tribal life. By granting this privilege under striking ceremonial accompaniment and vivid exhortation of fealty, the candidate is made to feel dependence upon the society for this right.

Certain pleasurable activities, such as smoking and drinking, are also withheld from the individual until this period. These acts, which are so precious, are made to depend again upon the feelings of adhesion and conformity. Among the Jibaros of Ecuador great festivities are celebrated when the child is initiated into the art and mysteries of smoking. All the family is gathered together and the eldest member delivers an oration in praise of the glorious valour of the child's ancestors and expresses the ardent hope that the latter may follow in their meritorious footsteps. Thereupon the child is given a pipe to smoke. This soon becomes a most treasured habit. All the members of the family on this occasion smoke with him.[64] Among the natives of the Bondei country in East Africa, smoking is one of the essential folkways, the practice of which is only allowed to those initiated into the men's society : " If a man was asked ' Who gave you leave to smoke ? ' he answered, ' I smoked strong tobacco in the *galo* ' " (or men's club). [65]

A revealing insight into the meaning of societal forms is reflected by the solemn duty assumed by the youth upon this formal entrance into the tribe of blood revenge—that is, of exacting the penalty of blood from the enemies of the family or the group. The close unity in blood which was often mythical, was one of the most ancient binding forces in the creation of the social solidarity and cohesion which gave protection to the individual. This alleged association by blood was also probably the basis of the origins of political organization. [66] To take an instance, among the Samoans, at the *Una* festival of initiation, the boy is solemnly introduced into the blood-brotherhood with an accompanying address by a near male relative. " The meaning of the *Una* festival consists in the fact that thereby a bond is sealed with the chief or head, who promises to revenge every evil that may be committed against the youth thenceforward. This accord amounts to a sort of life-insurance for the accepted candidate." [67] Thus the surety of life itself and the redress of personal grievances are the advantages of the existence in folk-association.

As the initiation is the most serious single occurrence in the individual's life in the primitive culture, it is severly impressed upon the novice that revelation of its secrets will be met with the direst, most horrible consequences for him. The utmost secrecy prevails as to the movements within the bush or place of ceremony. The candidates are especially warned to keep their tongues from wagging to the women. The women are often kept in subjection by the secretive halo thrown about these rites. As for a stranger, it is very unusual for him to gain admittance to the proceedings and where this is achieved, it is a sign of the deep regard with which he is held, for this admittance is tantamount to partaking of the innermost spirit of the mores. The continuity and prosperity of the folk hinge about the initiation. It would never do for an outsider to be present. The paucity of information we have on the actual proceedings in the ceremonies is due to this fact.

In British East Africa, a man even inquiring about the ceremony is fined one bull. The informants of Europeans have often been killed. Intruders are mishandled and even killed. [68] In Liberia, the unfortunate woman who either blunders or pries into the mysteries of the boy's school is killed—in some districts, eaten [69]—a certain way of preventing the information from being divulged. The Bambara boys are warned, that if they tell, " their bellies will swell, Komo will kill them, he will tear them to pieces, tear out their hearts, crush their heads so that their brains will not grow and their blood cease to course." [70] Toward the close of the Australian ceremonies, similarly, the headman and other armed warriors step up to the youths with uplifted tomahawks and spears, " and warn the novices that if they reveal what they have just seen, or any of the secret ceremonies which have taken place in their presence or in the bush to the women or uninitiated, their own lives and those of the persons to whom they confide the mysteries, will be required at the hands of the tribe." [71]

An atmosphere is created of continuous excitement and novelty that catches the unabated and fervid attention of all the youth's senses. He is aroused and put on edge so as to furnish a helpless receptivity to the precepts, admonitions and didactic pageantry there set forth. It is all arranged to capture his attention and become engraved indelibly with a severe, unmitigated decisiveness that time will never erase nor circumstance expunge. This is effected by an accumulated discipline of sleeplessness, ingenious torments and trials, nerve-wracking frights and vigils of an amazing variety. The child's will is rendered supine ; his mind is rendered hypersensitive and photographic to the impressions which the headmen and elders wish to transmit to the new generation.[72] The primitive man discerns little efficacy in the subtler, longer-continued and reiterated moulding of the personality. Crude, objective and gross measures are employed, particularly as this is the only type of treatment which can be of avail in the society where strength and physical prowess are of the greater moment for success in life. In addition, the absence of a written language that could convey the customs, traditions and lore left no other way open to induce the needful personal sentiments and to immortalize the deeds of the ancestors. The text is therefore acted graphically and symbolically in pageant and pantomime.

The youth is allowed no comfort or rest and kept rather in a state of uncertainty and anxiety. In addition he is secluded as a mark of the extraordinary transition in his life-experience. " . . . . He has no precise knowledge of what is in store for him and the sense of something out of the ordinary being about to happen to him—something moreover which is of a more or less mysterious nature—helps to impress him strongly with a feeling of the deep importance of strict compliance with the tribal rules and further still with a strong sense of the superiority of the older men who know and are familiar with all the mysterious rites. . . ."[73] So, among the Papuans, large smoky fires are kept going to make the boys sweat and steam. They are not permitted to talk much and then only in a low voice.[74] Among the Fuegians, also, strict silence is enforced : there must be no movement, speaking or laughter. The candidates must learn to sleep seated and crouched up in the narrow confines of the initiation-hall. At night there are watchmen installed to double up forcibly the legs of those who seek to extend them.[75] Among the Ba-thonga of South Africa, the boys " lie naked in their shed, heads turned toward the central court, and suffer bitterly in the cold. Shepherds watch them during the night and beat them if they lie on the side. . . ."[76] Nor are the boys allowed to go into the water and bathe during the probationary period, " lest the influence with which the ceremonies have filled them should be washed off."[77]   In this way the stage is set and the youth kept on the *qui vive*, alert and painfully aware of all that proceeds.

The whippings and torments are sometimes of incredible severity.   They also attest to the crude " impressionistic " manner in which the culture is brought to bear upon the young. The Bechuana boys are arrayed in a state of nudity, each morning.   " The men of the town, all armed with long thin wands of a tough, strong, supple brush . . . are engaged in a dance named ' *Khoa* ', in which questions are put to the boys, as, ' Will you guard the chief well ? ' ' Will you herd the cattle well ? ' and while the latter give an affirmative answer, the men rush forward to them, and each aims a full-length blow at the back of one of the boys . . . . causes the supple wand to descend and bend into his back and every stroke inflicted thus makes the blood squirt out.   At the end of the dance, the boys' backs are seamed with wounds and weals, the scars of which remain through life. . . ."[78]   Thus arises the common saying that the neophyte learns the law while he is thrashed.[79] The ordeals to which the Nandi boys are exposed are of this sort : " Each boy holds the one in front of him round the waist and stoops down so as to place his head against the other's buttocks. . . . At the entrance and exit of this cage stand warriors armed with stinging nettles and hornets.   With the former they beat the boys on the face and private parts, the latter they drop on the boys' backs.[80]

Among the Melanesians of the New Hebrides, likewise, the boys were tormented exceedingly.   They were forced to take live embers in their hands.   In the words of a participant : " We lay down on the ground and they trod upon us ; they all ran over us, one of them taking the lead, and when he had stamped on us as he ran they all stamped on us."[81]   In the Gilbert Islands, the boy's adoptive grandfather sets ablaze a large shrivelled coconut leaf in the fire, and standing behind the lad, shakes over his naked shoulders and head a continuous shower of burning morsels. " The heaviest of these were fanned away by the uncles, but the lesser sparks were allowed to burn themselves out on the bare skin, and if the lad flinched or attempted to wipe his streaming eyes he was taunted, pushed and thrashed by his stern guardians."[82]   Fortitude was induced by the Indians of Southern California by beating the naked body of the boy with stinging nettles until he was unable to move.   After that, " he was placed upon the nest of a species of virulent ant, while his friends irritated the insects by stirring them up.   The infuriated ants swarmed over every part of the sufferer's body, into his eyes, his ears, his mouth, his nose, causing indescribable pain."[83]   Whipping with switches was commonly employed among the Amerindians. According to old chroniclers among the Powhatan of Virginia, the boys were actually rendered unconscious, " the declared purpose being to take away the childish things so that they should wake up as men."[84]

By means of such torments and ordeals, the lesson was adequately enforced.   The boy, to claim mature rights in the folk-life, must curb his individuality in adjustment with the folk-ways.   The fact was driven into him by torture of the flesh that power rested in the hands of the elders and that his success as a man depended upon conforming and respecting it.   The boy who winced or demurred at the tortures perpetrated upon him would never attain to the status of a grown-up in the tribe. He was forced to endure such tests as walking on hot pebbles and crushed palm-nuts, passing naked through thorny thickets, and if he allowed a murmur to escape him, he would be exposed to the derision and insults and jests of the crowd.[85]

The social forces thus produce in the child a yielding and cringing conformity.   The entire folk gathered about shout cries of encouragement and hope among the Bambara, as the boys are whipped. The men spit on the boy's sandal, dip it in sand and strike the boy on the thigh with it, so that the sand scarifies the skin. " Or, a stick is spun with friction on a boy's skin, till it raises a blister. Or, a boy is struck across the throat with the outer edge of a man's extended hand. Or, a stick is laid across a lad's head and drummed with another stick, to the agony of the boy. . . ." The boys of six and seven years endure all this stoically after the second blow, and seem to be of bronze.[86] Should a boy show signs of fear, he would be so scorned and mocked that he would, unless restrained, commit suicide. Even a father would scorn such a son and would not prevent him from killing himself.[87] The Basuto would kill the boy who attempted to flee, and among the Euahlayi tribe of Australia, the timid boy would be returned to his mother as unfit for initiation, " and sooner or later, sympathetic magic would do its work, a poison-stock or bone would end him. . ."[88]

The most important activity to which all must contribute is the search for food. Where animals or plants are not yet domesticated, particularly, this food-getting is the most engrossing concern of the folk and upon this their welfare securely rests. The pre-eminent duty of the mature individual is to contribute to this supply of food and, as we have seen, the chief benefit he derives from social life is the right to draw upon its food-supply. At the initiation ceremony, therefore, it is essential that the novice be made to feel the social importance of food, the fact that the satisfaction of the basic desire for food is bound in relationship to the other individuals of the group and that by custom all are obliged to share the catch or yield in common. Food and drink, like fire, may thus serve, above all other objects, to arouse continuously the feeling of dependence and relation to the folk-fellows. To impress this most important fact, the novice is placed, for example, among the Australians, in the midst of plenty, and forced to

abstain from food for an extended period of time.   The feeling
of self-restraint is thus encouraged, and " the pride of flesh
brought down ", as is said of the Tasmanians.[89]   To further
indicate the close dependence of the individual upon the efforts
of his fellows as to the satisfaction of his hunger, among the
Papuans, the boys are taught economy in eating.   At the
initiation they are handed out food but told only to bite the
food and set it aside.[90]   In the Andaman Islands, it is the chief
who tests the endurance of the youths by withholding food from
them for days.   In fact, exceptional cases are cited in which
the probationer has expressed a desire to prolong the time of
abstinence, it being a cause for boasting when the average
period has been exceeded."[91]   This is a clear evidence of the
building of a social sentiment.   As food is the prime concern,
so the most skilful hunter or provider maintains a commanding
position and the natural impulse to stand out and receive
praise is channelized into those lines that best promote the
success of the entire group.

A similar custom has been found among the Fuegians.   To
receive the confidence of the older man, a probationary period
often extending over two years is instituted, during which
the boy abandons the protection of his family.   " He must
eat lean hard meat, with no fat—a real privation even for
whites in that bitter climate . . . not even the luxury of
' hard tack ' offered him privately and backed by a ravenous
appetite will induce a boy to break his self-imposed abstinence. . . ."[92]   It was common among the Amerindians that,
before becoming a warrior, the boy was forced to fast.   For
example, the Omaha youth was to fast four days and nights
and no matter how hungry he became, he was forbidden to
use the bow and arrows put into his hands by his father when
he left home for his solitary test of endurance.[93]

Not only the withholding of food but the serving of it along
with disgusting and nauseating admixtures is a feature of

puberty rites. The intention is again to test the mettle of the youth and pulverize his will into submission or to befuddle his mind so as to work a permanent remembrance in the recesses of his consciousness of this most memorable occasion. These horrors of the palate are thenceforward forever associated with the force behind the elders and the folk. As a striking instance, allusion may be made to the custom in the Gilbert Islands of giving the youth a mixture of fresh water, sea water and cocoanut oil to drink, stirred together in a cocoanut shell with the barb of a sting ray. This disgusting potion is administered to the recitation of a charm. At the same time the boy's scalp is lacerated with a shark's tooth until the blood streams over the eyes and cheeks.[94] Among the Australians the boys are compelled on this occasion to " eat the most revolting food that it ever entered the mind of man to eat or to offer to a fellow-creature, such as the prophet Ezekiel, in a vision, was commanded to eat (ch. 4, 12)."[95] The food is served often underdone and the boys are allowed to drink water only by sucking it up through a reed[96]—perhaps as a sample of the lack and want that often befalls these people. In the Torres Straits, we are told that during the course of instruction, the initiates are compelled to eat the flesh of corpses ; " one effect of this diet is to make them wild so that they care for nobody, and all affection temporarily ceases for relatives, wife and children . . . ."[97] In North Carolina, likewise, before the Indian youths graduated into man's estate, they were " husquenaughed. " This consisted first in half-starving the boys and then administering pellitory bark and intoxicating plants, " that make them go raving mad as ever were any people in the world . . . all which continues about five or six weeks, and the little meat they eat is the nastiest, loathsome stuff, and mixt with all manner of filth it is possible to get. . . . Several die under this terible purgation."[98] All the evidence points toward an effort to produce a total revolution at this point in the attitude of the individual toward his cultural environment : all that is to follow is supposed to be uncompromisingly fresh and unmistakably lasting.

Under this sort of treatment, it is not strange that many of the boys collapse mortally, and as far as their folk-existence is concerned no memory exists at all. The details of their deaths are kept secret and the body buried in the vicinity without benefit of mourning or funeral ceremony, for such individuals had never attained a complete independent personality. The deceased are considered simply to have disappeared, as among the Basutos and other folk in Africa.[99] When a Papuan boy succumbs to the trials of the initiation (which is not unusual), the faces of the survivors are painted one side red and the other side black, " and if a mother does not see her son among the emerging batch she knows by these signs that he is dead, but she is not permitted to comment or complain."[100]   In this way, a crude selection of those best fit for their social environment is carried out. The weaklings are mercilessly thrown aside as incapable of assuming the position of head of a family and food-getter and hence undeserving of the protective rights of the cult and the prestige as a descendant of renowned ancestors.

There is still another more formidable means used to overawe and intimidate the youth.   This consists in exposing the candidates to all the invisible frights and hair-raising terrors of the supernatural workings of the ghosts and spirits. It is this terrifying element of the unknown which casts its shadow over so large a province of primitive life because experience and collected facts of life are so scanty. The elders often draw upon this with a cynical manipulation of the superstitions. Gross force, threats and duress are clothed with mysterious trappings ; weird noises and dim forebodings are explained as emanating from ghostly ancestral spirits. All this is used to immolate the youth's will and to banish from his mind all doubts and questionings as to the proceedings through which he is to pass. In his resultant distress and quaking, the boy or girl is eager to turn to his personal guide or the headman for aid and yield unconsciously to his sway, and that of the ways of the folk forever after.

Thus, in Port Stephens, New South Wales, it was the awful sound of " the *goonanduckyer*, the voice of *Goolumbra*, which impressed the boys with the solemnity of the occasion and rendered their minds better fit to learn the society's lessons."[101] Bull-roarers are used to frighten the boys, but this mystery is later explained to them when they have satisfactorily passed the other ordeals. Large hot stones are sent coursing down the hills and pass immediately before the boys, scorching the grass in their passage. All this is said to be the work of *Dhurramoolun*, the angry spirit. A simpler device is also used : the guardians or sponsors of the boys direct the attention of the latter to the sun, which momentarily impairs their vision so that when they look down before them again it is all the more unearthly and demoniacal. The men who crouch down before the novices are painted jet black, pull down their lower eyelids with their hands and glare fiercely at the novices, who, blinded by the sun are frightened all the more by these fierce apparitions.[102] Among the Papuans, if a boy runs away in fright, trees are thrown across the road and he is told that this is the spirits' doing.[103] In New Guinea, a whining noise which the children were taught to regard as the voice of a demon (which was produced by a bull-roarer), absolutely terrorized them.[104] In Ceram, among the Malays, the boys were seated in darkness and then exposed to all manner of howls, yells, rattling of weapons and arms that made their hair stand on end.[105] On Florida Island in Melanesia, a screen, ten feet long and nine feet high, made of bark, painted and ornamented, is carried into the open to bulldoze the uninitiated, who believe it to be the work of the ghosts.[106]

A most remarkable and convincing case of the employment of these means of flabbergasting and stupefying is that used by the Fijians. The lads are brought to the eastern gate of an enclosure. " Here a dreadful sight appalled them. Right across the entrance lay the naked body of a dead man, smeared with black paint from head to foot, with his entrails protruding. Above him, stretched stiff, with his head upon one pyramid and his feet upon the other lay another body, and under this hideous arch . . . they were made to crawl. Within the inclosure their hearts turned to water, for the dead men lay in rows, smeared with blood and entrails, and over every body they had to crawl. . . . Suddenly (the chief) burst out with a great yell ; the dead men started up, and ran to wash off the blood and filth. . . . They are playing the part of the dead Ancestors. . . ."[107]

After this petrifying terror has been installed into the candidates, the elders usually pretend to beat off the monstrous forces. While in this chastened and receptive frame of mind, the lads, now impressed with the power of the men, will pay strict heed to the instruction given them. An expert observer states that " the entire process so beats down the will of the novices and terrorizes them, that even those who have been forced into it against their will, when they emerge at the close of the rite, must inviolably preserve its secrets, and express themselves as pleased."[108] The sociological character of the initiation is revealed by the fact stated by another informed reporter of the Africans, that what the boys actually dread is not always the physical suffering involved, but the fearful mystery and the heavy responsibilities which the ceremony entails for them.[109] The assumption of the full social personality for the youth in the simpler society is truly celebrated in a climactic, demonstrative manner.

These harrowing and turbulent performances are preliminary to the actual course of instruction meted out to the candidates. All that the child should know to qualify him for full participation in the folk-life, and for enjoyment of its precious privileges are thus found to depend upon an obedient reverence of age and tradition and an acceptance of the personal restrictions and tabus of conduct that are contained in the folk-ways. In this lies the core of the initiation ceremonies. Many of the folk-ways, particularly those of a more tangible nature, as we have seen, have already been acquired imperceptibly by the child during his infancy and adolescence. At the initiation, therefore, the instruction is usually confined to the more involved or developed folk-ways and to the mores, the less tangible aspects of the social heritage. These latter include the emotional disposition and the body of sentiments that cluster about the folk-ways and deem them "right" and "moral" and worthy of being cherished and defended. This conditioned behaviour hinges always about the acquiescent respect for elders and the traditions and lore of the tribe and respect for the unseen, supernatural forces which sanction the usages. The cohesion and continuity of the folk is thus insured.

At the initiation there can be witnessed overtly a didactic display of the characteristic features of the culture of the folk being handed down to the younger generation. In New Guinea, for instance, a procession wends its way along the beach, composed of young-men drummers, conch-shell blowers, dancing girls, groups of masks and totem-effigies, forming a tableaux representing every phase of the folk-life. "Its masks were traditional reminders of their obligations to their ancestors; its totem-effigies symbolised the sources of everything that made life possible to them. Nothing and nobody was overlooked, not even the missionary's wife, who was represented by a clever imitation of her white sun umbrella."[110] Often a series of pantomimic performances, akin to morality plays, are put on to impress the child with his " moral " duties—all of which are merely aspects of the mores. Howitt declares that " if one were to imagine all sorts of childish mischief mixed up with the cardinal sins represented in burlesque and ironically recommended to the boys on their return to the camp and afterwards, it would give a not unapt representation of what takes place."[111]

The queer nature of this use of irony is mentioned also by Mathews. The guardians of the boys joke with each other all the time. " If any of them see an iguana going up a tree, they say he is coming down ; if a small bird is seen they say it is very large ; if the day is cold, they remark that it is hot, and so on. At each of these statements . . . a shout is given and all the men laugh. The novices are not permitted to laugh at anything that is said or done no matter how amusing or preposterous it may be."[112] This is symptomatic of the extraordinary state in which the initiates are supposed to be, or it may be merely an aspect of the attempt to confuse the boys.

In Nyasaland, an essential part of the rites was an exhibition of representations of animals and other things, made of mounds of earth outlined in flour. One such mound pictured a whale, another Lake Nyasa ; and a third was called " the little hill of debt ", indicating a kind of abstract idea signifying that everyone owes a debt to his *unyago*, a debt to his ancestors and progeny.[113] Combined with this pageantry, there are symbolical dances performed by the elders, in which the youth begins to partake towards the end of his term in the bush. Dancing in the primitive society is an affirmation of the solidarity of those taking part. In a sense, the dance is a symbol of the organic unity of the folk. The song is a similar vocal expression of folk-life. As the youth hears these and later begins to take part in the dances and the songs, he is becoming inwardly conscious of the new relationship between himself and the group.[114] These methods are employed characteristically as they serve to arouse the emotions of the child and endear in his memory this prominent occasion. A diploma or degree certainly would not be nearly as effective in their stead.

So, among the Australians, the folk-spirit seems to come to a focus and the feeling of social cohesion most vivid at the corroborees or dances, which the initiate learns on this occasion. Dances and performances to illustrate the magical powers of the spirits are indulged in along with others, " to enforce tribal morality or to perpetuate tribal legends ".[115] In the Congo region, likewise, the mythical traditions and dances are learned at initiation.[116] The sacred matters relating to the totem or animal ancestors are displayed under mysterious guises to the novices at the Australian *bora*. By means of graphic dances and performances, the traditions dealing with this most hallowed part of the mores are impressed upon the youths. It is believed that " it is as a reincarnation of the never-dying spirit past of one of these semi-animal ancestors that every member of the tribe is born."[117] Such animals as bandicoots, grasshoppers, wallabies, turkeys, iguanas, bears, kangaroos, fish, bees, wood-ducks, are the subject of the play, one animal being selected for the evening.[118]

Among the Becwana of Africa, " songs of law " are chanted to the candidates which clothe native points of morality and correct conduct. For example, such songs exhort the boys to protect the cattle while the men are away ; to give the bones of killed cattle to the men, to kill the hawk that feasts on the doves, to refrain from disturbing the chief's fire, to respect the father's younger brother, to learn the hereditary refuges, etc. A specimen refrain is the following :

> " At home ! One's father ! One's father !
>   Should one curse him
>   He will be afraid,
>   Afraid of the tooth,
>   Even the long tooth
>   Which eats tripe
>   And chitterlings
>   The meat of old men."[119]

The Cahuilla Indians on the Pacific coast also taught the boys how to dance and use the gourd rattle as an accompaniment. Beside, " enemy songs ", which played an important part in the clan life, were taught. The force of custom is illustrated, for these songs had been in this way handed down for generations, " and while there may not have been any real enmity felt toward the people about whom the songs were composed, it was a sacred duty to sing them because their fathers had done so ".[120] Archaic elements are in this manner carried on long past the circumstances in the life-conditions of the folk which gave them survival-value. It is not unusual, in fidelity to the past, to find things done at the initiatory rites in the archaic way. The Nandi boy in East Africa is compelled, for example, to eat out of honey barrels instead of plates and to drink out of gourds instead of cups. The Sotho boy is forced to make the fire according to the ancient method rather than the current way.[121]

The initiation serves thus as a vehicle for the perpetuation of tradition by its transfer from the older generation which has lived in its light and to whom it has become extremely precious unto the younger generation which is to assume the burden of carrying it forward. But it is also essential that the youth be instructed in those ways that best promote the group-solidarity and internal peace, here and now. The instruction meted out to the candidates reflects the culture-traits of the folk. Each tribe has a programme of strictures, admonitions and lessons best suited its own needs. Among the Ba-thonga, for example, a veritable school is conducted to which the youths are brought each morning during their term. A special instructor, who holds his office by heredity, climbs on a tree and teaches the boys. He begins in this way : " Little boys, do you hear me ? I say ", etc., etc.[122] Among the Yao, the principal person at the " mysteries " is called " the rattler of the tails ". He it is who communicates to the initiates information about the customs of the tribe and delivers moral lectures.[123] The headman of the village tells the boys of their customs and history, among the Bageshu ; he also tells them who are the friends and the enemies of each clan. In the Congo basin, the medicine man teaches the dances, traditions and the art of making huts, baskets and medicine.[124] The man chosen for this important office as chief or medicine man embodies above all others the cohesive power behind the folk.

The instruction given often appears to be a hodge-podge of hygienic precautions, moral enlightenment and training in the daily occupations and concerns of life. A sample is that of the natives of the Torres Straits. The following is addressed to the boys : " If two boys are mates they may not marry each other's sisters, or by and bye they ashamed ; they like brothers, they may marry two sisters along another man. If man ask for food or water or anything else, you give, if you have a little, give little, suppose you got plenty you give half. Look after mother and father, never mind if you and your wife have to go without. Give half of all your fish to your parents ; don't be mean. Don't speak bad word to mother. Father and mother all along same as food in belly ; when they die you feel hungry and empty. Mind your uncles too and cousins. If your brother go to fight, you help him, go together ; don't let him go first."[125] From this one may infer that the bulk

of the admonitions are calculated to fasten upon the youth
a host of duties and obligations to his parents and relatives.
In each instance there is an evident curbing of the individual
selfish impulses and restriction of conduct, in order to produce
feelings of duty and obligation in the initiate. The network
of folk-relationships that are set up by life in society require
some such body of advice. The following additional information also relates to these same people and illustrates the
attempt to procure order and peace in the folk-life. The
novice was told " not to stand upright in the presence of the
old men ; not to swear, *bagai ;* not to talk scandal, that is,
if he heard about anyone committing adultery he was to remain
silent and not to talk about it and so make it worse ; not to
steal food ; that he should carry things for the old men ; he
ought to give food to the *maidelaig* (sorcerer) should he want
any . . . a man might not marry his *maidelaigau kazi* (the
child of a sorcerer) nor might he marry the sister of his *kaimi*
(mate) as she is all same sister."[126] Trivialities of deportment
are thus intermixed with graver, more serious folk-ways in
the unordered manner of the primitive's experience. But of
the greatest importance are the rules regulating intercourse
with the other sex, for here a veritable imbroglio of social
relationships is potentially possible. So that, finally, " the
characters of various girls were made known to the youths
that they might be forewarned. They were, for instance,
taught magical practices that the women might fall in love
with them."[127]

In Papua, the moral code runs as follows : " It is wrong
to steal. It is wrong to commit adultery, for if you do you
will die quickly. It is wrong to beat your wife, if you do,
other people will say, you are like a dog. It is wrong to steal
food from gardens. . . . It is good to make big gardens, in
order that your wife may be faithful to you. When you take
a wife, live with the single men until your gardens have plenty

of food ; until they are ready, let your wife live with your father and mother. If you have connection with your wife and she becomes pregnant before your gardens are ready, you will incur the contempt of the village."[128] There is exhibited in this a recognition of the remarkably intimate connection between marital and economic relations and the manner in which the success of the former is dependent upon that of the latter—how a fruitful garden will bring a faithful wife, and progeny. The youth's eyes are thus turned forward to the serious concerns of the adult experience with food and women.

Various other safeguards against the insidious feminine influences are also advanced, as among the Yaos of Africa. A drunken native supplied this information drawn from his own experience at initiation. The preceptor says : " You, my pupils, you are now initiated. Your mother and father fear (respect) them. See that you do not enter the house (un-announced) lest you should find them embracing. . . . You must be afraid (take care) when you see the (new) moon, you might get hurt. Beware of women during their courses, this is dangerous (it causes) many diseases." All the matters concerning sex are explained unreservedly.[129] In Australia, likewise, the boys are cautioned not to go near a woman *enceinte*, nor to let a woman's shadow fall across them, nor to permit a woman to make bread for them. . .[130] Other dangers of female wiles, less recondite perhaps, are inferred in the Torres Straits : " If a woman walk along, you no follow ; by and by man look, he call you bad name. If a canoe is going out to fight another place, you go in canoe ; no stop behind to see woman."[131]

The girls usually undergo a series of rites and ceremonies analogous to the initiatory experiences of the boys and often in imitation of them. The period of instruction is usually shorter and the girl does not always undergo organized formalities witnessed by the entire tribe. The wholly mysterious functional characteristics of puberty in the girl are, however, so dangerously alarming that the girl is often thrust outside the society altogether for this period. The experience of the natives, however primitive and simple, soon recognized these signs as premonitions of maturity and recognized also the social implications involved ; so that, at the time of the girl's removal from the folk, she is fully instructed in the necessary concerns and imbued with the attitudes and behaviour most fitting for an adult woman, in the light of the folkways. For example, in the Gilbert Islands, at puberty, the girl was thrust into a small cubicle, " deprived of sunlight and unseen by the people.   Only her parents and grandparents were allowed near her ; her only constant companion was her adoptive grandmother who attended to all her wants. She was allowed to wash and perform her toilet between the outer screen and the cubicle. . . . Thus she was obliged to live in utter manual idleness, since there was not enough light to guide her fingers at work, but to compensate for this she learned all the spells that her grandmother could teach her, most of them being connected with love, healing and the culinary arts."[132]   This isolation and course of initiation may, in some instances, as in the Riff Islands, occupy upward of two years.[133]

The girl also on this occasion may be forced to undergo an ordeal.   At the first signs of puberty, in the Amazon River region, all the friends and relatives of the girl assemble, "bringing each of them, pieces of *sipo* (an elastic climber) ; the girl is then brought out perfectly naked, into the midst of them, when each person present gives her five or six severe blows with the *sipo* across the back and breast, till she falls senseless, and sometimes dead."[134]   The tabus and restrictions upon her food during this period are extensive. Among the Stseelis of Canada, for example, " she might not eat any fresh meat or fish of any kind, only that which had been long killed and dried. These restrictions had a two-fold purpose. First, to prevent her from becoming a greedy and sensual woman, and second, because of the ' bad medicine ' of the malign influence she was supposed to exercise at this time upon animals because of her condition."[135] She was forced to dig trenches to inure her to hard work ; when carrying home fir branches with which to strew the floor of the hut, she had to stroke her back and head with a branch praying that those members might never get tired carrying heavy burdens. She made miniatures of every article which women were in the habit of making, as baskets of root and birch-bark, mats, ropes and thread.[136]

The girl's curriculum, then, included these things prominent in the life of the mature woman. Among the head-hunters of Borneo, elaborate dances and medicinal preparations were taught.[137] Among the Ila people of Rhodesia, the old woman instructress holds her pupils by the ear and dilates upon the proper conduct of the married woman : " Man has to be reverenced and well looked after in the house ; your parents-in-law also." The girl is not supposed to speak, but to nod her head and signify assent.[138] The essential things in the folk-ways of the Amazon Indians for the mature girl were a knowledge of the dances and songs and the festival-painting. These were secured at this time.[139] The girls were naturally more seriously involved in matters of sex. At the girls' houses in Papua, the old women gave thorough courses in prevention of conception, procuring abortion and other matters of sexology.[140] All this explains the common idea that it was by virtue of the initiation rites alone that the girl could bear a child. The rites were essential preliminaries and in the ordinary exaggerated way by which folk-thought often draws within its fantasy conclusions from erroneous premises, it was believed that propagation was also consequent upon the fulfilment by the girl of these ordeals and ceremonies. Pregnancy became thus a ghostly or spiritual, rather than a physical function.[141]

P

The immense accumulative force of these ordeals, privations, admonitions and instructions which in some instances are protracted for months, if not years at a time, is astounding in its effect upon the character of the youth. He emerges truly recast into a new mould, that of the mores of his folk. No longer indifferently interested in the life about, but keenly alive to the seriousness of his duties and the solemnity of his responsibilities, he emerges inwardly transformed. It is this conception of the supreme value of the initiation which moves the New Guinea native to declare that upon return from the bush to his village the youth carries with him, " the other fellow inside ", that is the consciousness of his bonds to the eternal past.[142]

Therefore, upon returning from the rites, the boy affects to treat everything with surprise as one come into a new life, to recognize no one, not even his own parents. In fact, the " new-comer " is treated with every mark of kindness until it is supposed that he has become accustomed to his surroundings and is shaken down into his place in life. He is often given new clothing, has his head shaved and is bathed, all to celebrate the birth of a new existence. Presents are also exchanged amid great festivity. The boy is now regarded as an adult and his spirit will live after death, and on his death, his name will be given to a member of his family, signifying thereby a complete recognition for ever of his individuality in the folk-life.[143] The boys cry out triumphantly (among the Mundombe of South Africa) on emerging, "Here we are!" upon which the entire folk who are assembled exclaim, "Truly ye are men!"[144]

A turnover of generations is thus greeted. This paraphernalia of pageantry and ceremony is typical of most of the social instruments or institutions which are pieced and woven together in culture-evolution. The machinery is awkward and creaking, as the product of innumerable individual efforts, yet tremendously effective as a pedagogical device. Such institutions are empirical products but as society becomes more closely knit and differentiation of groups begins to appear, the puberty rites along with the other institutions, which are merely aggregated folk-ways about a central folk-interest, become more coherent, and are consciously employed. The state or political organization, for example, arises out of the military organization. The chief or headman with the council of elders seize upon the puberty ceremonies as grist for their own mill. Thereafter the state forces obedience upon its subjects by imposing upon the youths these ordeals for the more selfish aims of the rulers. Among the Bechuanas, all the boys who attend the initiation ceremony at the same time form upon their return a regiment or contingent in the field under the command of a son of the chief.[145] Thus, a new " society " or societal sub-division is purposefully created through the medium of the initiation institution.

The men's societies among some of the peoples of simpler culture have also taken over the machinery to intimidate the women, as in Melanesia ; or in order to separate off distinct economic classes, as in certain districts of Polynesia. In many parts of Africa, the continued domination and tyranny of petty chiefs is due to this same instrument. In later culture-history, the church employed like tactics. As a matter of fact, the most vigorous employment of initiation to-day lies in the confirmation ceremonies of the older ecclesiastical organizations.

Contemporary vestiges occur also in the " ritual " of fraternal and benefit organizations. In no instance do they assume the significance, the universality characteristic of the initiation rites in the simpler cultures. That is because the initiation is there the salient episode in the knotting of individual to society. These rites centre about the period of puberty, which in organic evolution is also the turning-point between the individual and the race-life.

CHAPTER XI

INHERITANCE AND SUCCESSION

IT is not to be supposed that each child shares equally in the
social heritage even in the primitive society. In the main,
the initiation ceremonies serve to mould each youth without
distinction into a fixed cultural stereotype. The innate
physical and mental qualities differ among the individuals
even in the simpler societies, and in imperceptible ways that
may result in the development of variable aptitudes toward
the social life as a consequence. The mental and educational
discipline of the initiation period may not altogether erase
these individual distinctions, and to certain youths more may
be said to accrue then to others. Yet in the more primitive
culture the sense of solidarity and cohesion is of immeasurable
strength as it would have to be in order to insure the survival
of the folk. The various departments of culture, particularly
ways of food-getting and material support, are yet so fragile
and meagre that the tribe is forced to use stringent means
in imposing an undeviating conformity on the part of its
members. We have seen the dramatic manner in which this
is accomplished by the mingled physical and mental chastening
of the young. The spirited nonconformist or the quivering
weakling among them is summarily dispatched as unworthy
of assuming the toga of maturity and the benefits of the mores.
The new generation is thus composed of individuals all un-
differentiated and decisively beaten into line.

The purpose of the present chapter is to describe the manner
in which some of the tangible assets of a culture are transmitted to the children. It will be observed that objects of

property, real and personal, assume material value, and that through a gradual process of evolution of the forms of bequest and inheritance individuals receive the exclusive right and benefit of them. Possession of objects that enhance one's material standing, including human beings such as slaves or wives, are gradually assumed by stipulated heirs. The initiation is calculated to produce a type of behaviour and a body of sentiments alike for each child as the very basis of effective folk-existence, but the folk-ways of inheritance reveal the opening wedge of distinctions of an economic sort. These differences soon reverberate through the social field and carry in their train differences of prestige, rank, and position. Children are then able to benefit directly from the experience of their own particular family-group, as well as that of the entire folk. This motive, to endow the children, had a decisive effect upon narrowing of family-groups from the original horde to the exclusively monogamous family.

In the simpler cultures property is thought to follow blood. Determination of the heir or heirs is of a piece with the mores. The continuity of the economically developing society is dependent upon a habitual mode of succession, the nature of which is derived from the essential make-up of the folk-ways. Even where there have not yet appeared any fixed testamentary forms and procedure, a tacit feeling of " legality " only surrounds inheritance by the customary heir or group of heirs. This feeling is strong where the matter in dispute involves property which is of great importance. Even if the dying man specifies his heirs, as among the Mossi of Africa, once he is buried, " nothing more or less is done than is usual and customary which is often contrary to the expressed orders of the deceased."[1] The force of custom is unyielding in this matter. This is also illustrated in the case of the West African boy who claimed to inherit part of his father's property. The defendant was the uncle who had seized the goods and who pleaded in the administrative court to the effect that the son could not inherit the father's property because his parents had married for love ![2] Such frivolous considerations were not the binding force of durable sex-unions among these people and the issue of a love union were unrecognized and hence, "immoral". Purchase-marriage was the correct form of acquiring a wife and the children of such a union alone could have claim to the fruits of the father's toil and thrift, that is, his property.

The primitive ideas on inheritance are influenced also by the strong feeling entertained by primitive man as to the continuance of personal existence. "Death", to his mind, is a hazy notion of a temporary unconsciousness or transition of the person to a less palpable but very real presence in the imaginary environment of ghosts and spirits. We have examined the beliefs in ancestral reappearance in the child. Inheritance is easily adjusted for the child who is believed to be an ancestral reapparition and who is evidently also entitled to carry on the ownership of the property of the deceased. Thus, among the Ila natives of Rhodesia, " to succeed a person is *Kudyaizhina* (to eat the name), the successor is called *Mudyezhina* ('Eater of the name') and actually adopts the deceased's name. Eating the name involved inheriting a portion of the property but not all."[3] It is very striking, indeed, as displayed in the final note of this citation, that where matters of economic importance are concerned, the hazy ideology of the primitive man clears up instantly. The heir is considered to be a continued appearance of the individual who has fled his earlier physical body and in that capacity carries on with his former possessions. Or, the heir who is chosen is thought thereafter to become the dead individual. Under some circumstances this line of thought cannot be carried too far, as the property and belongings are so valuable that many others would like to enjoy them.

That the heir is supposed to perpetuate the deceased is shown also by the fact that he is set exactly in the latter's position. The social relationships are not disrupted but rather reaffirmed and the " eater of the name " is reinvested with them. The feeling of social disruption caused by the removal of an active adult into the imaginary spirit environment is healed by placing the heir into the vacant niche and thus resuming the social cohesion toward which inevitably the folk-life always contributes. Thus in the ceremony of the Baganda, " the heir is brought out and stands at the door of the house, and his uncle (a brother of the deceased) comes and throws over him a bark-cloth, and announces to all present : ' This is the heir of the deceased '. Each person then comes and ties on his right wrist a few cowrie shells, and all those who have unpaid debts come to him and announce the amount the deceased owed them. The heir is next presented with a shield, a spear and a large knife, and a girl is also given him as a wife."[4] The uncle officiates before the tribe as a representative of the blood-group or family and a bark-cloth is used probably as a symbol of an ancient form of dress, which lends solemnity to the occasion. The ancestral spirits are always associated with hoary age and the folk-ways of the past are jealously guarded by them. The heir is also duly accoutred with the tools, significant of one of the chief types of property of a self-respecting Baganda.

The mode of sealing the inheritance varies in the folk-ways. Among the Bakitara, " a few beans, like dwarf beans, or some millet, were placed in the dead man's right hand, and the son took them out of it with his lips, and after munching them up, puffed them over the body and round the room, thus proclaiming himself the legal heir to any property there might be "[5]

Originally, most immovable property was held in communal fashion. At the death of the individual, the survivors continued to enjoy in common such things as the yield from the land and the game and wild vegetable food on it. This inheritance devolved upon the children, as a group, without any set allocation among them. Actual use might tend, however, to cause certain parts of this " bequest " to gravitate into the hands of those of the children who could make most use of it. The needs of everyday existence might in this way divide the property along the lines of the sexes. Thus, among the Yoruba, " when a man dies his sons divide all the property between them. The daughters have no inheritance in their father's house, but they divide between them the property of their mother."[6] In Guam, the bequest comes unawares, and is none the less beneficent and real, but its enjoyment by the children is in common. When the father dies, " the wife and children are not left destitute, as would be the case if they depended on the results of his handiwork alone. The crops continue to ripen and are gathered in due time by the family ; the weeds and worms are kept out of the tobacco ; the coffee-bushes bend each year under their weight of berries ; and the cocoanuts, as usual, yield their annual dividend."[7]

Discrimination is bound to arise, however, if merely on the lines of sex, as above. In Borneo the male children inherit the land, cattle, buffaloes, ponies, gongs, etc., while the women receive the household goods, " perhaps a little brass-ware— anything, in fact, which is used by the women only. . . ." The male slaves go to the sons, the female slaves to the daughters. Birds' nest caves and bee trees, in the nature of the case, might be divided or shared among all the children.[8] On the island of Ambon in Melanesia, the hunting and fishing utensils left by the deceased were taken by the boys, the house-utensils and silver-work was bestowed on the girls. In Buru, the division was also by sex, the girls receiving the articles of clothing and personal property of the mother, the boys, the house and cultivated lands.[9]

Traces of a more purposive division on the basis of social position and relationship soon arises out of the broader division of sex. In Timor-Laut, in Melanesia, the goods were divided among the children, " those living in a large house getting more than those in a small one."[10] A rough division took place upon the death of the male head of the family among the Thompson River Indians in Canada, for the female children inherited all the kettles, baskets, cooking utensils and some of the blankets and robes. The dogs became the property of the male children. " The horses were divided among all the children, both male and female ; the former, however, taking twice as many as the latter."[11] But even this rough allocation among the survivors is an advance on the most primitive ways, as those of the Bushman who feared to disturb the possessions of the deceased in any way.[12] It was thought by the latter that the individual in his spirit-guise would need these objects, and to confiscate them for use by the survivors would be so to provoke and annoy the deceased that calamity and misfortune would result for the living.[13] This conception worked for long against social advance, as the fruits of past experience in the material form were always sacrificed for the uses of the dead.

The regulating modes of inheritance are derived from the ideas of descent in primitive society. The need of establishing the exact relationship of children to parents is felt most insistently as it concerns the property and possessions which have been accumulated by dint of the toil and self-abnegation of the elders. Few of them would have undertaken the pains involved if there had not been some prospect that the fruits would be transmitted to the children. Inheritance rules, therefore, follow the kinship-bonds or notions as to consanguinity.[14] One of the most primitive, perhaps the original kin-relationship, was based on a community of blood reckoned through the mother. Property was therefore transmitted in the female line, the nephew or son of a sister receiving the bequest of an adult man, rather than his own proper child. On one occasion, a Congo chief offered an explicit reason for this : " It is beyond any doubt that my sister and myself are derived from the same mother, consequently the child of my sister certainly has my blood. My son will inherit from the eldest brother of my wife who is of the royal blood."[15] Among the Ewe of the Slave Coast, also, if a man has no brother, his heir is the eldest son of his eldest sister.[16] It is to be observed in this case that the brother has the priority in the inheritance which is an evidence of the fact that the older males in the kinship group may seize the property, due simply to their strength and maturity. Perhaps this is one of the ways in which the idea of male dominance, based on force and duress, superseded the more ancient matriarchal system.

Bosman, the ancient chronicler, records the fact that on the Guinea Coast of Africa, " the right of inheritance is oddly adjusted ; and as far as I could observe the brother's and sister's children are the right and lawful heirs, in the following manner : They do not jointly inherit, but the eldest son of his mother is the heir to the mother's brother or his son, as the eldest daughter is heiress to her mother's sister or daughter ; neither the father himself nor his relations . . . have any claims to the goods of the defunct . . . "[17]   On the Loango coast, similarly, the movable property, including the slaves, descends to a nephew.[18]   The reason for this system of bequest is simple.   According to Macdonald, " a man's children are purposely set aside . . . They want to be sure that the heir really has the family blood in his veins and they cannot trust that a man's sons answer to this description."[19]   In the New Hebrides, land is heritable solely through the mother, and in the Gazelle peninsula, inheritance also follows in the " mother-right ", that is, " sons succeed not to their father, but to the maternal uncle if there is one."[20]   In Ponapé, the relations on the mother's side divide all the movable property and each takes what pleases his fancy.[21]   As a result of this system of kinship, the following remark of the Dagbamba youth is not entirely unexplainable : " If our maternal uncle dies, we become his heirs, not the sons, therefore we love our maternal uncle more than our father."[22]   This is an example of economic determinism.

With the entrance of the economic domination of the male, the other traits of the culture, to maintain a consistency, are slowly swung about.   Change in the branches of folk-activity other than food-getting and self-maintenance, are apt to lag behind, since they are not directly connected with the material concerns of life.   Religious ideas and beliefs, as the most remote, are the least amenable to verification and hence the least liable or the last to change.   The nature of inheritance, however, as part of the economic folkways exhibits the transition to the male system in a striking fashion. This change consisted of gradual transitional steps.   In many instances, generations elapsed before the full effect was felt. The difficulty of up-rooting customary prejudices as to rights based on the more ancient, tried system, in this case the maternal, are not insuperable, however, as is witnessed in these most illuminating instances of the mores of the Banks Islanders. It is not unusual that " a man before his death begs his brother not to disturb his son in his garden ; he agrees, and the son takes the father's place ; but the father was there of right, and the son has strictly no right ; he therefore gives money to the natural heirs, his father's sister's children.   In order to make a transaction of this kind secure, the son will put the money for the redemption of the garden upon his father's corpse when he is laid out for the burial ; the nephews and heirs of the deceased take the money from their dead *maraui* in the presence of the assembled people and never can deny that they have given up their right."[23]   Although the right of the sister's children as heirs is still regnant, a man is allowed to make a sort of testament distributing his personal property, as canoes, ornaments, and weapons among his own children, and they will not be disturbed in their inheritance.[24] The major economic means as land and cattle, it will be observed, are still omitted as being the communal possession of all those partaking of the kin, or blood-community which is reckoned through the female line.

Among the Bana, if the man's son is already mature physically (which is determined by the growth of the pubic hair), he receives the entire bequest and the uncle is let off only with a few cows and the child's mother. Otherwise the uncle, or guardian, receives half of the wives, daughters and cows as his own.[25] There are other methods of retaining the property in the family among one's own children. In British Columbia, among the Salish, many of whose clans are organized on the matrilineal basis, " a father often married his son to his own sister, that is to the boy's aunt, without taking into account the disparity of their ages, for she may be fifty and he but fifteen. There was a special object in this ; it permitted the father to pass over, through his sister, his own property and belongings to his own son, which under the matrilineal rule could not be otherwise done."[26] The uncle's position, particularly the maternal uncle, takes on the character of a bridge whereby the matrilineal descent shades off into the patrilineal order.

A complete compromise in the folkways are those of the people of the Kitui country in East Africa, with regard to a minor as heir. His inheritance is put into the custody of his uncles, who are given a small share of the cattle. The boy spends half his time with his mother's brothers and half with his father's brothers thereafter as representatives of both his ties and claims with the preceding generation.[27]

The development of important forms of economic means as

opprerty and capital and the elaboration of the patrilineal
system of reckoning descent through the father are aspects
of the same tendency in the history of culture. The domestication of animals and the tillage of the soil, created types of
valuable property which become desirable forms of inheritance. As the legacy became more valuable the heirs were
more definitely assigned. In New Guinea, to illustrate patrilineal descent, " the house is inherited in the male line . . .
so that if a man dies his eldest son becomes the ' master ' or
' owner ' . . . of the house. If he is a small child at his
father's death the title is latent (the father's younger brother
being considered ' owner ' or ' master ' for the time being),
but as soon as the boy is grown, he comes into his rights."[28]
In South Africa, among the Xosa, at the death of the father,
the sons and mother divide the property, the daughters claiming nothing and remaining with their mother or brother.[29]
The male system is widely prevalent among the cattle-raising
peoples of Africa.[30]

The natives of Brazil exhibit a more primitive condition of
inheritance, although through the male line. A Siusi youth
of ten years of age was observed on the death of his father to
carry two thin black marks under the eyes as sign of mourning.
In addition, as a legacy, there remained the oars, bows and
arrows, blow-guns and feather ornaments which belonged to
the father.[31]. These things became his possessions only after
the medicine-man had torn them out of the grasp of the now
" spirit-father " by erasing the " uncleanness " that con-
taminated them. This is redolent of the earlier system of
consigning with the dead all of his personal property, which
were considered to be integral parts of the man's personality.[32]
The importance of these tools soon militated against such
wasteful custom and the children were enabled to benefit by
them while the enraged spirit parent was calmed by the convenient hocus-pocus of the medicine-man. This tore the

weapons and ornaments from his grasp and alienated his influence in them.

A most lucrative form of property under the paternal system is the wife or group of wives. These perform valuable auxiliary service in food-getting and its preparation, and in supplying further effective material support, in the form of children.[33] As such, the women are passed on to the male heirs and included with the rest of the property. The purpose of this is unmistakable, as among the folk of Benin in West Africa : " His father's widows, especially those who have not had any children, the son takes home if he likes them, and uses as his own, but those which he does not like, he also takes them home with their children, and sets them to work in order to subsist them the more creditably . . . "[34] Among the Baele and numerous other African tribes, the son is accustomed to inherit his father's wives, excepting his own mother.[35] The heir takes all the children of his father's widows and these children regard him thereafter as their father.[36] In the same way, it is the custom among the Araucauns of Chile for the son to inherit his father's wives as so much working capital.[37] Under the paternal system, the woman's status deteriorates to that approximating a chattel of the male head of the family, and as inheritance is chiefly concerned with property, the women are awarded the children also. These women will aid materially in conserving the fruits of the labour of the deceased, and in enhancing the material position of the heirs.

The heir is looked upon as the representative of the dead father, and takes upon himself the duties and responsibilities as well as the property and privileges attached to his position. The idea of the blood—or family—solidarity is so firmly embedded in the mores, however, that it is only after a course of gradual changes that one son out of the many children was entitled to the sole possession of the inheritance. If the children do receive a definite portion of the valuable property, it is shared with all the other children. Thus in the African Bondei country, it is said that " if there are many children, they divide equally ; even in the case of polygamists the children inherit equally. . . ."[38] The communal nature of the inheritance is also displayed by the natives of the D'Entre-casteaux group of islands. It is there felt that each child should have the honour of guarding the family heirlooms for a time. Property which is left descends in the first instance to the eldest son, who retains possession of it for a time, then hands on the more valuable portion to his younger brother, and he in turn to the third son and so on, all enjoying the ownership for a period of time.[39] Among the natives of the Philippines, each of the children inherits the personal property from his own mother in consistency with an older custom. This inheritance is probably a more ancient and less valuable type of property. They also inherit equally the father's property at his death, and this is usually of more economic value to the descendants.[40] The family is in each instance the social unit and the children share almost equally in the legacy of their parents.

Irresistibly, however, a tendency arises towards endowing the children unequally by means of favouring one son above the others. Or else, the exigencies of life produce the set of conditions under which one of the children must assume the office of direct and acknowledged heir to the deceased. The son who is chosen is not necessarily the oldest one but one who may have distinguished himself more than the other brothers, as in Uganda. The heir may thus be the youngest or the oldest of the sons.[41] The natural way in which this custom arises is illustrated in the Sumatra practice : " When a man dies his effects, in common course, descend to his male children in equal shares ; but if one among them is remarkable for his abilities above the rest, though not the eldest, he usually obtains the largest proportion, and becomes the head

of the *tungguan* or house ; the others voluntarily yielding him
the superiority."[42] The eldest son if passed over in some
instances and not allowed to inherit at all as among the
Banyankole, must have possessed some mental or physical
disability, or " some known evil habit."[43] In Sumatra,
again, an eldest son was asked " how it happened that the name
of distinction passed over him and was conferred on his younger
brother . . . answered with great naîveté : ' because I am
accounted weak and silly '."[44] A system of primogeniture
has not yet been evolved ; inheritance by the eldest son is still
dependent upon the possession of favourable personal qualities
that fit him for these responsibilities. Where such do not
appear, other sons may take the helm. Succession by the
eldest male has not yet taken on the usualness of a conventional
usage.

The slow accumulating force of many individual instances
soon serves to create a customary usualness which amounts to a
folk-way namely, favouring the eldest son with a larger share
of the inheritance. Experience attests to the beneficial nature
of this usage and in its wake the folk sets its stamp of approval
and it is then " just " and " right " and even " moral "
perhaps, that the eldest son carry off the largest portion of the
father's effects. The other children are not, however, to be
forgotten in the distribution of economic goods. On the
Congo, " the eldest son takes the father's title and also inherits
a larger proportion of the property than his brothers. The
amount depends on the number of sons—if there are three
sons, the eldest takes a half, the second son, two-thirds of the
remaining half, and the last son the rest."[45] Among the Bana,
the eldest son receives two-thirds of the property, which
includes the wives and daughters of his father. The rest go
to the remaining sons. The brothers of the deceased are given
a few cows and one receives the widow as " presents " from the
principal heir, recalling the obsolescent custom of uncle-

inheritance.[46] Many of the Bantu tribes practice a similar system of equity, the eldest son always receiving the lion's share. In Theraka he is given one animal of each kind more than the other.[47] The preference is of some consequence as cattle are the principal form of wealth. In South Africa, the eldest son is entitled to a certain proportion of the movable property. "The residue may be divided between other members of the family in any proportion."[48] The latitude here implied argues for the informality and freshness of this usage in the experience of the folk.

Likewise, the originating causes for the development of divided inheritance are illustrated by the Thompson River Indians of British Columbia. All the male children inherit the deer-fences, fishing stations and eagle eyries but the eldest had the right of dividing these and taking his choice. " If he was a hunter, he generally took the deer-fence, leaving the fishing station to his next or some other brother who might be a fisherman, and *vice versa*."[49]

The eldest son, who inherits all the property of his father, does not have the sole use and benefit of it. He has acquired, rather, the prestige as head of the family-unit. The ties that unite the members of this group are very binding. Within the family, the property is considered a common good, the benefits and use of which are enjoyed communally. The eldest son is simply the director or representative of his family, and the younger sons with their dependents also partake of the inherited goods. In East Africa, we are informed that " natives will often say that the eldest son inherits everything, but this is not so in actual fact. He will claim outstanding debts, and so long as the brothers live together he will be called the owner, in the sense that he is the representative of the family. The property is, however, divided among all the brothers, legitimate or illegitimate. . . ."[50] Each of the sons may be mature and have his own dependents, which often accounts for the fact that the eldest son's position is a titular one only.   Among the Wa-Giriami, "on the death of a man, his land belongs nominally to his eldest son, but in reality all the sons have an equal share in it.   They all work the land, and the produce from it is equally divided among them. . . ."[51] The Wanyamnezi son likewise inherits everything including the wives, but must make provision for his younger brothers.[52] In East Africa, the necessity of arranging the economic relationships dictated the division of the legacy.   The eldest son, if an adult, took possession of the property, which included the women, houses and goats.   "He inherits all his father's widows, but only takes as his wives any in excess of three, and these only if they have not borne more than one child. . . . ."   To take more for his own use would create an enormous discrepancy in means—in wives, children and goats—between him and the younger brothers.   Therefore, the bulk of the property is merely held by him on behalf of the family, and in the long run the younger sons receive a share equal in value to that of the eldest.[53]

Where polygamy prevailed, there existed also, in many instances, a first or chief wife.   This has been interpreted as one of the lines by which the system of monogamy, or single-wife marriage, arose.   The eldest son of the chief wife became the chief heir or was designated in some manner to be the direct follower of the father in prestige and power within the family. Thus, his descendants by the chief wife occupied a position distinguishing them from the descendants of the other wives, who were cast into a less pretentious rôle.   Among the Wad-schagga, only male descendants inherit.   The eldest son of the chief wife is the chief heir ; the next largest share of the heritage is given to her second son, and after him, the son of the last-wedded wife receives the next largest share.   The other sons receive equal shares of what remains.[54]   Among the Kingsmill Islanders in Polynesia, the son of the mother of the highest rank also succeeds to the position and property of the father. " If all the children should be equal in rank, the eldest would receive twice as much land as the others ; or if the father does not choose to divide his property, the eldest son would receive the whole, and is obliged to support his brothers and sisters, who in turn are expected to work for him, and cannot marry without his consent."[55]

As a result the eldest son was placed in a commanding position, outranking and outstripping his brothers in wealth and power. This position was thus built up solely upon a superiority in years and the approval of the folk came to cluster about this arrangement as the most satisfactory one. Thereafter it became incumbent upon the younger children of the father to obey the dictates of their older brother. The line of primogeniture was fully developed among the Maoris, and the eldest child ruled the others. There were even separate terms to indicate his importance. A man thus never said, " my brother ", he either said, " my elder brother " (*tukana*), or " my younger brother " (*teina*).[56] The oldest male was regarded as the owner or master of the Hew Hebrides household, and to this position his oldest male child succeeded.[57] Among the Pangwe of West Africa, the eldest son inherits the largest capital, that is, wives, and becomes one of the " rich men " of the neighbourhood.[58] Among the Bassari, he becomes head of the family succeeding his father and obtains the latter's privileges and standing in the folk-life, including a place at the tribal council.[59] Among the Hudson Bay Eskimo, this drawing apart of the children in status is already revealed during the lifetime of the old man, for " when the father becomes superannuated or his sons are old enough to enable him to live without exertion, the management of affairs devolves on the eldest son and to the second is delegated the second place . . . " etc.[60] In this way the lot of the child is made to depend upon priority of birth and a personal inequality is set up.

The culture of these peoples is as yet on a fragile and unstable foundation which calls for a decisive preparation of the young for the task of perpetuating and carrying it on. Regard for children is influenced by the feeling that repose and peace in the otherworldly life is dependent upon a rigorous conformity on the part of the surviving children. Ambition and affection for one's own children enhance this motive of provision for them. The adage of the Maori puts the idea tersely : " when the seive is worn out with age, the new net encircles the fish ", which means that " When a man grows old, his son takes his place."[61]   During the advancing years of the father, therefore, he anticipates on various occasions the eventual succession of his children. This is illustrated by the habit in the Torres Straits Islands of the father in going over his gardens with his children and pointing out to each child the portions that are to be their respective shares after his death.[62]   The considerate action of the Yakut father is shown by dividing his property among his sons during his lifetime.[63]

These kinds of productive wealth have been toilsomely won and must be jealously preserved by the children for their own weal and comfort, which, in primitive thought, is intimately associated with the well-being of the parent as well. In fact, after the father is already dead and gone, he still surveys the scene of his son's activity and in a literal sense broods over the latter's rôle as his successor. In New Guinea, for instance, it is believed that a dead father longs for his son to join him. Yet he exhibits matchless consideration and restraint, for it is further declared that at times the father purposely allows his son to live on for a while in order that he may get some work done. The father muses : " I leave him boy little time. Who look out coconut ? Let him make plenty pickaninny

first time.   By and by I take him."[64]   It is truly remarkable
how closely the well-being of the living and the dead are inter-
twined in primitive thought.   The Pangwe of West Africa
believed that the father could continue to provide for his son
in a very effective manner after death.   If he were particularly fond of his son, he would be able to transform himself
into a great, beautiful leopard and contrive to have himself
shot by his son, thereby securing to the latter a skin and bones
with which to purchase a wife.[65]   The bond between father
and son is thus knotted securely during the life of the two by
economic chains making for the comfort of the descendant
in this life and the peace of the ghost of the parent in his
imagined existence.

There are also objects of signal importance in the life of the
family and folk which descends out of a hoary past into the
keep of the incoming generation.   Such tools, implements
and amulets also form part of the child's heritage.   A glamor-
ous aura of superstition clings to these and preserves them.
Traces of fetichistic power or ghostly attributes are bound to
infest them as age wipes out the memory of their origin.
Inherited property, tools and instruments actively used are
consumed or sub-divided, but sacred bundles, idols, and the
like have an increased potency with age.   The spirit-essence
of the ancestors have accrued to these objects by actual
contact in the past.   Nassau was, for example, informed in
West Africa by " a very intelligent woman " that, " when
she was a child she possessed a fetich supposed to be very
valuable, which she had inherited from her father.   She says
that when she would be going into the forest or where she
expected difficulty or danger or trouble . . . she would hold
the fetich in her hand. . ."[66]   An investigator was able to
obtain possession of " the family circumcision knife, which is
ordinarily handed down from father to son, and must not be
used for any other purpose. . . "[67]   In Samoa, it was the club

which was solemnly inherited ; among the Pueblo Indians, the cradle, " a sacred object, handed down in the family, and the number of children it had carried was frequently shown by notches on the frame."[68]

These are the heirlooms which invoke the precious tradition-ary records of folk and family. A cynical employment of this type of legacy is assuredly the use of the Kamba boys, who upon succeeding to the father's property, also become invested with the latter's brass bracelet which is worn on the right wrist. Upon the mother's death they wear the iron bracelet worn by her. Once invested with these, the boy is quite safe for ever after from the effect of any *kirume* (curse) from his parents."[69]

Not merely the residences of these immediate spirit influ-ences but vague personalities themselves, and the power they wield are inherited by the children. The purpose is clearly revealed in the New Guinea case, cited by Landtman. It is the custom there that " a father will from time to time bring his son with him to his garden and take him near the tree of the *etengena* so that the spirit may learn to know the boy and become kindly disposed to him, it will understand, ' This ground belong that boy, when father he finish, that boy he look out ground '."[70]   On the island of Ponapé, in the Pacific, the family religious secrets and paraphernalia are handed down to the sons, in case the maternal uncle has also died.[71]   Among the Eskimo of Greenland, the belief existed that " the souls of ancestors remained guardian spirits to their descendants, having left them their amulets and serrats as pledges ".[72] Among the Plains Indians in America, " property rights to the sacred bundles are transmitted exclusively in the paternal line, the method being for children to buy each ceremonial privilege jointly from their own father."[73]   These instances allude to the impressive rôle played by the appurtenances of the ghostly elements. To assure the child's rightful claim to succession in the place of the father, the spirits, especially those of ancestral origin, must be rendered complacent and favourable. There is no more effective way of insuring this than by gaining possession of the hallowed fetiches and the technique of placating the ghosts.

The solemn duty of blood revenge also formed part of the legacy bequeathed to the child. All the members of the group claiming blood-relation and allegiance were bound by the mores to revenge the shedding of blood by a fellow. Other outstanding feuds and unrepaid affronts were perpetuated in the same way. In New Zealand, for example, among the Maoris, it is said that " too often, the last words calmly spoken, would be of dire revenge on enemies—a legacy of blood to the children."[74] That this is no mere conventional play is the conclusion one derives from the account of the heritage acquired by the child in the Fiji Isles. There, " the dying man mentions his foe, that his children may perpetuate his hatred—it may be against his own son—and kill him at first opportunity. The name of the hated one is uttered aloud, if not as the object of immediate vengeance, yet of gloomy and disastrous predictions, which never fail to reach the ears where they are least welcome. Deep concern is often excited by these dying words, and the impressions made on the minds of those to whom the carrying out of their dark purport is entrusted is indelible."[75] The slights and grievances of the fathers are communicated to the sons as their just heirs. A case is recorded of an Eskimo boy in the Bering Straits region, of fourteen years of age, who shot and killed a man who had murdered his father when he himself was an infant. This is explained as the duty of blood revenge which belongs to the son. If he is an infant at the time, it rests with him to seek revenge as soon as he attains maturity.[76]

The child's inheritance may thus be on the side of the parents' unpaid debts, or unrequited ills. Among those people whose ideas of property are highly developed, the folk-ways surrounding inheritance and bequest are correspondingly definite. The actual debts of the father are then placed upon the shoulders of the child-heirs. An incident related of the Igorots of the Philippines is an unusual illustration. "At the mission of Quiangana, a young neophyte came to tell me that he was going down to the villages. 'What are you going to do there?' 'I am going to work in order to pay my debts, otherwise they will kill me or sell me.' 'What debts are those?' 'Those which my father contracted when he was sick in order to pay for the pills and powders he used to cure himself.'"[77] The child is placed in the vice of circumstances built by the parent and must work himself out of the obligations assumed by his sire, in this instance, commitments of which the son would be entirely unheedful and uninfluenced were it not for the force of the mores by which he is bound.

Under the matrilineal system the child succeeded to a less confined and individualized position. But under the patrilineal, he succeeds to a distinct niche in society left vacant by his father. The development of economic folk-ways, with property of greater consequence, serves to define more rigidly and narrowly the individual status. So, property, spirit-contacts, and even hates and enmities, are all taken over because of the inherent conservatism of the struggling society. The station of the parent is also transferred if class-divisions have appeared. For example, in the case of children of slaves, their status is determined by the folk-ways. Slaves are property and are owned by the adult man in a different way from which he owns and can sell his own children. Among West African tribes, children succeed to the position of slaves occupied by the mother. The man has absolute power over them.[78] A perfect transitional form between succession to the mother and succession to the father is to be observed in the Philippines : " If the father or the mother is free, so the son is half free and half slave ; with many tribes the first child inherits the father's position, the second the mother's, and where there are an odd number, the last is half free and half slave."[79] Under the full paternal system, the child achieves the father's position solely —if the former is a slave, he becomes a slave also.[80]

The " father " was regarded as the owner of the child rather than the progenitor. All traces of inheritance on the female side disappeared. For instance, among the Ewe people of West Africa, " neither of the words now used to express ' father ' has then any relation to the act of begetting. They do not mean ' he who begets ' but ' he who owns ' and ' he who maintains '." Among the neighbouring Yoruba, like-wise, the word for " father " relates to ideas of violence, power and strength rather than to the progenitor.[81] Children are thus considered valuable working capital and as such it is not very much to the point to distinguish between children of lawful, or slave, wives. In some instances, among the Tshi people, the slave is considered a member of the family and succeeds to the property in default of other heirs. Slaves are called " sons " and " daughters " by their owners among the Ewe-people.[82] The custom in this connection of the Maoris is extremely enlightening. When a man of rank marries a slave-woman, she has no power or *mana* in the tribe, " but the children would not only be free, but would inherit the rank, etc., of their father."[83]

There are few individuals whose personality protrudes out of the mass in primitive society. The deadening compulsion of forces making for conformity is so great that it is rare to discover the individual making his influence felt. Each person is absorbed into the folk-type because of the intensive need for solidarity and cohesion to preserve the life of all. The solitary man or the extreme individualist would apparently disrupt the group and endanger the successful struggle for self-maintenance in the societies of simpler culture. The one office in which the germs of individual specialization are apt to appear is that of the medicine man, sorcerer or shaman. He stands head and shoulders above the ordinary native because of the important function he performs. This is the manipulation of the countless unseen ghostly spirits who are held accountable for all the ill-fortune of life such as death, sickness, disease, famine, drought, etc. To procure protection from these abuses and also to wring concessions of good fortune from their grasp, it is found essential to employ a person who for one reason or another has gained some sort of contact or rapport with these spirits and so could deploy to desirable ends. The medicine-man who devotes his time to the hocus-pocus of the folk-life often becomes the sole repository of the medical knowledge and assorted wisdom of the tribe. He becomes a specialist in magical practices which are often forms of self-delusion but which may also be used by the more scheming shaman for private ends. Ordinarily to attain to this eminence, the person must either be abnormal physically or mentally, or pretend to have received a " call " to this service from the spirits themselves.[84]

It is not strange to find, however, that the established medicine-man seeks to transmit his privileged station with all his paraphernalia and sleight-of-hand to his own children. To placate the tribesfellows who are not inclined to regard this position as a hereditary one, the old Uganda sorcerer goes about it in this way : " When a witch-doctor becomes the father of a son he generally contrives to practise the following clumsy mystery : On the third night after the son is born the baby disappears, and everyone affects to bewail its loss and search for it ineffectually. At dawn it is found outside the door of its mother's house with the tail of an ox tied round its neck (by the father, of course). This is a sign that the child is intended to be a sorcerer when he grows up."[85]   Among the

Nandi, the child is found after a few days to have in its hand some hairs of a cow's tail, some grass, and a tick.[86] This species of mummery is necessary to reconcile the claims of custom that the spirit manifest itself within the person and the natural tendency of the medicine man to bequeath the office with its prestige and emoluments to his own son.

A man, " who knows a ceremony and incantation for raising the wind, or for making yams grow big and thick, or the wild pig entangle itself in the net ", occupies a very important place in the life of the natives of the D'Entrecasteaux Islands. If such a person is once successful he is forever after retained for this special service when called upon. Then the song and ceremony are handed down from generation to generation, " the eldest son usually succeeding to the father's practise ".[87] This is a lucrative profession, as it looms so important in folk-life.

Among the Kafirs, the trade of medicine is also hereditary— a doctor communicating his secrets only to his children. And " were he to teach the art to a younger son, the eldest would be entitled to the brother's fees ",[88] which indicates again the strength of the primitive family-bond. In Ceylon, among the Veddahs, the shaman is responsible for the initiation of his successor, who is, in all probability, his son or the son of his sister.[89] The allied profession of rain-maker is hereditary among the Wakamba.[90] The selfish motives which are the powerful incentives toward making this office heritable can be divined from the case of the natives of the Gold Coast. It is customary among these people that the Fetishman should train his own grandchildren for his calling. " He passes over his own children, rightly judging that one of a family is sufficient for all the purposes of a fraudulent livelihood ; and he concludes that his grandchild will be ready to carry on the game of deceit by the time his own age will preclude him from taking an active part in the Fetish ceremonies."[91]

To succeed in this practice, however, the child must be suitably trained and prepared.   Although inheriting the office, the Yuki child in California had to be poisoned and cured, which, in their opinion, rendered him invulnerable afterward, and fit to be the " poison-doctor " of the people.[92]   In Guiana, when the medicine man begins to feel that he is too weak to cope longer with the ghosts, he transfers his office to his son under all manner of ceremonies and ordeals, which include the swallowing of enormous quantities of tobacco juice.[93]   In Australia, the investiture of the medicine-man is vivid and prolonged.   The older medicine-men, in one region, stand away from the novice and go through the motion of projecting stones into the body.   In this manner they communicate their power of bringing up crystals, which is the folk's way of treating a sick man.[94]   In South Australia, a boy related the occurrences at his initiation into the shamanistic craft.   "My father showed me a lot of shining bright things, like grass on the walls, and told me to take some.   When we went out again, my father taught me how to make these things go into my legs, and how I could pull them out again.   He also taught me how to throw them at people. . . .   The old men came out with fire-sticks, and when they reached the tree, I sat down. . . .   It was like glass and we call it *Kini*.   I told the old men about it and they said that I was a doctor.   From that time I could pull things out of people."[95]   Some of the Siberian shamans communicate their power by blowing into the eyes or the mouth of a novice, or stabbing a candidate with a dagger which had been previously plunged into his own body.[96]

One had to exhibit qualifications for this office.   This was an obstacle originally standing in the way of making it a heritable position.   The custom of surrounding his work with secrecy enabled the shaman, nevertheless, to consign his office to the one whom he desired to succeed him, and in most cases this would probably be his own son.   In the Amazon region, the medicine-man always has a small boy with him, " who may be his son, actual or adopted ". Only to him does he confide his professional secrets.[97] On the Thompson River, in British Columbia, only a son, " strong in medicine " could succeed his father in this craft.[98] The father may teach his child but eventually the spirits choose the occupant according to the ways of many people. Thus in Guiana, the son may be trained for the position but one with an epileptic tendency seems to be preferred.[99] But after custom has hardened, it is then sufficient to obtain the office by right of birth alone. The child of the shaman is given some symbol (such as a small black stick used to cure the sick among the Siusi of Brazil),[100] and thus perpetuates the paternal rights and privileges undisturbed.

The political office of the chief borders on that of the partly religious, partly medical one of the shaman. This position was assumed originally by the man of unusual prowess or ability who was able to accumulate by hook or crook greater possessions than his fellows. Before long, the position became more than an informal ranging up of a crafty fellow out of the group. In due time, the chief will, by the tacit approval of the folk alone, have his position surrounded with the prestige given by the sanction of the mores. Until such habituation, the chief's son had to look to it to be deserving of the father's office. If regarded as incompetent, his claim by descent would not be listened to at all. In West Africa, for example, " kingship has connected with it the great honour that a son may inherit it if he is the right kind of a man ; but it is possible for him to be set aside and another chosen. A son may lose his place by foolishness and incompetency."[101] In Nigeria, there were two kinds of chiefs. The more important were succeeded by their sons, probably because they were able to enforce the rule, but generally the chief's son had no special claim and the office was sold by the king to the highest bidder.[102] Evidently the qualification for holding the office is an economic one only.   An extremely fluid condition is demonstrated in the New Hebrides also.   A chief's son is more apt to succeed his father in his chieftainship because he is richer as the son of a man with many tusk pigs, but it is added, " any man can acquire tusk-pigs through thrift and care. . . ."[103]   In some such manner the source of hereditary succession can be traced to the inheritance of economic means.

Inevitably the chief's son will succeed him.   But in order to accomplish this, the folk must be given some intimation of the competency of the son.   This necessitates a training for the specialized tasks of the headman.   All manner of fictions are gathered about the son's person to award him unusual distinction among men, whereas, as seen above, the original distinction may often have been simply an economic one.[104] In Tahiti, the son of the chief, immediately upon birth, is covered with a " sacred cloth ", to indicate that he has been admitted to the society of the gods and exalted over common men and in Melanesia he is not allowed to fraternize with the other boys that he may not fall low.[105]   Masai chiefs are believed to have " second sight " which is transmitted to their sons by a drug whose nature is known only to the royal family.[106]   In short, the son who is to succeed the chief is brought up to be considered a " cut above " the other people.[107] A curious custom in Polynesia is that by which at the birth of a son, the power and office of the father who is chief reverts to the babe, who then outranks the father.   All lands, insignia, etc., are also immediately transferred to it.[108]   Probably this was a means whereby the father could definitely establish a hereditary succession in the family where hitherto elective or informal.   Through habituation, tacit approval of this rule will have become effective even before the chief himself has passed away.

In arts and crafts, outside of the smith's, there was little specialization in the simpler cultures.   The ironworker was regarded with superstition everywhere and held a distinct position, in some cases feared and in others exalted. This was due probably to the fact that the dexterity of this single specialized craftsman was thought to be magical and derived from commerce with the spirits or because of the foreign origin of the smith in some instances.[109] The smiths formed a close endogamous group, therefore, often speaking a different language from that ordinarily employed by the folk. The occupation was strictly hereditary, passing from father to son or nephew, and guarded from falling into the hands of outsiders.[110] In addition to imparting the trade, the smith would initiate his child with the aid of divers magical practices, as in some cases the office of smith was closely allied to that of the medicine-man.

Among the women there arose in a few instances specialized crafts and occupations which their daughters also followed exclusively. Such was the craft of the tatooer in New Guinea. The woman who followed this had her profession by birthright ; she was skillled in her art because her mother trained her in it from childhood.[111] In East Africa, generally, if the mother is of a family skilled in pottery, basket-making or any other female craft, the girls follow the hereditary art.[112] Among the Fijians, " the abortionist's craft was in the hands of a few professional experts, who made too good a thing of their trade to trust their secrets to any but their daughters who were to succeed in their practice." Also, native midwives were generally the medical practitioners. Their craft was kept secret and as a consequence it became family property, being handed down from mother to daughter.[113] In the Baganda temples young girls were dedicated to the service of the gods as keepers of the holy fire and other fetiches. The girls set aside for this function were the children of mothers who had conceived after supplicating the gods to remedy their condition of barrenness.[114] Specialization among women is, however, unusual as the economic importance of woman's work decreased with progress in the ways of self-maintenance, such as the domestication of animals and agriculture, which, in most cases, became the exclusive employment of the men.

With the aid of the folk-ways of inheritance, the child is assured of a favoured position in life as compared with that of his ancestors. The social continuity is promoted by the effective steeping of the child in the mores which, as we have observed, also endow him with the necessary psychological outlook for a life in peaceful cohesion with that of his folk-fellows. The inheritance to which he may fall heir, however, elevates his lot above that of others who are not likewise benefitted. The inheritance of, and succession to property and craft has a double effect ; on the one hand, it marks a rise of the material welfare of the entire succeeding generation ; on the other it allows creation of individual distinction and inequality in material circumstance among children. In fact, it has been theoretically assumed by many that the elevation of standards of life are closely dependent upon the rise of inequality in the distribution of wealth and privilege. Certain it is that one of the fundamental incentives toward the creation of capital and exploitation of resources, such as land, has been the selfish appeal contained in the need and ability to bequeath to one's children the fruit of one's toil and thrift.

This line of development gave rise to interesting consequences in the evolution of the family and marital institutions. As the economic values of property became enhanced and fell under private control, particularly in the case of land, it became increasingly evident that definitely ordered provision had to be outlined for the children for whose enjoyment and use much of this property had been developed and accumulated. The same holds true of the passing down to the children of the industrial pursuits or crafts with their trade secrets. These incidents prolonged over generations, had the accumulated result of endowing sexual relations with a greater permanence and durability as the offspring were to be variously involved in succession to important and productive forms of wealth. To insure that the child should succeed to this desirable heritage, the rules of inheritance became increasingly fixed and invariable. The lot of children then differed in response to their heritage. Ideas of incipient standards of life or comparative ways, not merely living, but living well or in comfort, slowly produced the ferment of competitive striving on the part of the parents which had the unforeseen result of restricting sex relations more definitely into conformity with established, later, written codes of conduct. Property and its movement to the children was the great stabilizer of the institutions built about the relationships of the sexes.

CHAPTER XII

SOCIAL FORCES AND THE CHILD

THE mores condition the child's behaviour. The social pattern guides the innate, broadly appetitive, acquisitive interests of the young into a conformity with the habits of the older members of the tribe. In the history of culture, as regards the relatively primitive stages here treated, we have traced the generally casual nature of this process of socialization. Where the social heritage is bare and unsophisticated, harsh necessities force an early acquisition of the arts of life upon the child. Little tutoring or actual training is needed. Complete maturity, in the social sense, of independent activity in the struggle for subsistence is easily attained. The organization of these groups is extremely nebulous, and revolves about a supposed blood-tie through the maternal line of each individual. The status of the child is distinguished merely by his relative physical ineptness and weakness, as compared with his elders ; but he trails along with him fancied connections with the ancestral spirits and the entire imaginary environment from which he is thought to spring at birth.

Societal development is drab, gradual, and often imperceptible. There are occasional spurts of development and at times devastating setbacks through natural calamity. The environment may be of a nature that makes for progress, calling insistently for adjustment on pain of extinction, but there are other conditions which result in a static society. Development, therefore, is not uniform or clear-cut throughout primitive society. Nevertheless, there is a perceptible general drift of development which is quickened considerably as male

dominance emerges. This occurs through the enrichening of
the food supply by the domestication of animals and plants
which was a characteristic male talent or prerogative, in the
history of culture. Thereafter, institutions which had been
but vaguely outlined in the matrilineal societies are slowly
differentiated and take shape.

This momentous trend is recorded variously in the treatment
of the child and the folk-ways surrounding infancy and childhood. The position of the child in the life of the folk is
enhanced as a material aid in the struggle for the incipient
standards of life or degree of " right " living made possible by
the superior economic system. His status becomes more
clearly defined in the measure that his economic worth is
increased. Mere personal whim on the part of parents is then
buttressed by material interest in their offspring. The threat
of quick dispatch through abortion and infanticide is lessened
and the child acquires a closer tie to an older male, i.e. to a
" father ". In addition, the child's station in life is enhanced
by his ability to ease the life of the parents in the spirit-world
and to nurture and tend the ancestral spirits that lurk everywhere. Children acquire a tenure on life and a distinctive
worth that redounds to the material comfort and peace of
mind of the elders.

Under the influence of this elaborated body of folk-ways,
various social forces impinge upon the child to produce in
him the typical attitudes and behaviour of the group. The
" social personality " is thus chiseled out of the raw material
furnished by nature. The strongest influences of this type
originate unconsciously out of the folk-life and work their
way into the conduct of the child unperceived. But inevitably
a dim recognition of the importance of the young in preserving
the mores makes itself felt. This tendency reinforces the
selfish motives of the parent in acquiring interest in the child.
As a result, sporadic attempts are made to harden and dis-

cipline the child and actually to train him in the ways of life
that are considered " fit " and " good ", because materially
expedient.

Social consciousness may be stimulated by the particular
events in the tribal history which result in a quickened appreciation of the position occupied by the child. Migration from
the ancestral seat may so definitely cut off contact with the
past that the lore and traditions, in order to be preserved, must
be assiduously recounted to the younger generation. Contact
with other tribes or with a superior type of culture may produce a necessity for definitely instilling the social pattern into
the young. Short of this, however, the rapidly flowering
society develops ways that are not easily appreciated or
divined by the young unaided. Nor can the entire body of
tradition and experience be completely assimilated without
direction.

This groping need for compelling conformity and equipping
the young culturally becomes definitely connected with the
physical evidences of maturity in the youth. The potential
nexus of social relationships at this period, particularly those
revolving about sex, becomes apparent in all its gravity for
the welfare of the folk. As a result, the initiation ceremony
is evolved with a remarkable world-wide range among the
most diverse and scattered groups and tribes. The youth, as
we have seen, is battered into position as the recipient and
active preserver of the old and tried ways. The ceremonial
induction features a regime of force, duress, cajolery and
intimidation, utterly annihilating and " trimming " the will
with a savage vindictiveness. Selected elements of the
mores are at this time unmistakably taught to the
children.

The forces which make for a rigid conformity to the culture-
pattern on the part of the child rule from the cradle on. The
child always stands out as the recipient of a tried body of

folkways or as an object of control and manipulation. Nothing else could be expected. Primitive man is not a free-thinker nor an inquirer into new and untried things. He lives in eternal fear of the contingent ills of life, sickness, famine, starvation, accident. These harass him continually and lurk everywhere, inhabiting all things otherwise inexplicable in the primitive's limited body of experience. The unfamiliar is thus steeped with malignant powers : the usual and habitual, on the other hand, is to be adhered to with pitiful insistency. To the primitive man what was once done was done for all time.

And it does not do to peer into the meaning of the habitual. Among the Bechuana, for example, " as things were in the days of long ago, so they are to-day, so they must remain. That which is gone has gone. The wicked one is he who tries to get behind them. A man must do as his forebears did, speak as they spoke, and speak whatever it may be, even though it may be very wrong. Nor must any question be asked of the elders or any things new and strange said to them which might reveal their ignorance. To do so is *Tshita*—that is, to ask about or speak something too great for the younger generations. Things remain ; they don't pass away ; they don't change. As the parents found them, so will the children strike against them. As the saying is . . . ' The unconquerable things have been ever since the beginning '."[1]

The initiation ceremony is in this light to be thought of only as a final decisive attempt to rivet certain mores with a final, all-compelling blow. But this " fundamentalism " also streams in unawares to fix conduct and thought throughout the impressionable years. In Rhodesia, the child learns bit by bit " what he may eat and what he may not eat, say and not say, do and not do. As he grows he shapes his conduct according to the thinking and doing of his fellows and in turn leads the steps of the younger generation along the path he has followed."[2] So that " a child soon comes to see that a custom is one of those fundamental things which it is useless to examine. A custom is its own justification."[3] Later in life, for instance, " they are asked who first taught them circumcision, and to believe menstruating women unclean ; they reply that they do not know themselves, but that these customs are traditionally handed down to them by their ancestors ; and this is the common answer of all the Blacks."[4] If the Madagascar native is asked why he observes a particular custom, he replies : " ' Our ancestors practised it and we do the same ', and should he be still further importuned, ' But why did your ancestors do it ? ' the trenchant reply is thrown back on the too inquisitive inquirer, ' Who can tell that ? ' "[5] Truly, the wisdom of the ancient is too esoteric and profound. The social life seems to be built on immutable, or " natural " foundations—a cry that the privileged (who in the simpler societies are most often the elders), have always proclaimed.

The natives of the Daly River region of Australia also weary of examination into their customary ways of life, according to Mackillop. They believe among other things, that an old man residing in a neighbouring hill attends to all the births in the vicinity. " Laughing once over this matter, I said to a young man, ' Well, if all this be true, you were once in the hill yourself.' ' O, yes,' he answered, ' What sort of a place is it there ? You should know.' ' Ah ! too much long time ; me been lose'm,' ie. I have forgotten."[6]

No practice is horrible or wrong if it has been followed from childhood ; on the contrary it appears as the basis for well-being and prosperity. In Borneo, head-hunting is condoned in this way. The native argues that it is " an ancient custom, bequeathed to us by our fathers and our father's fathers ; it brings us blessings, plentiful harvests and keeps off sickness and pains."[7] The revolting brutality perpetrated on occasions by the Papuan woman on her children are regarded by her as an unquestioning necessity simply " because it is the custom to practise it ",[8] and for no other apparent reason.

The old, tried folkways are adhered to with extreme religiosity on the part of the old men. When they die, it is believed that in the nebulous form of spirits they dog the movements and actions of the living to enforce jealously allegiance to the ways they had followed in their life in the tribe. To stray from the beaten path on the part of the youths would therefore arouse the ire of the ancestral ghosts. As all the ills of life are in their control, they would see to it that the rain would cease to fall, crops and cattle would fail, and all manner of calamity would be visited on the living. Any tendency to burst these iron bonds of conservatism would be suppressed by fear of being charged with the working of witchcraft.[9] The principal function of the priesthood often reduces, therefore, to " the reinforcement of already static tendencies, to bind more firmly the fetters of superstition by making what is wonderful more wonderful still, what is awful more awful still, and what is mysterious more mysterious still. . . . The one desideratum is the acquirement of a certain amount of dexterity or skill in doing just the things his ancestors have done century after century before him. Indeed, in all their occupations requiring skill, such as building, weaving, basket and pottery making, the forms have become so conventionalized by their beliefs that a religious sanction is placed upon them, which it would be a serious desecration to disregard."[10]

Customs may be looked upon, therefore, as being transmitted to the new generations among peoples of less developed culture with practically the same allegiance and fidelity as the physical characters.

Inevitably, however, murmurs of dissent and strainings at the leash on the part of the young will occur. In spite of the stringent training of the behaviour along ancient grooves, the wilfulness or irrepressible spirit of the youth will

assert itself. Though the son learns the ritual and repeats the
formulas of the elders, he is bound to regard the social life
from a slightly variant angle. Conditions of life are not apt
to be exactly the same in successive generations. There is
that insuperable but subtle individual difference in the young
so hard to capture yet so precious which escapes the severest
regimentation. Youth is more apt to stray. The Ewe
peoples of West Africa are cognizant of this. They have a
proverb which declares : " The stranger's son makes people
angry." The reference is to the offending foreigners who
laugh at the customs of the natives. The young are also
prone to do this more than the old ; hence the " stranger's "
son is mentioned as the chief offender.[11]

The contact of a new culture makes the heaviest inroads
upon the youths who have not yet been hardened into conformity.   In Melanesia, an instance is recorded of the collapse
of the entire social super-structure upon the arrival of the
whites. " The sacred precincts were explored, bull-roarers
became the playthings of the boys, and the old men sat and
wept over the profanation and loss of their power and prestige."[12] A contamination of this type may come with
demoralizing abruptness. In Samoa, the young were ready
to laugh at the old fogies, their progenitors, ' *Samoa valea* ',
foolish Samoans, ' *oletausaga pouliuli* ', it was the end of
darkness, they pathetically remarked."[13]

The pathos involved in this juncture of culture is of course
the inspiration for the most moving tragedies in every folk-
history. All the endearing sentiments bred by habituation
are severely jolted by this rude upheaval which is surrepti-
tiously wrought in the young. A cleavage between the generations in this way yawns abysmally. Ordinarily there is a fine
insensible thread of continuity which wraps the fading activities and interests of the old in their children. In the Gran-
Chaco the story is related of the very old Indian who sat at the

fire recounting the great exploits of antiquity and the fables filled with marvellous tales of bird and animal. " He talked with his mouth, his eyes, hands, and feet." One by one the youthful listeners fell asleep while the ancient mumbled on to himself of the fox-god and the armadillo-god. This was truly symbolical : " The young listen for a while, but soon it bores them. They have new interests. They have begun to dance the great dance called civilization by the Christians, but which is mainly danced about the golden calf."[14]

Among the African Bakongo, boys who attend the mission schools contrary to their parents' wishes, are called " children of the curse ". They may, like other children, acquire knocks and cuts at play. These are caused by the ancestral spirits, the elders are convinced, whom the children have offended by their waywardness.[15]

It does not always require the catastrophic invasion of a superior material culture to shake the fealty of the youths. There are those who attempt to introduce minor innovations rather spontaneously, unheedful of the gravity of their actions. Most instances of this kind must remain unrecorded, for they are repressed with bitter savagery by the elders of the tribes. An investigator in West Africa, however, elicited from the natives some inkling of their feeling on this subject. He reports that in answer to a suggestion for alleviation of the cruelty of the folk-ways : " They were terribly aroused, and swore, ' Never ! Never ! You can't change them.' ' No, not I ; but they will be changed ? ' ' Never ! Who can or will do it ? ' ' Your own sons.' ' Then we will kill our own sons.' "[16] Among the Labrador Eskimo, a child who does not obey willingly, it is said, will become a " bad-hearted " man, that is, a murderer.[17]

The perils associated with youthful lapses from rigid allegiance to the folk-ways are disastrous indeed. Such breaches are punished by the ghosts (to whom the sanctity of the old and tried is most appealing), " with sickness, bad luck, bad dreams, depression, sterility, sickness of dear relatives ; and also the minor worries of life ; the hunter will miss an easy shot, the pot-maker will break a nearly finished pot, the wife will spoil her husband's food, and so on."[18] All grievances, great and small, can thus be laid at the door of disobedience or irregularity of conduct.

Actual instances are available of the fate of those youths who dared to be wilful or wayward.   In the Torres Straits region there were once four boys who tired of the isolation and irksome discipline of the initiation ceremonies which they were undergoing at the time.   Seeing their mothers pass with some yams and sweet potatoes they shouted and asked for some food, of which they had been deprived for days.   They were all immeditaely killed by the officiating tribesmen.[19]   A youngster in the Andaman Islands once persisted in partaking of a forbidden article of food.   Shortly after he fell sick and died.   Thereupon the natives were fully convinced " that he had incurred his fate by failing to comply with the ancient rites and ceremonies as handed down by their fathers."[20] At an initiation among the Arumafu of New Guinea, one of the candidates for manhood boasted that he was not scared and intended to fight the spirit.   Somehow, he was bitten in the finger and a few years later died (while at work on a plantation).   But this event had been long anticipated and surprised no one.[21]   In the Fiji Islands, it is also recounted, that a boy on one occasion, in passing a cooked bird intended for his father's consumption, broke off part of its tail.   " A dark scowl covered his relation's face at this, and at an early opportunity, he slew his son, having first told him that he could not brook the insult put upon him by the breaking of the guana's tail ! "[22]

In 1872, a Fanti youth in West Africa was about to be put to death for taking a leaf from a tree sacred to and overshadow-

ing a tutelary deity in the town of Coomassie.   He had been
to the Cape Coast and there acquired a bit of scepticism.   Only
with difficulty was the native ruler appeased with a substitute
of sheep.[23]

This uncompromising passion for comformity which is
exercised by the elders spreads into the most minute detail
of life.   But it is effectively supported by the pressure exerted
by the group of youths themselves upon the hesitant or
obstreperous individuals of their own generation.   The
repressing spirit is easily caught by the young and thus made
doubly insistent.   It assumes the proportion of a social force
and the form of ridicule.   For example, in Rhodesia, the boy
or girl who wavers before undergoing the rite of extraction
of the teeth is ridiculed unmercilessly.   The youth who has his
teeth is the butt of the village.   " ' Beware the zebra, he bites ',
they call after him, and sooner than face the scoffing he sub-
mits."[24]   Similarly, those who quail before circumcision are
jeered and ridiculed.   Such expressions as " You are a
woman ", " Your eyes are unopened " and other taunts are
used to chide him.   The boy who consorts with the girls after
the puberty ceremony is also ridiculed without end.[25]   Again,
the boy who becomes frightened at any stage of the tatooing,
in Polynesia becomes " the butt of the jokes and taunts of his
own sex, and the object of the jeer and ridicule of the other."[26]

With the development of society the pressure toward
conformity increases.   This pressure is exerted by the social
forces which we have reviewed, forces which are ultimately
derived from the material or fancied spiritual interests of the
parents, or group elders.   Often these interested groups may
include the chieftains or the medicine men but always stress
toward the inculcation in the child of the conventional folk-
ways and sentiments springs from those persons who have
prerogatives or interests bound up with the conservation of
things as they are.   In societies that have acquired superior

economic instruments, the " education " becomes less casual and more purposive in the degree that individuals acquire these vested interests and status.

In the history of primitive educational methods, however, the most remarkable phenomenon is rather the casual, yet decisive manner in which the social continuity is preserved by the fashioning and tutoring of the sentiments and attitudes of the child. The tribes-people are forced to build up suitable adjustments to their environment in order to carry on the struggle for maintenance and in order to be able to propagate themselves. The young inherit this complex of adjustments which have been tested by trial, particularly the ways of procuring food and shelter. There is little visible enquiry or dissidence on the part of the child of the simpler society because the struggle for self-support is too insistent. His world, which is very small indeed, hangs together by ties of personal relationships and folk-ways which may appear to us unintelligible, capricious and perhaps even absurd. Nevertheless, in the light of the tribal history they have proved adequate and sustaining.

Progress in the later stages, however, has been impeded by the overweening prestige of the old and tried ways. " Institutions ", or protective rationalizing beliefs in the ancient usages, have collected round the selfish interests and material prestige of the heads of the cult, the political rulers, the patriarchal heads of the family, the traders and the like. The growing child is then purposefully stereotyped in a world of conventions which serve to enhance the power and interests of these individuals. The social world is construed as an immemorial normality to which the young are to be adapted by " educational " devices, which, too often, have operated to stultify, to discourage, or even to eradicate their personality.

To watchwords and catchwords like " the church ", " the

state ", " the family ", " the blood ", the child has had to submit. These are the institutional devices which are the thin veneers by which powerful groups have, unconsciously and self-deluded perhaps, sought to amalgamate their interests with that of the entire folk. These folk-ways live vividly in the lives of the youths, who are forced into allegiance, but their original meaning becomes overclouded and blind as unthinking allegiance is produced. Nevertheless, such notions as the " church " and the " state " have had their value at one time undoubtedly in serving to secure a better adjustment for life-purposes for the child in his social life.

In historical times, too, this " primitive " education of the child has predominated. Its spirit still broods behind our modern pedagogy, as a cursory examination will reveal. Institutional devotion is still stressed as the actuating motive for a world of pure convention much of which is unbelievably crass and stupid. A morality for example is held up for acceptance which is antiquated, a lag from vastly different conditions of life that prevailed in the past. Character is moulded and personal behaviour and sentiments encouraged in the light of the allegiance to old institutions. The child is always sacrificed to the welfare and glory of ephemeral and often vague social survivals behind which it is only too easy for the vested interests to hide. And because of this un-intelligent schooling we find ourselves to-day in a confused chaos and welter in our social relationships. Pedagogy, which too often differs but slightly from demagogy, can offer nothing but empty symbols in the light of which we accomplish merely a tampering, tinkering and patching of the social texture.

The tendency has been to omit consideration of the internal life of the individual. Social stereotypes require little or no appreciation of individual differences. Unthinking, blind acceptance of tattered institutional norms are best conveyed when standardized. Variation, improvement and progress have therefore been limited practically to the field of the art of self-maintenance, or the economy of life, because in this field institutional slogans are soon tested by actual experience. But in the superstructure of sex, family, and religious life the indomitable pressure of emptied slogans and symbols has too often perverted or distorted the child's individuality.

Values, in the life of society, are artificial and the danger arises from their persistence. The "state", the "school", the "community", are mere artifices that should forever be tested and given worth and meaning in the individual's life, because his life is the most precious good, and only as the mores conduce toward the best and fullest expression of individual differences may these symbols remain anything but terrifying scarecrows held up by vested interests of some kind. The suffering, the privation, the screwing up and shrivelling of talent and promise that have been produced in children's lives can be accounted in the main to-day to the inertia produced by the vestiges of this "primitive" education.

With the tremendous growth of population and the eventual exhaustion of natural resources, technical education calls for more inventive genius. But it is to-day, rather, in the field of social relations that inertia and the conventional must be replaced by intelligence and discretionary control, as, for example, in sex relations. The massive lumbering social "forces" of the past must be reinterpreted in the terms of individuals. Man has unleashed enormous forces rather casually and it is yet to be decided whether these are to be employed to glorify a moribund phantasy like the "state" or whether they are to be employed to enrich the lives of the great masses. Individuals are the ultimate and only reality in social life. A realization of this truth may alone be sufficient to purge our educational systems of primitive survivals and may, perhaps, prevent the recurrence of such abysmal horrors as have recently gripped the world.

The present study has been confined to an interpretation of the primitive origins of education. It has revealed above all the position of the child in a simple culture as the perpetuating organ of society. Through the conformity of the child the continuity of the tribe is assured. To secure this most desired goal the primitive man resorts to the employment of such elaborate and convincing usages as the initiation rites. It is not, however, the conscious wish of the parents and elders to perpetuate the mores as such, but rather the natural inclination to preserve peace and comfort and prosperity for themselves in this life and in the spirit-world to come. To accomplish this the child must be duly impressed and his behaviour demonstrably conditioned for this leading purpose.

The prevailing curricula and the spirit underlying educational systems has departed but little from this norm. It still contains much of the " primitive " element in education. In many ways the child and the youth is still exposed to the primitive view that he is the perpetuating organ of this institutional myth or that antiquated cult. And it is by inculcating a conforming allegiance that these aims, half-understood even by the orthodox educationalists themselves, can be secured. In the light of reason, at least, it is time that this pressure making for conformity and perpetuation of outworn symbols should be replaced by a desire to allow the child to express *himself* and perpetuate *himself* by the development of *his* individuality. Education is only a means to an end. In the past it has been used more or less consciously as the vehicle by which the elders or the privileged have perpetuated their hold through conventional fictions. Perhaps it will be used in the future as an instrument by means of which the child may enrich the culture of his age by the simultaneous development of his own life as well.

NOTES

NOTE TO CHAPTER I.

1 : Sumner and Keller, *Science of Society*, I, pp. 6-7.

NOTES TO CHAPTER II

1 : cf. Lippert, *Kulturgeschichte*, I, p. 76 ff.
2 : cf Sumner and Keller, I, p. 419.
3 : Sumner, *Folkways*, p. 30.
4 : Torrend, *Specimens of Bantu Folk-lore*, p. 12, note ; Casalis, *Les Bassoutos*, p. 217 ; Kropf, *Kafir-English Dictionary*, pp. 237, 385.
5 : Ellis, *Yoruba-Speaking Peoples*, pp. 181-182.
6 : See above, Chapter X.
7 : Junod, *Life of a South African Tribe*, I, p. 56.
8 : Fletcher and La Flesche, *B.A.E.*, XXVII, p. 117.
9 : Hose and McDougall, *Pagan Tribes of Borneo*, I, p. 79 ; Webster, *Primitive Secret Societies*, p. 25.
10 : Radin, *University of California Publications*, XVI, p. 385, note.
11 : Spencer, *Principles of Sociology*, I, chs. X-XI.
12 : Henry, *Les Bambara*, pp. 57, 168.
13 : Tauxier, *Le Noir du Yatenga*, p. 385.
14 : Cardinall, *Northern Gold Coast*, p. 66-67.
15 : Smith and Dale, *Ila-Speaking Peoples*, II, p. 153 ; cf. Ellis, *Ewe*, p. 115 ; *Yoruba*, p. 152 ; Treager, *Maori Race*, p. 42 ; Roscoe, *J.R.A.I.*, XXXII, p. 31.
16 : Lindblom, *Akamba*, pp. 30, 179, 180 ; Hobley, *Bantu Beliefs*, p. 159.
17 : Jochelson, *Memoirs Amer. Mus. of Nat. Hist.*, XIII, pp. 97, 105 ; Czaplicka, *Aboriginal Siberia*, p. 130.
18 : Weeks, *Bakongo*, p. 115.
19 : Melland, *Witch-Bound Africa*, pp. 150, 166 ; cf. also Codrington, *Melanesians*, p. 154 ; Pritchard, *Polynesian Reminiscences*, p. 107 ; Partridge, *Cross River Natives*, p. 273.
20 : Spencer and Gillen, *Proceed. Royal Soc. Victoria*, X (N.S.), pp. 24-25.
21 : Roth, W. E., *North Queensland Ethnography*, Bulletin 5, p. 23
22 : Spencer and Gillen, *Native Tribes of Central Australia*, p. 337.
23 : Schulze, *Transac., Royal Soc. South Australia*, XIV, p. 237 ; Kingsley, *Travels in West Africa*, p. 460 ; Czaplicka, *Aboriginal Siberia*, p. 129 ; Stoll, *Internationales Archiv für Ethnographie*, I, p. 67 (supplement).
24 : Skeat and Blagden, *Pagan Races of Malay Peninsula*, II, pp. 194-195.
25 : Weeks, *Among Congo Cannibals*, pp. 129, 291 ; cf. Hartland, *Primitive Paternity*, I, p. 244 ff.
26 : Mackillop, *Proceed. Roy. Soc. South Aus.*, XVII, p. 262.

27 : cf. Van Gennep, *Rites de Passage*, p. 60 ; Ploss, *Das Kind*, I, p. 52.

28 : Ploss, op. cit., I, p. 252 ; Pfeil, *Studien und Beobachtungen*, p. 17 ; Nieuwenhuis, *Quer durch Borneo*, I, p. 69.

29 : Kropf, *Kafir-English Dictionary*, p. 141 ; cf. also pp. 310, 402.

30 : Finsch, *Ethnologische Erfahrungen*, III, p. 131.

31 : Fritsch, *Eingeborenen Südafrikas*, p. 334 ; Holub, *Seven Years in South Africa*, I, pp. 401-402 ; Stuhlmann, *Mit Emin Pasha*, pp. 37, 82, etc.

32 : Chrisman, *The Historical Child*, pp. 239-240, 112-113.

33 : Hooper, *Univ. of Calif. Publ.*, XVI, p. 351 ; cf. Bogoras, *Mem. Amer. Mus. Nat. Hist.*, XI, p. 509 (Chukchee) ; Low, *Sarawak*, p. 307.

34 : Thomson, *Fijians*, p. 209 ; cf. Lindblom, *Akamba*, p. 31 ; Collins, *Account of English Colony* (1804), p. 364 ; Parkinson, *Südsee*, p. 160 ; Lumholtz, *Unknown Mexico*, I, p. 272 ; Aldea, *Los Araucanos*, p. 39.

35 : Nansen, *Eskimo Life*, p. 151.

36 : Bancroft, *Native Races*, I, p. 391 ; cf. Rochefort, *Histoire des Îles Antiles*, p. 550 (Caribs).

37 : Roscoe, *Bakitara*, p. 240.

38 : Kidd, *Savage Childhood*, pp. 7-8.

39 : Smith and Dale, op. cit., II, pp. 3-5.

40 : Parkinson, *Südsee*, p. 398.

41 : *Cambridge Expedition*, V, 197 ; cf. Hose and McDougall, II, p. 153 ; Whiffen, *North-West Amazons*, p. 146, etc.

42 : cf. below, pp. 227 ff.

43 : Lindblom, *Akamba*, p. 36.

44 : Smith and Dale, op. cit., II, p. 5.

45 : Du Chaillu, *Explorations and Adventures*, p. 163.

46 : St. John, *Forests of the Far East*, I, p. 160.

47 : Quoted by Ploss, *Kind*, I, p. 35 ; cf. also Thomson, *Fijians*, p. 179 ; Ling Roth, *Natives of Sarawak*, I, p. 97 ; Jacobs, *Groot-Atjeh*, I, p. 109.

48 : Klose, *Togo*, p. 251 ; Parkinson, *Südsee*, p. 189 ; Codrington, *Melanesians*, p. 229 ; *J.R.A.I.*, XVIII, p. 309 ; Seligmann, *British New Guinea*, p. 487 ; Wilken, *Verspreide Geschriften*, II, pp. 143-159 ; Riedel, *De Sluik-en kroesharige Rassen*, I, p. 278 ; Batchelor, *Ainu of Japan*, p. 44 ; Nordenskiöld, *Indianerleben*, p. 206 ; Bancroft, *Native Races*, I, p. 391.

49 : Simson, *Travels in Ecuador*, pp. 92-93.

50 : Tylor, *J.R.A.I.*, XVIII, p. 256.

51 : Von den Steinen, *Naturvölker Zentral-Brasiliens* (1897), pp. 291-294.

52 : Ploss, *Das Kind*, I, p. 156.

53 : Weeks, *Congo Cannibals*, p. 132.

54 : *Cambridge Expedition*, VI, p. 106 : Krieger, *New Guinea*, p. 294.

NOTES TO CHAPTER III

1 : Sumner and Keller, *Science of Society*, I, pp. 69 ff.

2 : Vaiene and Bernard, *Bul. Soc. Roy. Belge de Geog*, XXXIV, p. 201 ; cf. Delhaise, *Les Warega*, p. 147 ; Colle, *Les Baluba*, p. 259 ; Weeks, *Bakongo*, p. 108 ; Johnston, *Grenfell and the Congo*, II, p. 671·

3 : Weiss, *Völkerstämme im Norden Deutsch Ostafrikas*, pp. 166-167 ; Merker, *Petermann's Mittheilungen*, XXX, pp. 12-13 ; Eschlimann, *Anthropos*, VI, p. 260,

4 : Jenks, *Bontoc Igorot*, p. 60 ; cf. Sigoyan, *Costumbres de los Indios Tirurayes*, p. 66.

5 : Bonwick, *Daily Life of Tasmanians*, p. 76 ; Landor, *Hairy Ainu*, p. 296.

6 : Steller, *Beschreibung Kamtschaka* (1774), pp. 294, 349 ; Czaplicka p. 129.

7 : Jenness-Ballantyne, *D'Entrecasteaux Islands*, p. 106 ; Hunt, *J.R.A.I.*, XXVIII, pp. 11-12 (Murray, I) ; Grabowsky, *Globus*, LXXII, p. 270 (Samoa) ; Hahl, *Ethnologisches Notizblatt*, bd. II, heft. ii, p. 11 (Ponapé) ; Haddon, *J.R.A.I.*, XIX, p. 359 (Torres St.) ; Ribbe, *Kannibalen*, pp. 144, 271 ; Sarfert, *Kusae*, II, p. 309 ; Elton, *J.R.A.I.*, XVII, p. 93 (Solomon I) ; Erdland, *Marshall Insulaner*, p. 124 ; Finsch, *Ethnologische Erfahrungen*, III, p. 31 (Gilbert I) ; Williams and Calvert, *Fiji*, p. 141.

8 : Thomson, *Fijians*, p. 222.

9 : cf. Danks, *J.R.A.I.*, p. 291 (New Britain) ; Parkinson, *Südsee*, p. 267 (New Mechlenburg) ; Rosenberg, p. 454 (New Guinea), etc.

10 : Nieuwenhuis, *Quer durch Borneo*, I, p. 70 ; Mayer, *Javaansche Volksleven*, I, p. 303 ; Perelear, *Beschrijiving der Dajaks*, p. 37 ; Riedel, *De sluik-en kroesharige Rassen*, pp. 24, 72, 136, 208, 449.

11 : Charlevoix, *Journal of a Voyage*, II, p. 52 (1923 ed.).

12 : Gibbs, *Contributions to North American Ethnology*, I, p. 199 ; Powers, *Contributions to North American Ethnology*, III, p. 207 ; Von den Steinen, *Zentral-Brasilien*, p. 289.

13 : Knoche, *Zeitschrift für Ethnologie*, XLIV, pp. 660-661.

14 : Nordenskiöld, *Indianerleben*, p. 38.

15 : Nieboer, " Der Malthusianismus der Naturvölker," *Zeitschrift für Socialwissenschaft*, VI, p. 716. For additional cases, consult Carr-Saunders, *Population Problem*, pp. 145, 168, 178, 189, 196 ; Ploss, *Das Kind*, II, pp. 245 ff.

16 : cf. below, Chapter IV.

17 : Delhaise, *Bul. Soc. Roy. Belge de Geog*, XXXIII, p. 123.

18 : Schmidt, *Les Baholoholo*, pp. 145, 135.

19 : Skeat and Blagden, op. cit., II, pp. 23-24.

20 : Smith and Dale, *Ila-Speaking Peoples*, II, p. 6.

21 : Brincker, *Mittheilungen des Seminars für Orientalische Sprachen*, III, p. 82 ; cf. Maass : *Durch Zentral-Sumatra*, I, p. 436.

22 : Velten, *Sitten und Gebräuche der Suaheli*, p. 101 ; Merker, *Petermanns Mittheil*, XXX, p. 11.

23 : Lindblom, *Akamba*, p. 38.

24 : Codrington, *Melanesians*, p. 229.

25 : Maugham, *Zambesia*, p. 339 ; Johnston, *Brit. Central Africa*, p. 417 ; Azara, *Voyage dans l'Amerique*, II, p. 116 ; von Martius, *Beiträge Brasiliens*, I, p. 121 ; Thomson, *Fijians*, pp. 222-223.

26 : Hyades and Deniker, *Mission Scientifique au Cap Horn*, VII, p. 376 ; Curr, *Australian Race*, I, p. 76.

27 : Lindblom, op. cit., p. 30 ; cf. Williams and Calvert, *Fiji*, p. 142 ; Jacobs, *Groot-Atjeh*, I, p. iii ; Schomburgk, *Reisen in Britisch-Guiana*, II, p. 313, etc.

28 : Sumner, *Folkways*, pp. 313, 316 ; cf. Kulischer, *Zeitschrift für Ethnologie*, XV, p. 193.

29 : cf. Kulischer, *Zeit. für Ethn.*, XV, pp. 191-193 ; Carr-Saunders, *Population Problem*, pp. 146 ff ; Ploss, *Das Kind*, II, pp. 243 ff ; Sumner, *Folkways*, pp. 314 ff.

30 : Eschlimann, *Anthropos*, VI, p. 263.

31 : Smyth, *Aborigines of Victoria*, I, p. xxi ; II, p. 386 ; cf. Spencer and Gillen, *Native Tribes*, p. 51 ; Stretton, *Trans. Roy. Soc. South Australia*, XVII, p. 231 ; Curr, I, p. 272 ; II, p. 37, 46 ; III, p. 164 ; Eylmann, *Eingeborenen Südaustralien*, p. 261, etc.

32 : *Cambridge Expedition to Torres St.*, VI, p. 109.

33 : Williams and Calvert, op. cit., p. 142.

34 : Ellis, *Polynesian Researches*, I, pp. 251, 253 (Tahiti) ; cf. ibid, I, pp. 250, 255 ; IV, p. 328 (Hawaii).

35 : Grubb, *An Unknown People*, p. 169 ; cf. Gumilla, *El Orinoco Illustrado*, p. 343 ; Hawtrey, *J.R.A.I.*, XXXI, p. 295 ; *Handbook of American Indians*, I, p. 110 (" Athapascan ").

36 : Bonney, *J.R.A.I.*, XIII, p. 125 ; cf. Wilhelmi, *Aus Allen Weltiheilen*, I, p. 121 ; Howitt, *S. E. Australia*, p. 749 ; Spencer and Gillen, *Native Tribes*, p. 264, etc.

37 : Turner, *Samoa*, p. 333.

38 : Ellis, *Polynesian Researches*, IV, p. 329 ; Grubb, *Unknown Peoples*, pp. 143, 233, 234.

39 : Chrisman, *Historical Child*, pp. 114, 115, 143, 193.

40 : Curr, I, p. 76 ; cf. Malinowski, *Trans. and Proceed. Roy. Soc. of South Australia*, XXXIX, p. 573 ; Abel, *New Guinea*, p. 43.

41 : Skeat and Blagden, *Malay Peninsula*, II, p. 11 ; cf. Sebbelov, *A.A.* (N.S.) X, p. 757 (New Hebrides) ; Parkinson, p. 161 (Jazelle Peninsula).

42 : Powers, *Contribut. to North American Ethnology*, III, p. 328 ; cf. ibid, III, p. 222.

43 : Whiffen, *North-West Amazons*, p. 151.

44 : Hill-Tout, *Natives of Brit. North America*, p. 205.

45 : Grubb, in Hambly, *Origins of Education among Primitive Peoples*, p. 27.

46 : Eschlimann, *Anthropos*, VI, p. 266-267.

47 : Venegas, *History of California* (1759), I, p. 82.

48 : Roscoe, *Bakitara*, p. 246 ; La Herisse, *L'anciene royaume du Dahomey*, p. 230 ; Delhaise, *Soc. Roy Belge de Geog.*, XXXII, p. 193 ; Johnston, *Liberia*, II, p. 1051 ; Cardinall, *Gold Coast*, p. 69.

49 : Thomson, p. 175-177, cf. Seemann, *Mission to Viti*, p. 191.

50 : *Jesuit Relations* (1925 ed.), p. 113.

51 : Krieger, *New Guinea*, pp. 294, 390.

52 : *Cambridge Expedition*, VI, p. 109 ; cf. Hunt, *J.R.A.I.*, XXVIII, p. 11.

53 : Seligmann, *British New Guinea*, p. 86 ; cf. Hinde, *Last of the Masai*, p. 75.

54 : Cole, *J.R.A.I.*, XXXII, p. 312.

55 : Smyth, II, op. cit., p. 290.

56 : Turner, *Samoa*, p. 286.

57 : Muller, *Südsee Expedition*, II, p. 224.

58 : Grinnell, *The Cheyenne Indians*, p. 149.

59 : Decle, *Three Years in Savage Africa*, p. 160 ; Stuhlmann, *Emin Pasha*, p. 38 ; Hobley, *Bantu Beliefs*, pp. 114, 154, 157 ; Strehlow, *Aranda und Loritja-Stämme*, IV, p. 2 ; Hovelacque, *Les Nègres de l'Afrique sus-Equatoriale*, p. 110 ; Klose, *Togo*, p. 350 ; Holmes *Primitive New Guinea*, p. 64 ; Kingsley, *West African Studies*, p. 455, etc.

60 : Weule, *Native Life in East Africa*, p. 283.

61 : Lindblom, op. cit., p. 38.

62 : Mockler-Ferryman, *Up the Niger*, p. 38 ; cf. Ploss, *Das Kind*, II, pp. 265, 266 ; Spencer and Gillen, *Native Tribes*, p. 52 ; Chalmers, *Pioneering in New Guinea*, p. 165, etc.

63 : Junod, *Life of a South African Tribe*, II, p. 395.

64 : Johnston, *Liberia*, II, 1050 ; Rivers, *Melanesian Society*, I, p. 313.

65 : Holmes, op. cit., p. 49.

66 : Kingsley, *Travels in West Africa*, p. 473.

67 : Hollis, *Nandi*, p. 68.

68 : Merker, *Masai*, p. 51.

69 : Krapf, *Travels and Missionary Labours*, pp. 193-194 ; cf. Kidd, *Savage Childhood*, p. 49 ; Fritsch, *Eingeborenen Süd-Afrikas*,

p. 334 ; Mangin, *Anthropos*, IX, p. 489 ; Maugham, *Zambezia*, p. 327.
    70 : Routledge, *Prehistoric People*, pp. 149-150.
    71 : Tremearne, *Hausa Superstitions*, p. 93 ; Roth, *Sarawak*, I, p 101 ; Powers, *Contrib. to No. Amer. Ethn*, III, p. 382 ; *Handbook Amer. Indians*, I, p. 266 (art. " Child Life ") ; Gumilla, *Orinoco Illustrado*, p. 344 ; Medina, *Aborijenes de Chile*, p. 289, etc.
    72 : Russell, 26th *A.R.B.A.E.*, p. 185.
    73 : Kingsley, *W. African Studies*, p. 487 ; Livingstone, *Missionary Travels*, p. 577 ; Roscoe, *J.R.A.I.*, XXI, p. 120 ; Volkens, *Kilimandscharo*, p. 252 ; Ellis, *Ewe*, p. 116, etc.
    74 : Skinner, Memoirs of Bernice P., Bishop Museum, IX, p. 44.
    75 : Chrisman, *Historical Child*, p. 193 ; cf. ibid., pp. 97-98 (Hindus) ; 143 (Japan) ; 238-239 (ancient Rome).
    76 : Holmes, op. cit., pp. 49-50.
    77 : Hagen, *Unter den Papuas*, p. 230.
    78 : Cureau, *Savage Man in Central Africa*, p. 158 ; Smyth, *Victoria*, I, p. 52, etc.
    79 : Whiffen, *N. W. Amazons*, p. 155.

NOTES TO CHAPTER IV

    1 : Smith and Dale, op. cit., II, p. 1.
    2 : Wilson, *Western Africa*, p. 269.
    3 : Low, *Sarawak*, p. 197 ; cf. van Ophuysen, *Kykes en het Huiselijk Leven der Bataks*, pp. 10-11.
    4 : Thomson, *Fijians*, p. 218 ; cf. Radiguet, *Les Derniers Sauvages*, p. 181 ; Krämer, *Samoa-Inseln*, II, p. 55, etc.
    5 : Jenks, *Bontoc Igorot*, pp. 59-60.
    6 : Nachtigal, *Sahara und Soudan*, II, p. 685.
    7 : Smith and Dale, op. cit., II, p. 71.
    8 : Weeks, *J.R.A.I.*, XL, p. 419.
    9 : cf. Spiess, *Baessler-Archiv.*, II, p. 68 ; Tauxier, *Le Noir du Yatenga*, p. 636 ; Christol, *Au Sud de l'Afrique*, p. 82, etc.
    10 : Cator, *Everyday Life among Head-Hunters*, p. 68.
    11 : Stevenson, 5th *A.R.B.A.E.*, p. 545.
    12 : pp. 44 ff., above.
    13 : Delhaise, *Les Warega*, pp. 153-154 ; cf. Stuhlmann, *Emin Pasha*, pp. 83, 185, 391, 504 ; Johnston, *Uganda*, II, p. 748 ; Baumann, *Durch Massailand*, p. 190 ; Bosman, *Pinkerton's Voyages* (1814), XVI, p. 526, etc.
    14 : Schmidt, *Les Baholoholo*, p. 141.
    15 : Weeks, *Congo Cannibals*, p. 136.
    16 : Lindblom, p. 86 ; cf. Hobley, *Ethnology of the Akamba*, p. 165.
    17 : Hollis, *Nandi*, pp. 55, 68 ; cf. Tremearne, *Hausa Superstitions*, pp. 498-499.
    18 : Roscoe, *J.R.A.I.*, XXXII, p. 38.
    19 : Jacobs, *Groot-Atjeh*, I, p. 101.
    20 : Weeks, *Bakongo*, p. 107 ; Livingstone, *Missionary Travels*, p. 412 ; Seligmann, *British New Guinea*, p. 704 ; cf. also, Delafosse, *Revue des études ethnographiques*, I, p. 483, etc.
    21 : Hinde, *Masai*, p. 72 ; Casalis, *Les Bassoutos*, p. 193 ; Magyar, *Reisen in Süd-Afrika*, pp. 23, 284.
    22 : Kidd, *Essential Kaffir*, p. 229.
    23 : Stuhlmann, *Emin Pasha*, p. 81 ; Theal, *Yellow- and Dark-Skinned Peoples*, p. 220, etc.
    24 : Batchelor, *Ainu of Japan*, pp. 43-44.
    25 : Sieroshevski-Sumner, *J.R.A.I.*, XXXI, p. 77.

26 : Merker, *Petermanns Mittl*, XXX, p. 20 ; Casalis, *Bassoutos*, p. 265.

27 : Roscoe, *Bagesu*, p. 105 ; Grabowsky, *Globus*, LXXII, p. 272 ; Czaplicka, *Aboriginal Siberia*, p. 132.

28 : Taylor, *Te Ika a Maui*, p. 213.

29 : Powers, *Contrib. No. Amer. Ethnology*, III, p. 318.

30 : Roscoe, *Bagesu*, p. 43.

31 : Thomson, *J.R.A.I.*, XXI, p. 141 ; Sieroshevski-Sumner, *J.R.A.I.*, XXI, p. 97 ; Seligmann, op. cit., p. 567.

32 : Finsch, *Ethnologische Erfahrungen*, pt. 3, p. 131.

33 : Hose and McDougall, *Pagan Tribes of Borneo*, pp. 77-79.

34 : Rivers, *History of Melanesian Society*, I, p. 55 ; Fletcher-La Flesche, 27th *A.R.B.A.E.*, p. 61.

35 : Chrisman, *Historical Child*, p. 242 ; cf. ibid., pp. 145, 146, 194.

36 : Kidd, *Essential Kaffir*, p. 200.

37 : Le Herissé, *L'ancien royaume*, p. 228 ; Reade, *Savage Africa*, p. 206.

38 : Man, *Andaman Islanders*, I, p. 450.

39 : Delhaise, *Bul. Soc. Roy Belge de Géog*, XXXII, p. 266.

40 : Erdland, *Marshall-Insulaner*, p. 127.

41 : *Cambridge Expedition*, VI, pp. 109-110.

42 : Turner, *Samoa*, pp. 81-82.

43 : Lindblom, *Akamba*, pp. 36-37.

44 : Shooter, *Kafirs of Natal*, pp. 91-92.

45 : Best, *J.R.A.I.*, XLIV, p. 141.

46 : Gibbs, *Contrib. to No. Amer. Ethnology*, I, p. 198.

47 : Ellis, *Yoruba-Speaking Peoples*, p. 157.

48 : Weeks, *Bakongo*, pp. 266-267.

49 : Roscoe, *Banyankole*, p. 108.

50 : Hobley, *Bantu Beliefs*, p. 30.

51 : Jochelson, *Memoirs Amer. Museum Nat. Hist.*, XIII, p. 107.

52 : Kidd, *Savage Childhood*, p. 142 ; Lindblom, *Akamba*, p. 173.

53 : Ploss, *Das Kind*, II, p. 131.

54 : Jenks, *Bontoc Igorot*, pp. 59-60.

55 : cf. above, ch. XI.

56 : Spieth, *Ewe-Stämme*, p. 217.

57 : Ellis, *Polynesian Researches*, I, p. 257.

58 : Russell, 26th *A.R.B.A.E.*, p. 185.

59 : Chrisman, *Historical Child*, pp. 112-113.

60 : Routledge, *Prehistoric People*, p. 123 ; Dobrizhoffer, *Abipones*, II, p. 97.

61 : Aldea, *Los Araucanos i sus Costumbres*, p. 39.

62 : St. John, *Forests of the Far East*, I, p. 165.

63 : Murdoch, 9th *A.R.B.A.E.*, p. 419.

64 : Finsch, *Zeitschrift für Ethnologie*, XII, p. 317.

65 : Van Ophuysen, *Kykes en het Huiselijk Leven der Bataks*, p. 11.

66 : Smith and Dale, op. cit., I, 385.

NOTES TO CHAPTER V

1 : Furness, *Borneo Head-Hunters*, p. 18.

2 : ibid, p. 32.

3 : Kropf, *Kaffir-English Dictionary*, p. 379.

4 : Clodd, *Magic in Names*, p. 230.

5 : Hunt, *J.R.A.I.*, XXVIII, p. 12.

6 : " Names and Naming," *Handbook of American Indians*, II, p. 16

7 : Dorsey, 15th *A.R.B.A.E.*, p. 241.

8 : Junod, *South African Tribe*, I, p. 37.

9 : Jenness-Ballantyne, *D'Entrecasteaux*, p. 91.

10 : Hawkes, *Labrador Eskimo*, p. 112.

11 : Willoughby, *Race Problems in the New Africa*, p. 72.

12 : Junod, *South-African Tribe*, I, p. 37.

13 : Morgan, *League of the Iroquois*, II, p. 239.

14 : Rink, *Tales and Traditions of the Eskimo*, p. 64.

15 : Hill-Tout, *J.R.A.I.*, XXXIV, p. 322.

16 : Roscoe, *Bakitara*, p. 246.

17 : *Captivity of Hans Stade*, p. 142 ; cf. von den Steinen, *Reisen*, p. 289 (1897 ed.).

18 : Willoughby, *Race Problems*, p. 72.

19 : Hollis, *Nandi*, p. 66 ; cf. Hurel, *Anthropos*, VI, p. 294.

20 : Taylor, *Te Ika a Maui*, p. 184.

21 : Riedel, *De sluik-en Kroesharige Rassen*, p. 73 ; van Ophuysen, *Kijkes en het Huiselijk Leven*, p. 14 ; Perelear, *Beschrijving der Dajaks*, p. 41.

22 : Bogoras, *Memoirs, Am Mus. Nat. Hist.*, XI, p. 512.

23 : Jenks, *Bontoc Igorot*, p. 62 ; Baumaun, *Durch Massailand*, p. 186 ; Roscoe, *Bagesu*, p. 24 ; Roscoe, *Banyankole*, p. 114.

24 : Roscoe, *Bagesu*, p. 59.

25 : cf. Sumner and Keller, *Science of Society*, II, pp. 784 ff.

26 : Werner, *Natives of Brit. Central Africa*, p. 104.

27 : Smyth, *Aborigines of Victoria*, I, p. 55 ; Chalmers, *Pioneering in New Guinea*, p. 164 ; Sebbelov, *Amer. Anthr.* (N.S.), XV, p. 273 ; Wilken, *Volkenkunde Nederlandsch-Indië*, p. 213 ; Bancroft, *Native Races*, VIII, p. 534 ; Rochefort, *Iles Antilles*, pp. 552-553.

28 : McDonald, *J.R.A.I.*, XIX, p. 267.

29 : Strehlow, *Aranda-und Loritja-Stämme*, p. 3-4 ; cf. Hagen, *Papuas*, p. 231.

30 : Russell, 26th *A.R.B.A.E.*, p. 188.

31 : Tessmann, *Die Pangwe*, II, p. 278.

32 : Tregear, *Maori Race*, p. 163.

33 : Krieger, *Neu-Guinea*, p. 294.

34 : Koch-Grünberg, *Zwei Jahre unter den Indianern*, I, p. 183

35 : Guevara, *Araucanía*, I, p. 209.

36 : Johnston, *Uganda*, II, p. 779.

37 : Hose and McDougall, *Pagan Tribes of Borneo*, II, p. 24.

38 : Green and Beckwith, *Amer. Anthr.* (N.S.), XXVI, p. 239.

39 : cf. Hartland, *Primitive Paternity*.

40 : cf. above, pp. 10 ff.

41 : Merker, *Die Masai*, pp. 56-58.

42 : Tessmann, *Die Pangwe*, II, p. 277.

43 : Johnston, *Uganda*, II, p. 553 ; Stuhlmann, *Mit. Emin Pasha*, pp. 38, 392, 503 ; Avon, *Anthropos*, X-XI, p. 102.

44 : Müller, *Südsee Expedition*, II, p. 227.

45 : Delhaise, *Bul. Soc. Roy belge de géog*, XXXII, p. 191.

46 : Dall, *Alaska*, p. 414.

47 : cf. below, pp. 191 ff.

48 : Hose and McDougall, *Pagan Tribes*, I, p. 80.

49 : cf. Decle, *Three Years in Savage Africa*, p. 76 ; Kidd, *Savage Childhood*, p. 34 ; Theal, *Yellow- and Dark-Skinned Races South of the Zambezi*, p. 210 ; Shooter, *Kaffirs of Natal*, pp. 220-221 ; Hinde, *Last of the Masai*, pp. 48-49 ; Hobley, *A-Kamba*, p. 127 ; Livingstone, *Missionary Travels*, p. 126 ; Merker, *Die Masai*, pp. 59, 235 ; Melland, *Witch-Bound Africa*, p. 54 ; Nachtigal, *Sahara and Soudan*, I, p. 450 ; Spieth, *Ewe-Stämme*, p. 217 ; Dale, *J.R.A.I.*, XXV, pp. 183-184 ;

Smyth, *Victoria*, I, p. 56 ; Furness, *Borneo Head-Hunters*, pp. 18, 55; St. John, *Forests of the Far East*, I, pp. 197-198 ; Perelear, *Ethnographische Beschrijving der Dajaks*, p. 42 ; Riedel, *De Sluik-en Kroesharige Rassen*, pp. 5, 238, 392, 450 ; Chalmers, *Pioneering in New Guinea*, p. 165 ; Ling Roth, *Sarawak*, II, pp. 273-274 ; Low, *Sarawak*, p. 197 ; Skeat and Blagden, *Malay Peninsula*, II, pp. 16-17 ; Hickson, *North Celebes*, p. 281 ; Jochelson, " The Yukaghir," *Memoirs of American Museum of Natural History*, XIII, p. 105 ; Czaplicka, *Aboriginal Siberia*, p. 132 ; Krause, *Tlinkit-Indianer*, p. 217 ; " Anthapascan," *Handbook of American Indians*, I, p. 114 ; " Names and Naming," II, p. 16, Wilken, *Volkenkunde*, p. 216.

50 : Wilken, *Volkenkunde Nederlandsch-Indië*, p. 219 ; cf. *Verspreide Geschriften*, I, pp. 109-111, 283-285.

51 : Tylor, *J.R.A.I.*, XVIII, pp. 249-250.

52 : Steinmetz, *Ethnologische Studien zur Ersten Entwicklung der Strafe*, II, pp. 240-242.

53 : cf. Lippert, *Kulturgeschichte*, II, pp. 341 ff.

54 : Wilken, *Verspriede Geschriften*, I, p. 284.

55 : Hollis, *Nandi*, pp. 67-68.

56 : cf. Schulien, *Anthropos*, XVIII-XIX, p. 89 ; Hutereau, *Bul. Soc. roy. belge de géog.*, XXXIV, p. 148 (Kafirs) ; Mathews, *Proceed. Roy. Soc. Victoria*, IX (N.S.), p. 171 ; Clodd, *Magic in Names*, p. 84 ff ; Morgan, *Iroquois*, II, p. 238 ; Nelson, *Indians of New Jersey*, p. 41 ; also below Chapter XI.

57 : Taylor, *Te Ika a Maui*, p. 326.

58 : " Names and Naming," *Handbook of American Indians*, II, p. 16.

59 : Smyth, *Aborigines of Victoria*, I, p. 58 ; cf. Bancroft, *Native Races*, I, p. 245.

60 : *Handbook of American Indians*, II, p. 16.

NOTES TO CHAPTER VI

1 : cf. Sumner and Keller, *Science of Society*, II, pp. 1292-1295.

2 : Rivers, *Melanesian Society*, I, p. 144.

3 : Skeat and Blagden, *Pagan Races*, II, pp. 9-10.

4 : Bogoras, *Memoirs, Am. Mus. Nat. Hist.*, XIII, p. 104.

5 : Skeat and Blagden, op. cit., II, p. 23.

6 : Pritchard, *Polynesian Reminiscences*, p. 140.

7 : Hahl, *Ethnologisches Notizblatt*, bd. II, heft. II, p. 10.

8 : Turner, *Samoa*, pp. 340-341.

9 : Erdland, *Marshall-Insulaner*, p. 125.

10 : Swanton, 26th *A.R.B.A.E.*, p. 429.

11 : Voth, *Field Columbian Museum, Anthrop. Series*, VI, p. 48.

12 : Parsons, *Man*, XXIV, p. 149, no. 112.

13 : Mayer, *Javaansche, Volksleven*, I, p. 285.

14 : Bleek, *Bushman Folklore*, p. 373.

15 : Kidd, *Savage Childhood*, p. 12 ; *Essential Kafir*, p. 201.

16 : Willoughby, *Race Problems*, p. 60.

17 : Howitt, *S. E. Australia*, pp. 747-748.

18 : Dorsey, 9th *A.R.B.A.E.*, p. 482 ; cf. Stevenson, 5ht *A.R.B.A.E.*, p. 545 (Zuñi).

19 : Nelson, 18th *A.R.B.A.E.*, p. 290.

20 : Owens, *Journal American Folklore*, II, p. 173.

21 : Roscoe, *J.R.A.I.*, XXXII, p. 30.

22 : Best, *J.R.A.I.*, XLIV, 161.

23 : Ellis, *History of Madagascar*, I, pp. 151-152.

24 : Parkinson, *Südsee*, p. 70.

25 : Mendez, *Indian Notes and Monographs* (Heye Foundation), IX, p. 187.

26 : Codrington, *Melanesians*, p. 230.

27 : Grabowsky, *Globus*, LXXII, p. 270.

28 : Bancroft, *Native Races of Pacific Coast*, I, p. 634.

29 : Kohl, *Kitchi-Gami*, pp. 7-8.

30 : Boas, *University of California Publications*, XX, p. 5 ; cf. Sebbelov, *Amer, Anthr.* (N.S.), XV, pp. 273-274 (New Hebrides).

31 : Swanton, 26th *A.R.B.A.E.*, p. 429.

32 : Sebbelov, *Amer. Anthr.* (N.S.), XV, pp. 273-274.

33 : Graafland, *De Minahassa*, II, p. 270.

34 : Cole, *J.R.A.I.*, XXXII, p. 307.

35 : Ploss, *Das Kind*, I, pp. 257, 288, 290, 336 ; Kulischer, *Zeitschrift für Ethnologie*, XV, p. 200.

36 : Cureau, *Savage Man*, p. 169.

37 : Smith and Dale, *Ila-Speaking Peoples*, I, p. 94 ; cf. Roscoe, *Bagesu*, p. 27 ; Baumann, *Massailand*, p. 186 ; Klose, *Togo*, pp. 250 507.

38 : Fritsch, *Eingeborenen Südafrikas*, p. 235.

39 : Weeks, *Congo Cannibals*, p. 141.

40 : Curr, *Australian Race*, II, p. 55.

41 : Buller, *Forty Years in New Zealand*, pp. 215-216.

42 : Parkinson, *Südsee*, p. 183 ; Brainne, *La Nouvelle Calédonie*, . 249.

43 : Cook, *Voyage to the Pacific*, I, p. 261.

44 : " Child Life," *Handbook of Amer. Indians*, I, pp. 265-266.

45 : Hill-Tout, *Tribes of British North America*, p. 40.

46 : Ploss, *Das Kind*, I, p. 289 ; Colenso, *Trans. and Proceed. New Zealand Institute*, I, pp. 355-356.

47 : Ploss, op. cit., I, pp. 288-289.

48 : See below, 187 ff ; also Wilken, *Verspreide Geschriften*, IV, pp. 205-246.

49 : Wilson, *Western Africa*, p. 399.

50 : Fison, *J.R.A.I.*, XIV, p. 23.

51 : Junod, *Life of a South African Tribe*, I, p. 56.

52 : Fletcher, La Flesche, 27th *A.R.B.A.E.*, p. 117.

53 : ibid, p. 116 (note).

54 : Rivers, *Melanesian Society*, I, p. 146.

55 : Turner, *Samoa*, p. 290.

56 : Stevenson, 5th *A.R.B.A.E.*, p. 546.

57 : Lumholtz, *Unknown Mexico*, II, p. 177.

58 : Casalis, *Les Bassoutos*, p. 202.

59 : Schmidt, *Les Baholoholo*, p. 140.

60 : Best, *J.R.A.I.*, XLIV, p. 149.

61 : cf. Ploss, *Das Kind*, I, p. 78.

62 : Roscoe, *Banyankole*, p. 114.

63 : Fritsch, *Eingeborenen Südafrikas*, p. 108.

64 : Tremearne, *J.R.A.I.*, XLV, p. 34.

65 : Jochelson, *Memoirs, Am. Mus. of Nat Hist.*, X, pp. 492, 747.

66 : Sumner and Keller, *Science of Society*, I, pp. 247 ff.

67 : Riedel, *Bijdragen Taal, Land-en Volkenkunde Neder. Indië*, XXXV, p. 92.

68 : Thurnwald, *Beihefte zur psychol. Sammelforschung*, VI, p. 119.

69 : Green and Beckwith, *Amer. Anthr.* (N.S.), XXVI, p. 234.

70 : Fletcher, La Flesche, 27th *A.R.B.A.E.*, p. 237 ; Schmidt, *Zentral Brasilien*, p. 317 ; Roth, 38th *A.R.B.A.E.*, p. 177.

71 : King, *Voyage of the Adventure and Beagle*, I, pp. 76-77.

72 : Tauxier, *Le Noir du Soudan*, p. 618 ; Codrington, *Melanesians*, p. 113, etc.

NOTES TO CHAPTER VII

1 : cf. Fiske, *Meaning of Infancy, Excursions of an Evolutionist*, p. 315 ; Spencer, *Sociology*, I, p. 630 (note).

2 : cf. above, pp. 70 ff.

3 : "Names and Naming," *Handbook of American Indians*, II, p. 16.

4 : Radin, *University of California, pub.* XVI, p. 385 (note).

5 : Webster, *Primitive Secret Societies*, p. 25.

6 : Ling Roth, *Natives of Sarawak*, I, p. 101 ; Hose and MacDougall *Pagan Tribes of Borneo*, I, p. 79.

7 : cf. Callaway, *Religious System of Ama-zulu*, p. 176 (note) ; Tessmann, *Pangwe*, II, p. 109.

8 : Sieroshevski-Sumner, *J.R.A.I.*, XXI, p. 80 (Italics ours).

9 : Lindblom, *Akamba*, p. 34.

10 : Shooter, *Kafirs of Natal*, p. 87 ; Kropf, *Ama-Xosa*, p. 122 ; Brunache, *Le Centre de l'Afrique*, p. 68 ; Schmidt, *Les Boholoholo*, p. 142, etc.

11 : Parkinson, *Südsee*, p. 71.

12 : Kidd, *Savage Childhood*, pp. 19, 22, 43 ; Kropf, *Kafir-English Dictionary*, p. 255.

13 : Bosman, *Pinkerton's Voyages*, XVI, p. 526.

14 : Czaplicka, *Aboriginal Siberia*, p. 305.

15 : Rosenberg, *Malayische Archipel*, p. 198.

16 : cf. Sumner and Keller, *Science of Society*, II, pp. 1076 ff.

17 : Hose and McDougall, *Pagan Tribes of Borneo*, II, p. 157.

18 : Snouck Hurgronje, *Atjehers*, I, pp. 433-434.

19 : Routledge, *Prehistoric People*, p. 11.

20 : Roscoe, *Bakitara*, p. 257 ; cf. van Ophuysen, *Huiselijk Leven der Bataks*, p. 15 ff.

21 : Owens, *Journal Amer. Folklore*, II, pp. 166-167.

22 : cf. Van Gennep, *Rites de Passage*, pp. 77, 275-276 *et passim*.

23 : Turner, *Samoa*, p. 82 ; Stair, *Old Samoa*, p. 177 ; Krämer, *Samoa-Inseln*, II, p. 55.

24 : Junod, *Revue d'Ethnographie*, I, p. 131.

25 : Williams and Calvert, *Fiji and Fijians*, p. 138 ; cf. Sieroshevski-Sumner, *J.R.A.I.*, XXXI, p. 80.

26 : Curr, *Australian Race*, I, p. 31 ; cf Hollis., *Nandi*, p. 12 ; Livingstone, *Missionary Travels*, p. 148 ; Nassau, *Fetichism*, p. 12 ; Gregory, *Great Rift Valley*, p. 350.

27 : Smyth, *Aboriginies of Victoria*, I, p. 75.

28 : Nieuwenhuis, *Quer durch Borneo*, I, p. 101.

29 : ibid., I, p. 76.

30 : Rawling, *New Guinea Pygmies*, p. 62.

31 : Charlevoix, *Journal of a Voyage*, II, p. 104.

32 : Aldea, *Araucania*, p. 40.

33 : Johnston, *Uganda*, II, p. 827.

34 : Cureau, *Central Africa*, p. 164.

35 : Hahn, *Globus*, XVIII, p. 122.

36 : MacCauley, 5th *A.R.B.A.E.*, p. 498.

37 : cf. Sumner and Keller, *Science of Society*, I, ch. V ; Routledge, *Prehistoric People*, p. 121.

38 : Furness, *Borneo Head-Hunters*, p. 8 ; Hose and McDougall, II, p. 163.

39 : Jochelson, *Yukaghir*, p. 106.

40 : Johnston, *British Central Africa*, p. 418.

41 : Hinde, *Last of the Masai*, pp. 52, 58.

42 : Mangin, *Anthropos*, IX, p. 485.

43 : Routledge, op. cit., pp. 121-122.

44 : Borgoras, *Memoirs, Amer. Mus. Nat. Hist.*, XI, pp. 37, 553-554.

45 : Mendez, *Indian Notes and Monographs*, IX, p. 177.

46 : *Tijdschrift voor Nederlandsch-Indië*, XXXV, p. 90; cf. further, Franke, *Geistige Entwicklung der Negerkinder*, p. 222 ff; Smith and Dale, II, p. 15; Dale, *J.R.A.I.*, XXV, pp. 187-188; Fritsch, *Eingeborenen Sudafrikas*, pp. 205, 208; Spieth, *Ewe-Stämme*, p. 595; Klose, *Togo*, p. 252; Gomes, *Sea-Dyaks*, p. 11; Maass, *Zentral-Sumatra*, I, p. 438; Junghuhn, *Battaländer*, pp. 130-131; Schadenberg, *Zeit. fur Ethnologie*, XIII, p. 136; Pfeil, *Studien*, p. 22; Kubary, *Globus*, XLVII, p. 72; Boas, 6th *A.R.B.A.E.*, p. 566; Crantz, *Greenland*, I, p. 151; Grinnell, *Cheyenne Indians*, I, pp. 110-111; Russell, 26th *A.R.B.A.E.*, p. 191; Stoll, *Inter. Archiv fur Ethnologie*, I (sup), p. 68; Schomburgk, *Britisch-Guiana*, I, pp. 167, 419, etc.

47 : Owens, *Journal American Folklore*, II, p. 163; Jenks, *Bontoc Igorot*, p. 61.

48 : Batchelor, *Ainu of Japan*, p. 43.

49 : French-Sheldon, *J.R.A.I.*, XXI, pp. 371-372; Weule, *Ethnologisches Notizblatt*, II, p. 48; Todd, *Primitive Family as an Educational Institution*, pp. 108-109.

50 : Chalmers, *Pioneering in New Guinea*, p. 168; St. John, *Forests of the Far East*, II, p. 115.

51 : Guppy, *Solomon Islands*, p. 42; Guevara, *Araucania*, I, pp. 209-210; Reade, *Savage Africa*, p. 206; cf. also Franke, *Enwicklung der Negerkinder*, pp. 133-137.

52 : Franke, op. cit., p. 133; Hagen, *Die Orang Kubu*, p. 130.

53 : Thomson, *Fijians*, XIV; Theal, *Yellow- and Dark-Skinned Peoples*, p. 264; Curr, *Australian Race*, I, p. 105; cf. Krieger, *Neu-Guinea*, p. 176.

54 : Cureau, *Savage Man*, p. 73.

55 : Torday, *Camp and Tramp*, p. 241.

56 : Man, *Andaman Islanders*, p. 27.

57 : Maugham, *Zambezia*, pp. 306-307; Torday, *Camp and Tramp*, p. 241; Torday and Joyce, *J.R.A.I.*, XXV, p. 412.

58 : Schmidt, *Les Baholoholo*, p. 463.

NOTES TO CHAPTER VIII

1 : cf. Eylmaun, *Eingeborenen Südaustralien*, p. 247; Rosenberg, *Malayische Archipel*, p. 199; Thurnwald, *Beihefte zur psychologischen Sammelforschung*, VI, p. 19; Girschner, *Baessler-Archiv*, II, p. 168; Parkinson, *Internationales Archiv für Ethnographie*, XIII, p. 41, etc.

2 : Batchelor, *Ainu of Japan*, p. 109.

3 : Baegert, *Smithsonian Report* (1863), p. 369.

4 : Gumilla, *El Orinoco Ilustrado*, pp. 73-74; cf. Von Martius, *Volkenkunde Brasiliens*, I, p. 124.

5 : Kidd, *Savage Childhood*, pp. 48, 52.

6 : Kidd, *Essential Kafir*, p. 90.

7 : cf. Ploss, *Das Kind*, II, p. 323; Todd, *Primitive Family*, p. 171.

8 : Werner, *Natives of British Central Africa*, p. 118; cf. Weule, *Ethnologisches Notizblatt*, II, p. 48 etc.

9 : Van Overbergh, *Les Mangbetu*, p. 308; Cruickshank, *Gold Coast*, II, pp. 205-206.

10 : Smyth, *Victoria*, I, p. 47 (note); Malinowski, *Family among Australian Aborigines*, p. 256; Colenso, *New Zealand Institute*, I, p. 374; Roth, *Aborigines of Tasmania*, p. 127; Mayer, *Javaansche Volksleven*, II, p. 394; Hose and McDougall, II, p. 165; Pfeil, *Studien*, p. 25;

Erdland, *Marshall-Insulaner*, pp. 127-128; Saville, *Unknown New Guinea*, pp. 147-199.

11 : Teschauer, *Anthropos*, IX, p. 23 ; cf. Murdoch, 9th *A.R.B.A.E.* p. 417.

12 : Camboué, *Anthropos*, X-XI, p. 859.

13 : Willoughby, *Race Problems*, p. 124 ; Weeks, *Congo Cannibals* p. 140.

14 : Turner, 11th *A.R.B.A.E.*, p. 202.

15 : Simson, *Travels in Ecuador*, pp. 102-103.

16 : Bastian, *Deutsche Expedition*, II, p. 20.

17 : Powers, *Contributions to North American Ethnology*, III, p. 271.

18 : Grinnell, *Cheyenne Indians*, I, p. 109.

19 : Fitzroy, *Voyage of the Adventure and Beagle*, II, p. 154

20 : Roth, 38th *A.R.B.A.E.*, p. 699 ; Mendez, *Indian Notes*, IX, p. 179.

21 : Seligmann, *Veddas*, p. 91.

22 : French-Sheldon, *J.R.A.I.*, XXI, p. 371.

23 : Weeks, *Congo Cannibals*, p. 143.

24 : Seligmann, *British New Guinea*, p. 264 ; cf. Weeks, *J.R.A.I.*, XXXIX, p. 130 (Congo).

25 : Quoted in Roth, *Natives of Sarawak*, II, p. 144.

26 : Stair, *Old Samoa*, pp. 249-250.

27 : Mangin, *Anthropos*, IX, p. 484 ; cf. Willoughby, *Race Problems* pp. 124-125.

28 : Poupon, *L'Anthropologie*, XXVI, p. 112 (Baya).

29 : Blair, *Indians of Upper Mississippi Valley*, II, p. 194.

30 : Buller, *Forty Years in New Zealand*, p. 216.

31 : Saville, *Unknown New Guinea*, p. 99.

32 : Parkinson, *Internationales Archiv für Ethnographie*, II, p. 36.

33 : Jenness and Ballantyne, *Northern D'Entrecasteaux*, pp. 92-93.

34 : Kidd, *Savage Childhood*, p. 153.

35 : Pfeil, *Studien u. Beobachtungen*, p. 23.

36 : cf. Lippert, *Kulturgeschichte*, I, pp. 226, 228 ; Keller, *Societal Evolution*, pp. 217-218 ; Franke, *Entwicklung der Nègerkinder*, p. 216 ; Schmid, *Geschichte der Erziehung*, I, p. 44.

37 : Weule, *Ethnographisches Notizblatt*, II, pp. 49-50 ; French-Sheldon, *J.R.A.I.*, XXVII, p. 374 ; Nachtigal, *Sahara and Soudan*, I, p. 454 ; Hovelacque, *Les Negres*, p. 138, etc.

38 : Roth, *North Queensland Ethnography*, IV, p. 15 ; Curr, *Australian Race*, II, p. 71.

39 : Seligmann, *Veddas*, p. 91.

40 : Malinowski, *Proceed. Roy. Soc. South Australia*, XXXIX, p. 576 ; Nieuwenhuis, *Quer durch Borneo*, II, pp. 139-140 ; Finsch, *Ethnologische Erfahrungen*, II, p. 34.

41 : Bogoras, *Memoirs, Am. Museum Nat. Hist.*, XI, p. 273.

42 : Murdoch, 9th *A.R.B.A.E.*, p. 383.

43 : Fletcher, La Flesche, 27th *A.R.B.A.E.*, pp. 363-364.

44 : Schmidt, *Indianerstudien in Zentral-Brasilien*, p. 311, 313.

45 : Whiffen, *North-West Amazons*, p. 108 ; cf. Ploss, *Das Kind*, II, p. 325 ; Sheldon, *American Antiquarian*, I, p. 397, etc.

46 : Fric and Radin, *J.R.A.I.*, XXXVI, p. 399.

47 : Smyth, *Aborigines of Victoria*, I, xxi.

48 : Schmidt, *Indianerstudien*, p. 177.

49 : Schmidt, *Les Baholoholo*, p. 463 ; cf. Groos, *The Play of Man*, p. 290.

50 : Felkin, *Journal Royal Society Edinburgh*, XIII, p. 746.

51 : Hollis, *Nandi*, pp. 83-84 ; cf. Merker, *Masai*, p. 55 ; Smith and Dale, *Ila-Speaking Peoples*, II, p. 38 ; Tessmann, *Baessler-Archiv.*, II, pp. 259-260 ; Hobley, *Akamba*, p. 56 ; Weeks, *J.R.A.I.*, XL, p. 404, etc.

52 : Weeks, *Congo Cannibals*, p. 74.
53 : Wollaston, *Pygmies and Papuans*, p. 118.
54 : Partridge, *Cross River Natives*, pp. 259-260.
55 : MacDonald, *Africana*, I, p. 124.
56 : Nordenskiöld, *Indianerleben*, pp. 64-65.
57 : Grinnell, op. cit., I, pp. 108-109.
58 : Delhaise, *Les Warega*, p. 67.
59 : *idem.*
60 : Saville, *Unknown New Guinea*, pp. 99-100 et seq.; cf. Rawling, *New Guinea Pygmies*, p. 286.
61 : Tessmann, *Baessler-Archiv*, II, p. 262.
63 : Grinnell, op. cit., I, p. 114.
64 : Kidd, *Savage Childhood*, p. 175.
65 : Mariner, *Tonga Islands*, II, p. 209.
66 : Kidd, op. cit., p. 166.
67 : Johnston, *Liberia*, II, p. 1078.
68 : cf. Ploss, *Das Kind*, II, p. 280 ; Chamberlain, *The Child*, p. 156 ; Lippert, *Geschichte der Familie*, p. 97.
69 : Gregory, *Great Rift Valley*, p. 342.
70 : Tylor, *Primitive Culture*, I, pp. 225-228.
71 : Gregory, op. cit., p. 342.
72 : cf. Hobley, *Bantu Beliefs*, p. 280.
73 : " Child Life," *Handbook of American Indians*, I, p. 266.
74 : Tessmann, *Baessler-Archiv*, II, pp. 261-262.
75 : Jenks, *Bontoc Igorot*, p. 65.
76 : Groos, *Play of Man*, pp. 280-281.
77 : " Dolls," *Handbook of American Indians*, I, p. 396 ; cf. Fewkes, *Internationales Archiv für Ethnographie*, VII, p. 70 ff.
78 : Malinowski, *Proceed. Roy. Soc. South Australia*, XXXIX, pp. 574-575.
79 : cf. Tylor, *Primitive Culture*, I, pp. 72-73 ; Chamberlain, *Child*, pp. 22-23.
80 : " Nascapee," *Handbook of American Indians*, II, p. 32.
81 : Nordenskiöld, *Indianerleben*, pp. 69-70.
82 : Veth, *Java*, II, p. 381 ; cf. van Ophuysen, *Huiselijk Leven der Batak*, p. 16.

NOTES TO CHAPTER IX

1 : Malinowski, *Family among Australian Aborigines*, pp. 241, 247-248.
2 : cf. Chap. VIII, above.
3 : Smyth, *Aborigines of Victoria*, I, pp. 49-50, xxi.
4 : Batchelor, *Ainu of Japan*, pp. 109-110 ; cf. von Siebold, *Zeitschrift für Ethnologie* (1881 supp.), p. 30.
5 : Hahn, *Globus*, XVIII, p. 122 ; Dornan, *J.R.A.I.*, XLV, p. 48,
6 : Weeks, *Congo Cannibals*, pp. 142, 144.
7 : Powers, *Contributions to North American Ethnology*, III, pp. 109-110.
8 : cf. Wissler, *Man and Culture*.
9 : Weeks, *Bakongo*, p. 119.
10 : Mendez, *Indian Notes and Monographs*, IX, p. 148.
11 : Mariner, *Tonga Islands*, II, p. 212.
12 : " Education," *Handbook of American Indians*, I, p. 415.
13 : McClintock, *Old North Trail*, pp. 235-236.
14 : Schomburgk, *Reisen in Britisch-Guiana*, I, p. 152.
15 : Catlin, *North American Indians*, I, p. 131.
16 : " Education," *Handbook of American Indians*, I, p. 415.

17 : Eastman, *Indian Boyhood*, p. 57 ; cf. Nelson, *Indians of New Jersey*, p. 43.

18 : Hose and McDougall, *Pagan Tribes*, II, pp. 160, 168.

19 : Jenness and Ballantyne, op. cit., p. 94.

20 : Knoche, *Zeitschrift für Ethnologie*, XL, p. 659.

21 : Batchelor, *Ainu of Japan*, pp. 109-110.

22 : Howitt, *Natives of South-East Australia*, p. 300.

23 : Russell, 26th *A.R.B.A.E.*, p. 191.

24 : Crantz, *History of Greenland*, I, p. 140.

25 : Hill-Tout, *J.R.A.I.*, XXXIV, p. 316.

26 : Hill-Tout, *Tribes of British North America*, p. 246.

27 : Dall, *Alaska and its Resources*, pp. 388-389.

28 : Krause, *Die Tlinkit-Indianer*, p. 251 ; cf. Teit, *Memoirs, Amer. Mus. Nat. History*, II, pp. 309-310.

29 : Jochelson, *Koryak*, p. 758 ; von Siebold, *Zeitschrift für Ethnologie* (1887 supplement), p. 32.

30 : Olden, *Tipi Sapa*, p. 52.

31 : Kidd, *Essential Kafir*, p. 207 ; Livingstone, *Missionary Travels*, p. 149 ; cf. Magyar, *Reisen in Süd-Afrika*, p. 25.

32 : MacDonald, *J.R.A.I.*, XIX, p. 268.

33 : Skeat and Blagden, *Pagan Races*, I, pp. 669-670.

34 : Miklucho-Maclay, *Tijdschrift voor Nederlandsch-Indië*, XXXVI pp. 298-299.

35 : Niblack, *Annual Report, U.S. National Museum* (1888), p. 370.

36 : Hill-Tout, *J.R.A.I.*, XXXIV, p. 32.

37 : Hooper, *Univ. of California Publ.*, XVI, p. 348.

38 : Furness, *Everyday Life among Borneo Head-Hunters*, pp. 62-63 (Italics mine).

39 : Martin, *Reisen in den Molukken*, p. 153.

40 : Williams and Calvert, *Fiji and Fijians*, p. 139 ; cf. Cook, *Voyage to the Pacific*, I, p. 300 ; Bancroft, *Native Races of Pacific Coast*, I, p. 704.

41 : Cremony, *Life among the Apaches*, p. 85.

42 : cf. Keller, *Societal Evolution*.

43 : Man, *Andaman Islanders*, p. 25-26 ; cf. Brown, *Andaman Islanders*, p. 276 ff.

44 : Batchelor, *Ainu of Japan*, p. 110.

45 : Eastman, *Indian Boyhood*, pp. 58-59 ; cf. Fletcher-La-Flesche, 27th *A.R.B.A.E.*, p. 329.

46 : Russell, 26th *A.R.B.A.E.*, p. 190.

47 : Grinnell, *Cheyenne Indians*, I, p. 121.

48 : Blair, *Indians of the Upper Mississippi Valley*, II, p. 164.

49 : cf. below, chap. X.

50 : Veth, *Borneo*, II, p. 239.

51 : Weeks, *Congo Cannibals*, p. 162 ; cf. Spieth, *Ewe-Stämme*, p. 211 ; Maughan, *Zambezia*, p. 369 ; Schmidt, *Les Baholoholo*, p. 154, etc.

52 : Colenso, *Trans. and Proceed. New Zealand Institute*, XIII, p. 57 ; cf. Best, *J.R.A.I.*, XLIV, p. 142.

53 : Kingsley, *Travels*, p. 453.

54 : Whiffen, *North-West Amazons*, p. 208.

55 : Jenness and Ballantyne, *Northern D'Entrecasteaux*, pp. 166, 168.

56 : Bleek, *Bushman Folklore*, pp. 192, 214, 247 ff.

57 : Kolb, *Beschreibung des Vorgebürges der Guten Hoffnung und derer darauf wohnenden Hottentoten* (1745), p. 147.

58 : Swanton, 43rd *A.R.B.A.E.*, p. 89.

59 : Russell, 26th *A.R.B A E.*, p. 206.

60 : Jarves, *History of Hawaiian Islands*, p. 37.

61 : cf. Torrend, *Specimens of Bantu Folk-lore*, pp. 5-6, 145 (note) ; Ploss, *Das Kind*, II, p. 331.

62 : Camboué, *Anthropos*, X, XI, pp. 847-848.

63 : Hose and McDougall, *Pagan Tribes*, II, p. 165.

64 : Ribbe, *Salomo-Inseln*, pp. 153, 273 ; Kubary, *Globus*, XLVII, p. 87 ; Thomson, *Fijians*, p. 315 ; Ellis, *Polynesian Researches*, I, p. 199, etc.

65 : Pritchard, *Polynesian Reminiscences*, pp. 119, 125.

66 : Batchelor, *Ainu of Japan*, pp. 109-111.

67 : Hambly, *Origins of Primitive Education*, p. 364.

68 : Kidd, *Essential Kafir*, p. 383.

69 : Weeks, *Congo Life and Folklore*, p. 370.

70 : Nansen, *Eskimo Life*, p. 73 ; cf. Crantz, *Greenland*, I, p. 159 ; Eastman, *Indian Boyhood*, p. 51, etc.

71 : Weeks, op. cit., p. 383.

72 : Riggs, *Contrib. to No. Amer. Ethnology*, IX, p. 209.

73 : Kidd, *Savage Childhood*, pp. 98, 108.

74 : Ploss, *Das Kind*, II, p. 338.

75 : Luiz de la Cruz, *Peguenches*, p. 63 ; cf. Schmid, *Geschichte der Erziehung*, I, p. 41.

76 : Erdland, *Marshall-Insulaner*, p. 172.

77 : cf. above, pp. 47 ff.

78 : Wilhelmi, *Aus Allen Welttheilen*, I, p. 122.

79 : Hose and McDougall, *Pagan Tribes*, II, p. 185.

80 : Dorsey, *Journal American Folklore*, XVIII, pp. 227-228 ; cf. Fletcher-La-Flesche, 27th *A.R.B.A.E.*, pp. 331-333.

81 : cf. Sumner and Keller, *Science of Society*, II, p. 748 ff.

82 : Werner, *British Central Africa*, p. 121.

83 : Henry, *Les Bambara*, p. 25.

84 : Dundas, *J.R.A.I.*, XLV, p. 258.

85 : Fletcher, La Flesche, 27th *A.R.B.A.E.*, pp. 331-332.

86 : Bleek, *Bushman Folklore*, p. 421.

87 : Willoughby, *Race Problems*, p. 130.

88 : Junod, *Life of a South African Tribe*, I, p. 84.

89 : Delhaise, *Les Warega*, p. 161 ; cf. Wilson, *Western Africa*, p. 118 ; Spieth, *Ewe-Stämme*, pp. 216, 700.

90 : Bogoras, op. cit., p. 561.

91 : Lowie, *Anthropological Papers, Amer. Museum Nat, Hist.*, IX, p. 219 ; Charlevoix, *Journal*, II, p. 106 ; Blair, *Upper Mississippi Valley*, II, p. 165 ; Morgan, *League of the Iroquois*, I, pp. 231-232.

92 : Kohl, *Kitchi-Gami*, p. 277.

93 : Russell, 26th *A.R.B.A.E.*, p. 191.

94 : Hobley, *Bantu Beliefs*, pp. 146-147 ; cf. Westermarck, *History of Human Marriage*, II, p. 351 ff.

95 : Smith and Dale, op. cit., I, p. 416.

96 : Johnston, *Uganda*, II, p. 879.

97 : Weeks, *Congo Cannibals*, pp. 299-300 ; Tessmann, *Die Pangwe*, p. 292.

98 : Weeks, *Bakongo*, pp. 155-156.

99 : Hose and McDougall, *Pagan Tribes*, II, p. 165.

100 : Poupon, *L'Anthropologie*, XXVI, p. 123.

101 : Spieth, *Ewe-Stämme*, p. 216.

102 : Kohl, *Kitchi-Gama*, p. 273.

NOTES TO CHAPTER X

1 : Howitt, *Natives of S.E. Australia*, p. 530.

2 : Van Gennep, *Rites de Passages*, p. 94.

3 : Webster, *Primitive Secret Societies*, p. 37.

4 : Weiss, *Völkerstämme Norden Deutsch Ostafrikas*, p. 336.

5 : Hose and McDougall, *Pagan Tribes*, II, pp. 168-169 ; Furness, *Borneo Head-Hunters*, p. 92.

6 : Beyer, *Zeitschrift für Ethnologie*, LVIII, p. 250.

7 : Roscoe, *Bagesu*, p. 74 ; Gusinde, *Zeitschrift für Ethnologie*, LVIII, p. 271.

8 : Stevenson, 5th *A.R.B.A.E.*, p. 553.

9 : Codrington, *Melanesians*, p. 87.

10 : Chalmers, *Pioneering in New Guinea*, p. 85.

11 : Stannus and Davey, *J.R.A.I.*, XLIII, p. 119.

12 : Martin, *Reisen in der Molukken*, p. 154 ; Fletcher, La Flesche, 27th *A.R.B.A.E.*, p. 118 ; Spier, *Univ. of Cal. Publications*, XX, 316.

13 : Mathews, *Proceedings Royal Soc. New South Wales*, XXVIII, p. 124 ; Laidler, *Man*, XXII, p. 13 (no. 7).

14 : Howitt, op. cit., p. 530.

15 : Fison, *J.R.A.I.*, XIV, p. 20.

16 : Melland, *Witch-Bound Africa*, p. 76 ; Smith and Dale, *Ila-Speaking Peoples*, II, p. 21.

17 : Lippert, *Kulturgeschichte*, II, p. 318 ff ; Wilken, *Volkenkunde* p. 232.

18 : cf. Brown, *Andaman Islanders*, p. 320.

19 : Schweiger, *Anthropos*, IX, pp. 54-55.

20 : Bugeau, *Anthropos*, VI, pp. 616-618 ; cf. Spieth, *Ewe-Stämme*, p. 626.

21 : Torday, *Camp and Tramp*, p. 135.

22 : Hinde, *Last of the Masai*, p. 41.

23 : Lindblom, *Akamba*, pp. 40, 42-43 ; cf. Eliot, *East African Protectorate*, p. 136.

24 : Miklucho-Maclay, *Tijdschrift voor Nederlandsch-Indië*, XXXVI, p. 299.

25 : cf. Bastian, *Deutsche Expedition an der Loango-Küste*, I, p. 177.

26 : cf. Van Gennep, op. cit., p. 161 ; Schurtz, *Altersklassen und Männerbunde*, pp. 104, 107 ; Todd, *Primitive Family*, p. 89 ; Junod, *Revue d'Ethn. et de Soc.*, I, p. 168 ; Kulischer, *Zeit. für Ethn.*, XV, p. 203.

27 : Hollis, *Nandi*, pp. 55, 58.

28 : Webster, *Primitive Secret Societies*, p. 39.

29 : Moszkowski, *Zeitschrift für Ethnologie*, XLIII, p. 340.

30 : " Ordeal," *Handbook of American Indians*, II, p. 145 ; Lafitau, *Moeurs des Sauvages Ameriquains*, I, p. 286.

31 : Smith and Dale, *Ila-Speaking Peoples*, II, p. 18 ; cf. Beyer, *Zeitschrift für Ethnologie*, XVIII, p. 251.

32 : Hovelacque, *Les Nègres*, p. 152.

33 : Kidd, *Essential Kafir*, p. 207.

34 : Lindblom, *Akamba*, p. 47.

35 : Chinnery and Beaver, *J.R.A.I.*, XLV, p. 77.

36 : Laidler, *Man*, XXII, pp. 13-14 (no. 7).

37 : cf. above, pp. 87 ff.

38 : Todd, *Primitive Family*, p. 89 ; cf. van Ekris, *Tijdschrift voor Nederlandsch-Indië*, XVI, pp. 302, 304 ; Ceston, *Anthropos*, VI, p. 752.

39 : Martin, *Reisen in den Molukken*, p. 155.

40 : Beaver, *Unexplored New Guinea*, pp. 186-187.

41 : Schurtz, *Altersklassen*, p. 104.

42 : Howitt, *Natives of S.E. Australia*, p. 532 ; cf. *Aus. Assoc. Advancement of Science*, III, p. 345.

43 : Mathews, *Proceedings American Philosophical Society*, XXXVII, pp. 59-60 ; *J.R.A.I.*, XXVI, p. 274 ; cf. Smyth, *Aborigines of Victoria*, I, p. 66 ; Curr, *Australian Race*, II, pp. 61-62 ; Mathews, *Proceed. Royal Soc. New South Wales*, XXXI, p. 132 ; *Roy. Soc. Victoria*, IX (N.S.), pp. 155, etc.

44 : Brown, *Andaman Islanders*, pp. 281-282.
45 : Mathews, *Roy. Society of Victoria*, IX (N.S.), p. 132.
46 : Webster, *Secret Societies*, p. 30.
47 : Howitt, *J.R.A.I.*, XIV, p. 320.
48 : Brown, *Andaman Islanders*, p. 324.
49 : Koppers, *Unter Feuerland-Indianern*, p. 101.
50 : Howitt, *S.E. Australia*, p. 558.
51 : Bugeau, *Anthropos*, VI, pp. 622-623.
52 : Thomson, *Fijians*, pp. 150, 153 ; cf. Deane, *Fijian Society*, p. 19.
53 : Holmes, op. cit., p. 120 ; cf. Henry, *Les Bambara*, pp. 94, 186.
54 : cf. Boas, *Univ. of California Publ.*, XX, p. 6 ; Fletcher-La Flesche, 27th *A.R.B.A.E.*, p. 122 ; Kohl, *Kitchi-Gami*, p. 47.
55 : Stevenson, 5th *A.R.B.A.E.*, p. 552.
56 : Brown, op. cit., p. 279.
57 : Man, *Andaman Islanders*, p. 134 ; Brown, op. cit., p 281
58 : Jenness and Ballantyne, op. cit., p. 93.
59 : Deane, *Fijian Society*, p. 19.
60 : Vormann, *Anthropos*, X-XI, pp. 171-172.
61 : Ridley, *Kamilaroi and Kurnai*, pp. 24, 156.
62 : Malinowski, *Proceed. Royal Society South Australia*, XXXIX, p. 573; Howitt, *S.E. Australia*, p. 626.
63 : Steinmetz, *Entwicklung der Strafe*, pp. 215-216.
64 : Simson, *Travels in Ecuador*, p. 92.
65 : Dale, *J.R.A.I.*, XXV, pp. 190-191.
66 : cf. Sumner and Keller, *Science of Society*, I, p. 449 ff.; Lippert, *Kulture-Geschichte*, II, p. 345 ff.
67 : Thurnwald, *Forschungen auf den Salomo-Inseln und dem Bismarck-Archipel*, III, p. 6 ; II, p. 262.
68 : Dundas, *J.R.A.I.*, XLIII, p. 523 ; cf. Lindblom, *Akamba*, p. 57.
69 : Johnston, *Liberia*, II, pp. 1030, 1032.
70 : Henry, *Les Bambara*, pp. 187-188 ; cf. Ceston, *Anthropos*, VI, p. 745.
71 : Mathews, *Proceed. Royal Soc. New South Wales*, XXI, p. 145 ; cf. Spencer and Gillen, *Native Tribes*, pp. 221-222 ; Beaver, *Unexplored New Guinea*, p. 186 ; Fison, *J.R.A.I.*, XIV, p. 23 (Fiji).
72 : cf. Schurtz, *Altersklassen*, pp. 97-98 ; Webster, *Secret Societies*, pp. 47-48 ; Todd, *Primitive Family*, pp. 192-193 ; Steinmetz, *Zeitschrift für Social-wissenschaft*, I, p. 626.
73 : Spencer and Gillen, *Proceed. Royal Society Victoria* (N.S.), X, p. 150.
74 : Chinnery and Beaver, *J.R.A.I.*, XLV, p. 75.
75 : Gusinde, *Zeitschrift für Ethnologie*, LVIII, p. 273 ; Koppers, *Unter Feuerland-Indianern*, p. 60.
76 : Junod, *Life of a South African Tribe*, I, pp. 82-84.
77 : Howitt, *S.E. Australia*, p. 557.
78 : Livingstone, *Missionary Travels*, p. 147 ; Macdonald, *Africana* I, pp. 131-132 ; Brown, *J.R.A.I.*, LI, p. 424.
79 : Willoughby, *J.R.A.I.*, XXXIX, p. 236.
80 : Hollis, *Nandi*, p. 54.
81 : Codrington, *Melanesians*, p. 89.
82 : Gimble, *J.R.A.I.*, XI, p. 39 ; cf. Haddon, *J.R.A.I.*, XIX, p. 405 (Torres St.).
83 : Bancroft, *Native Races of Pacific Coast*, I, p. 414.
84 : "Child Life," *Handbook of American Indians*, I, p. 266 ; Whiffen, *Northwest Amazons*, p. 157 ; Lafitau, *Moeurs des Sauvages*, I, p. 286 ; Stevenson, 5th *A.R.B.A.E.*, p. 553, etc.
85 : Cureau, *Savage Man*, pp. 170-171.
86 : Willoughby, *Race Problems*, pp. 129-130 ; Henry, *Les Bambara* p. 112.

87 : Roscoe, *Bagesu*, p. 75.

88 : Casalis, *Les Bassoutos*, p. 279 ; Webster, *Secret Societies*, p. 34.

89 : Howitt, *J.R.A.I.*, XIV, p. 321 ; Bonwick, *Daily Life of the Tasmanians*, p. 201 ; cf. Brown, *Andaman Islanders*, pp. 270 ff.

90 : Chinnery and Beaver, *J.R.A.I.*, XLV, p. 77.

91 : Man, *Andaman Islanders*, p. 62.

92 : Barclay, *Nineteenth Century*, LV, p. 99.

93 : Fletcher and La Flesche, 27th *A.R.B.A.E.*, p. 131.

94 : Grimble, *J.R.A.I.*, LI, p. 39 ; cf. Codrington, *Melanesians*, p. 89 (New Hebrides).

95 : Ridley, *Kamilaroi and Kurnai*, p. 154 ; Mathews, *Proceed. Royal Society of Victoria*, IX (N.S.), p. 128.

96 : Howitt, *S.E. Australia*, p. 674.

97 : Haddon, *J.R.A.I.*, XIX, p. 398.

98 : Lawson, *History of North Carolina*, pp. 381-382 ; cf. Hooper, *Univ. of California Studies*, XVI, p. 346.

99 : Wheelwright, *J.R.A.I.*, XXXV, p. 255.

100 : Chinnery and Beaver, *J.R.A.I.*, XLV, pp. 75-76

101 : Enright, *Proceed. Royal Society New South Wales*, XXXIII, pp. 118-119

102 : Mathews, *J.R.A.I.*, XXVI, p. 333 ; *Proceed. Roy. Soc. New South Wales*, XXXI, p. 145 ; *Proceed. Roy. Soc. of Victoria*, IX (N.S.), p. 157 ; *J.R.A.I.*, XXV, p. 331.

103 : Chinnery and Beaver, op. cit., p. 72.

104 : Holmes, *Primitive New Guinea*, p. 121.

105 : Rosenberg, *Malayische Archipel*, p. 318.

106 : Codrington, *Melanesians*, p. 96.

107 : Thomson, *Fiji and Fijians*, p. 152 ; Joske, *Internationales Archiv. für Ethnographie*, II, p. 264.

108 : Nassau, *Fetichism in West Africa*, p. 250.

109 : Roscoe, *Bagesu*, p. 24.

110 : Holmes, *Primitive New Guinea*, p. 130.

111 : Howitt, *S.E. Australia*, p. 532 ; cf. *J.R.A.I.*, XIII, p. 458 ; Webster, *Secret Societies*, p. 49.

112 : Mathews, *Proceed. Roy. Society New South Wales*, XXXI, p. 141.

113 : Stannus and Davey, *J.R.A.I.*, XLIII, p. 122.

114 : cf. Brown, *Andaman Islanders*, pp. 282-283.

115 : Howitt, *S.E. Australia*, p. 544 ; Mathews, *Royal Soc. New South Wales*, XXVIII, p. 120 ; *J.R.A.I.*, XXV, p. 310.

116 : Van de Velde, *Bulletin Société Roy. Belge de Géographie*, X, p. 398.

117 : Spencer and Gillen, *Native Tribes of Central Australia*, pp. 229-230 ; *Proceed. Royal Society Victoria*, X (N.S.), pp. 26, 155-156.

118 : Mathews, *Proceed. Royal Society Victoria*, X (N.S.), p. 35 ; IX (N.S.), pp. 129, 165, 166.

119 : Willoughby, *J.R.A.I.*, XXXIX, pp. 238-241.

120 : Hooper, *Univ. of California Publications*, XVI, p. 346.

121 : Hollis, *Nandi*, p. 55 ; Beyer, *Zeitschrift für Ethnologie*, LVIII, pp. 252-253.

122 : Junod, *Life of a South African Tribe*, I, p. 85 ; cf. Tauxier, *Noir du Yatenga*, p. 638 ; Laidler, *Man*, XXII, p. 14 ; Gottschling, *J.R.A.I.*, XXXV, p. 372 ; Mathews, *J.R.A.I.*, XXV, p. 310 etc.

123 : Werner, *British Central Africa*, pp 125-126.

124 : Roscoe, *J.R.A.I.*, XXXIX, p 185 ; Van de Velde, *Bul. Soc. Roy Belge de Géographie*, X, p 398.

125 : Haddon, *J.R.A.I.*, XIX, pp. 411-412.

126 : *Cambridge Expedition to Torres Straits*, V, p. 214.

127 : ibid., V, p. 211.

128 : Chinnery and Beaver, *J.R.A.I.*, XLV, p. 76.

129 : Weule, *Native Life in East Africa*, pp. 188, 304.

130 : Howitt, *S.E. Australia*, p. 633.

131 : *Cambridge Expedition*, V, p. 212.

132 : Grimble, *J.R.A.I.*, XL, p. 42 ; cf. Russell, 26th *A.R.B.A.E.*, p. 182 ; Holub, *Seven Years in South Africa*, II, p. 315 ; Fritsch, *Eingeborenen Südafrikas*, pp. 206-207 ; Lichtenstein, *Reisen in Süd-Afrika*, I, pp. 428-430 ; Shooter, *Kafirs of Natal*, p. 395 ; Schulien, *Anthropos*, XVIII, p. 101.

133 : Parkinson, *Südsee*, p. 440.

134 : Wallace, *Travels on the Amazon*, p. 496.

135 : Hill-Tout, *J.R.A.I.*, XXXIV, pp. 319-320.

136 : Teit, *American Museum of Natural History*, II, pp. 311-317.

137 : Cator, *Everyday Life among Head-Hunters*, p. 193.

138 : Smith and Dale, op. cit., II, p. 20.

139 : Whiffen, *North-West Amazons*, p. 157.

140 : Chinnery and Beaver, *J.R.A.I.*, XLV, p. 76.

141 : cf. Schulien, *Anthropos*, XVIII, p. 75 ff ; for additional cases illustrating the instruction given at initiation, see Roscoe, *Bagesu*, pp. 75-76 ; Kidd, *Essential Kafir*, p. 208 ; Lindblom, *Akamba*, p. 52 ; Weiss, *Deutsch. Ostafrika*, p. 295 ; Hutereau, *Bul. Soc. Roy. Belge de Geog.*, XXXIV, p. 20 ; Felkin, *Royal Soc. Edinburgh*, XII, pp. 325-326 ; XIII, p. 745 ; Johnston, *Brit. Central Africa*, p. 409, etc., etc.

142 : Holmes, *Primitive New Guinea*, p. 119.

143 : Hollis, *Nandi*, p. 57 ; Fritsch, *Eingeborenen Südafrikas*, pp. 206-208 ; Kingsley, *Travels in West Africa*, p. 531 ; Schmidt, *Les Baholoholo*, p. 159 ; Lindblom, *Akamba*, p. 64 ; Kropf, *Kafir-English Dictionary*, pp. 373-374 ; Delhaise, *Bul. Soc. Roy. Belge de Geog*, XXXIII, p. 128 ; Hagen, *Unter den Papuas*, p. 238.

144 : Magyar, *Reisen in Südlichen Afrika*, p. 24.

145 : Fritsch, *Eingeborenen Südafrikas*, p. 206.

NOTES TO CHAPTER XI

1 : Tauxier, *Le Noir du Yatenga*, p. 272.

2 : Kingsley, *Travels in West Africa*, p. 486.

3 : Smith and Dale, *Ila-Speaking Peoples*, I, p. 303.

4 : Roscoe, *J.R.A.I.*, XXI, p. 128.

5 : Roscoe, *Bakitara*, p. 174.

6 : Ellis, *Yoruba-Speaking Peoples*, p. 177.

7 : Safford, *American Anthropologist* (N.S.), IV, p. 727.

8 : Evans, *Primitive Peoples in Borneo*, p. 227 ; Hose and McDougall, *Pagan Tribes*, I, p. 83.

9 : Riedel, *De sluik-en kroeshaarige Rassen*, pp. 82, 28.

10 : Forbes, *J.R.A.I.*, XIII, p. 14.

11 : Teit, *Memoirs, American Museum of Natural History*, II, p. 294.

12 : Dornan, *Pygmies and Bushmen*, p. 55.

13 : cf. Lippert, *Kulturgeschichte*, I, p. 113 ff.

14 : cf. Sumner and Keller, *Science of Society*, III, pp. 1940-1941.

15 : Van de Velde, *Bulletin, Société Royale Belge de Géographie*, X, pp. 396-397.

16 : Ellis, *Ewe-Speaking Peoples*, p. 207 ; cf. Kingsley, *Travels in West Africa*, p. 485.

17 : Bosman, *Pinkerton's Voyages*, XVI, p. 421 ; cf. also Torday, *Camp and Tramp*, p. 94 ; Torday and Joyce, *J.R.A.I.*, XXXVI, p. 44, etc.

18 : Bastian, *Deutsche Expedition*, I, p. 165.

19 : Duff Macdonald, *Africana*, I, pp. 187-188.

20 : Sebbelov, *American Anthropologist*, XV (N.S.), p. 279 ; Burger, *Die küsten-und bergvölker der Gazellehalbinsel*, p. 31.

21 : Hahl, *Ethnologisches Notizblatt*, II, p. 9.

22 : Fisch, *Baessler-Archiv.*, III, p. 155.

23 : Codrington, *Melanesians*, pp. 64-65.

24 : ibid., p. 66.

25 : Von Hagen, *Baessler-Archiv.*, II, p. 103.

26 : Hill-Tout, *Tribes of British North America*, p. 182.

27 : Dundas, *J.R.A.I.*, XLIII, p. 56.

28 : Malinowski, *Proceedings Royal Society South Australia*, XXXIX, p. 638.

29 : Fritsch, *Eingeborenen Südafrikas*, p. 118 ; Kropf, *Ama-Xosa*, p. 150.

30 : See Torday and Joyce, *J.R.A.I.*, XXXV, p. 411 ; Klose, *Togo*, p. 515 ; Spieth, *Ewe-Stämme*, p. 785 ; Cardinall, *Northern Gold Coast*, pp. 40, 64-65 ; Tauxier, *Le Noir du Yatenga*, p. 272, etc.

31 : Koch-Grünberg, *Zwei Jahre unter den Indianern*, I, p. 164.

32 : cf. on " property," Sumner and Keller, op. cit., I, chap. XI.

33 : cf. above, pp. 52 ff.

34 : Bosman, *Pinkerton's Voyages*, XVI, p. 528.

35 : Nachtigal, *Sahara und Soudan*, II, p. 176 ; Ellis, *Ewe*, p. 205 ; Weeks, *J.R.A.I.*, XXXIX, p. 426 ; Decle, *Three Years in Savage Africa*, p. 348 ; Routledge, *Prehistoric People*, pp. 143-144, etc.

36 : Roscoe, *Bagesu*, p. 199.

37 : Guevara, *Araucanía*, p. 208 ; Medina, *Aboríjenes de Chile*, p. 280.

38 : Dale, *J.R.A.I.*, XXV, p. 224.

39 : Jenness and Ballantyne, op. cit., pp. 72-73.

40 : de Mas, *Estado de las Filipinas*, p. 13.

41 : Johnston, *Uganda*, II, p. 694.

42 : Marsden, *History of Sumatra*, p. 244.

43 : Roscoe, *Banyankole*, p. 151.

44 : Marsden, op. cit., p. 244.

45 : Weeks, *Congo Cannibals*, p. 111.

46 : Von Hagen, *Baessler-Archiv.*, II, p. 103 ; cf. Barrett, *J.R.A.I.*, XLI, p. 33 ; Hobley, *Akamba*, p. 82.

47 : Dundas, *J.R.A.I.*, XLV, p. 294.

48 : McDonald, *J.R.A.I.*, XIX, p. 277.

49 : Teit, *Memoirs, American Museum Natural History*, II, p. 294.

50 : Dundas, op. cit., p. 294.

51 : Barrett, *J.R.A.I.*, XLI, p. 25.

52 : Stuhlmann, *Mit Emin Pasha*, p. 93.

53 : Routledge, *Prehistoric Peoples*, pp. 143-144.

54 : Merker, *Petermanns Mittheilungen*, XXX, p. 1 ; cf. also Lindblom, *Akamba*, p. 153 ; Fritsch, *Enigeborenen Südafrikas*, p. 92 ; Casalis, *Les Bassoutos*, p. 196 ; Theal, *Yellow- and Dark-Skinned Peoples*, p. 180.

55 : Wilkes, *U.S. Exploring Expedition*, V, p. 85.

56 : Tregear, *Maori Race*, p. 125 ; cf. Best, *New Zealand Institute*, XXXVI, p. 29-30.

57 : Malinowski, *Proceed. Royal Soc. South Australia*, XXXIX, p. 521 ; cf. Riedel, *De sluik-en kroeshaarige Rassen*, p. 82 (Ambon).

58 : Tessmann, *Die Pangwe*, II, p. 208.

59 : Klose, *Togo*, p. 515 ; cf. ibid., p. 276.

60 : Turner, 9th *A.R.B.A.E*, p. 190.

61 : Buller, *Forty Years in New Zealand*, p. 175.

62 : *Cambridge Expedition*, VI, p. 163.

63 : von Middendorf, *Sibirische Reisen*, IV, p. 1614.

64 : Beaver, *Unexplored New Guinea*, p. 303.

65 : Tessmann, *Die Pangwe*, II, p. 102.

66 : Nassau, *Fetichism in West Africa*, pp. 97-98 ; cf. Du Chaillu, *Explorations and Adventures*, p. 337 ; Ellis, *Tshi-Speaking Peoples*, p. 89.

67 : Tessmann, *Die Pangwe*, I, p. 102.

68 : Krämer, *Samoa-Inseln*, I, p. 477 ; " Cradles," *Handbook of American Indians*, I, pp. 358-359.

69 : Hobley, *J.R.A.I.*, XLI, p. 429.

70 : Beaver, op. cit., pp. 309-310.

71 : Hahl, *Ethnologisches Notizblatt*, II, p. 3.

72 : Rink, *Traditions and Tales of the Eskimo*, p. 63.

73 : Lowie, *Anthropological Papers, American Museum of Natural History*, XXI, p. 40.

74 : Buller, *Forty Years in New Zealand*, p. 218.

75 : Williams and Calvert, *Fiji and the Fijians*, pp. 145-147.

76 : Nelson, 18th *A.R.B.A.E.*, p. 293.

77 : Ruiz and Sanchez, *Exposición General de las Islas Filipinas*, pp. 123-124.

78 : Kingsley, *Travels in West Africa*, p. 498 ; Ellis, *Ewe-Speaking Peoples*, p. 205.

79 : Jagor, *Reisen in den Philippinen*, p. 281, note.

80 : Hutereau, *Bulletin, Société Royale Belge de Géographie*, XXXIII, p. 48 ; Torday and Joyce, *J.R.A.I.*, XXXVI, p. 286.

81 : Ellis, *Ewe-Speaking Peoples*, p. 213 ; *Yoruba-Speaking Peoples*, p. 181.

82 : Ellis, *Tshi-Speaking Peoples*, p. 290 ; *Ewe-Speaking Peoples*, p. 219 ; cf. also Klose, *Togo*, p. 275.

83 : Best, *Transactions and Proceedings of New Zealand Institute*, XXXVI, p. 64.

84 : cf. Maddox, *Medicine Man ;* Hambly, *Origins of Primitive Education*, p. 216 ff.

85 : Johnston, *Uganda*, II, p. 882.

86 : Hollis, *Nandi*, p. 51.

87 : Jenness and Ballantyne, op. cit., pp. 72-74.

88 : Shooter, *Kafirs of Natal*, p. 353.

89 : Hambly, op. cit., p. 230.

90 : Krapf, *Missionary Travels and Labors*, p. 170 ; cf. also Smith and Dale, *Ila-Speaking Peoples*, I, p. 271 ; Spieth, *Ewe-Stämme*, p. 225 ; Colle, *Les Baluba*, p. 269 ; Kingsley, *West African Studies*, p. 171, etc.

91 : Cruickshank, *Eighteen Years on the Gold Coast*, II, p. 142.

92 : Powers, *Contributions to North American Ethnology*, III, p. 131.

93 : Schomburgk, *Reisen in Britisch-Guiana*, I, p. 172.

94 : Hambly, op. cit., p. 264.

95 : Howitt, *Natives of S.E. Australia*, p. 408-409.

96 : Czaplicka, *Aboriginal Siberia*, p. 181.

97 : Whiffen, *North-West Amazons*, p. 181.

98 : Teit, *Memoirs, American Museum of Natural History*, II, p. 328.

99 : Whiffen, op. cit.; cf. Hambly, op. cit, pp. 233-236 ; Maddox, *Medicine Man*, pp. 25-26.

100 : Koch-Grünberg, *Zwei Jahre unter den Indianern*, I, pp. 167-168.

101 : Nassau, *Fetichism in West Africa*, p. 15 ; cf. Roscoe, *Bakitara*, p. 172.

102 : Hambly, *Origins of Primitive Education*, pp. 277-278.

103 : Sebbelov, *American Anthropologist*, XV. (N.S.), p. 275.

104 : cf. Sumner and Keller, *Science of Society*, I, p. 491 ff.

105 : Hambly, op. cit., pp. 278-279.

106 : Hinde, *Last of the Masai*, p. 23.

107 : Somerville, *J.R.A.I.*, XXVI, pp. 394-395 ; cf. Mariner,

Tonga Islands, II, p. 98 ; Ellis, *Polynesian Researches*, III, pp. 99-101 ;
Tregear, *Maori Race*, p. 129, etc.

108 : cf. Sumner and Keller, op. cit., I, p. 489.
109 : cf. Lippert, *Kulturgeschichte*, I, pp. 604-630 ; II, p. 220.
110 : Hobley, *Akamba*, pp. 51, 167 ; Weeks, *Congo Cannibals*, p. 90.
111 : Holmes, *Primitive New Guinea*, p. 85.
112 : Willoughby, *Race Problems in New Africa*, p. 123.
113 : Thomson, *Fijians*, pp. 221, 206.
114 : Roscoe, *Baganda*, p. 275.

NOTES TO CHAPTER XII

1 : Brown, *J.R.A.I.*, LI, p. 427.
2 : Smith and Dale, *Ila-Speaking Peoples*, I, p. 344.
3 : Kidd, *Savage Childhood*, p. 123.
4 : Bosman, *Pinkerton's Voyages*, XVI, p. 527.
5 : Ellis, *Hist. of Madagascar*, I, p. 177.
6 : Mackillop, *Proceed. Royal Soc. South Australia*, XVII, p. 262
7 : Furness, *Borneo Head-Hunters*, p. 59.
8 : Abel, *Savage Life in New Guinea*, p. 42.
9 : cf. Weeks, *J.R.A.I.*, XXXIX, p. 108 ; Melland, *Witch-Bound
Africa*, p. 171 ; Koppers, *Unter Feuerland-Indianern*, pp. 233-234.
10 : Spencer, *Education of the Pueblo Child*, pp. 78-80.
11 : Ellis, *Ewe-Speaking Peoples*, p. 262.
12 : Codrington, *Melanesians*, p. 99.
13 : Pritchard, *Polynesian Reminiscences*, p. 109.
14 : Nordenskiöld, *Indianerleben*, p. 250 ; cf. McClintock, *Old
North Trail*, p. 507 ; Teit, *Amer. Mus. of Nat. Hist.*, *Memoirs*, II,
p. 181.
15 : Weeks, *Bakongo*, p. 156.
16 : Nassau, *Fetichism in West Africa*, p. 152.
17 : Hawkes, *Labrador Eskimo*, p. 135.
18 : Melland, *Witch-Bound Africa*, pp. 169, 299.
19 : Haddon, *J.R.A.I.*, XIX, p. 411.
20 : Man, *Andaman Islanders*, p. 64.
21 : Chinnery and Beaver, *J.R.A.I.*, XLV, pp. 74-75.
22 : Williams and Calvert, *Fiji and the Fijians*, p. 118 ; cf.
Seemann, *Mission to Viti*, pp. 402-403.
23 : Ellis, *Tshi-Speaking Peoples*, p. 85.
24 : Smith and Dale, *Ila-Speaking Peoples*, I, p. 96.
25 : Wheelwright, *J.R.A.I.*, XXXV, p. 254.
26 : Pritchard, *Polynesian Reminiscences*, p. 145.

BIBLIOGRAPHY

Abbreviations
    A.A.—American Anthropologist (n.s.), new series
    A.R.B.A.E.—Annual Reports of the Bureau of American Ethnology
    J.R.A.I.—Journal of the Royal Anthropological Institute of Great
               Britain and Ireland

Abel, Charles W., *Savage Life in New Guinea*, London, 1902
Ahlqvist, Aug., " Unter Wogulen und Ostjaken," *Acta Societatis Scientarium Fennicae*, xiv, 1885
Alberti, L., *Description physique et historique des Cafres*, Amsterdam, 1811
Aldea, P. Ruiz, *Los Araucanos i sus Costumbres*, Santiago de Chile, 1902
Andree, R., " Ueber die Spiele in ihrer ethnographischer Bedeutung," *Correspondenzblatt der Deutschen Gesellschaft für Ethnographie und Urgeschichte*, xix, 1888
Avon, R. P., " Vie sociale et familiale des Wabende au Tanganika," *Anthropos*, x-xi, 1915-1916
Azara, D. Felix de, *Voyages dans l'Amerique meridionale*, 3 vols., Paris, 1809

Baegert, Jacob, " An Account of the Aboriginal Inhabitants of the Californian Peninsula," *Annual Report of the Regents of the Smithsonian Institution for the Year* 1863, Washington, 1864
Bagge, S , " The Circumcision Ceremony among the Naivasha Masai," *J.R.A.I* , xxxiv, 1904
Bancroft, H. H , *The Native Races of the Pacific Coast* 5 vols., New York, 1875
Barclay, W. S., " Life in Tierra del Fuego," *Nineteenth Century*, lv., 1904
Barrett, W. E. H., " Notes on the Customs and Beliefs of the Wa-Giriama, etc. of British East Africa," *J.R.A.I.*, xli, 1911
Barth, Paul, " Die Geschichte der Erziehung in soziologischer Beleuchtung," *Vierteljahrsschrift für wissenschaftlicher Philosophie und Soziologie*, xxvii, 1903
Bastian, Adolf, *Die Deutsche Expedition an der Loango-Küste*, 2 vols , Jena, 1874
Batchelor, John, *The Ainu of Japan*, New York, n.d.
Baumann, Oscar, *Durch Massailand zur Nilquelle*, Berlin, 1894
Beardmore, Edward, " On the Natives of Mowat, Dandai, New Guinea," *J.R.A.I.*, xix, 1890
Beaver, Wilfred N., *Unexplored New Guinea*, London, 1920.
Best, Elsdon, " Ceremonial Performances pertaining to Birth, as performed by the Maori of New Zealand in Past Times," *J.R.A I.*, xliv. 1914
—— " Maori Marriage Customs," *Transactions and Proceedings of the New Zealand Institute*, xxxvi, 1904
—— " Tuhoe Land," *Transactions and Proceedings of the N.Z. Institute*, xxx, 1898

BEVERLEY, R , *The History of Virginia*, London, 1722

BIRD, W. H., " Ethnographical Notes about the Buccaneer Islanders, North Western Australia," *Anthropos*, vi, 1911

BLAIR, Emma Helen, *The Indian Tribes of the Upper Mississippi Valley and the Region of the Great Lakes*, 2 vols., Cleveland, 1911

BLEEK, W. H. I., *Specimens of Bushmen Folklore*, London, 1911

BLEY, P., " Sagen der Baininger auf Neupommern, Südsee," *Anthropos*, ix, 1914

BOAS Franz, " The Central Eskimo," 6th *A.R.B.A.E.*, 1888

—— " The Mythology of the Bella Coola Indians," *Memoirs of the American Museum of Natural History*, ii, 1900

—— " Notes on the Tillamook," *University of California Publications in American Archeology and Ethnology*, xx, 1923

—— " Some Traits of Primitive Culture," *Journal of American Folklore*, xvii, 1894

BOGORAS, Waldemar, " The Chukchee," *Memoirs of the American Museum of Natural History*, xi, 1907-1910

BELINDER, Gustaf, " Einiges über die Motilon-Indianer der Sierra de Perija, Columbien, Südamerika," *Zeitschrift für Ethnologie*, xlix, 1917

BONNEY, Frederick, " On Some Customs of the Aborigines of the River Darling, New South Wales," *J.R.A.I.*, xiii, 1884

BONWICK, James, *Daily Life and Customs of the Tasmanians*, London, 1870

BOSMAN, William, *A New and Accurate Description of the Coast of Guinea : Pinkerton's Voyages and Travels*, xvi, London, 1814

BRAINNE, Ch., *La Nouvelle Caledonie*, Paris 1854

BRINCKER P. H " Charakter, Sitten und Gebräuche speciell der Bantu Deutsch-Südwest-afrikas " *Mittheilungen des Seminars für Oriental-ischer Sprachen zu Berlin*, jahrgang, iii

BROWN, A. R., *The Andaman Islanders*, Cambridge, 1922

BROWN, J. Tom, " Circumcision Rites of the Becwana Tribes," *J.R.A.I.*, li, 1921

BRUNACHE, P., *Le Centre de l'Afrique autour du Tschad*, Paris, 1894

BUGEAU, Frederic, " Le Circoncision au Kikuyu," *Anthropos*, vi, 1911

BULLER , James, *Forty Years in New Zealand*, London, 1878

BURGER, Friedrich, *Die Küsten-und Bergvölker der Gazellehalbinsel*, Stuttgart, 1913

BURROWS, Capt. Guy, *The Land of the Pygmies*, London, 1898

CALLAWAY, Canon, *Nursery Tales, Traditions and Histories of the Zulus*, Natal, London, 1868

—— *The Religious System of the Amazulu*, Natal, London, 1870

CAMBOUE, Paul, " Education et Instruction en Madagascar," *Anthropos*, x-xi , 1916

CAMPBELL, J., *Travels in South Africa*, 2 vols., London, 1822

Cambridge Anthropological Expedition to Torres Straits, Reports of

—— Vol v, *Sociology*, " Magic and Religion of the Western Islanders," Cambridge, 1904

—— Vol vi, *Sociology*, " Magic and Religion of the Eastern Islanders," Cambridge, 1908

CARDINALL, A. W., *The Natives of the Northern Territories of the Gold Coast*, London, n.d.

CASALIS, E., *Les Bassoutos*, Paris, 1860

CATLIN, George, *Illustrations of the Manners, Customs and Conditions of the North American Indians*, 5th ed., 2 vols., London, 1848

CATOR, Dorothy, *Everyday Life among the Headhunters*, London, 1905

CESTON, Jean Marie, " Le ' Gree-Gree ' Bush (Initiation de la Jeunesse) chez les Nègres Golah, Liberia," *Anthropos*, vi, 1911

CHALMERS, James, *Pioneering in New Guinea*, London, 1887

CHAMBERLAIN, Alexander Francis, *The Child : A Study in the Evolution of Man*, London, 1901

CHAPIN, F Stuart, " Education and the Mores," *Studies in History, Economics and Public Law*, (Columbia U.) no. 10, New York, 1911

CHARLEVOIX, P. Pierre François-Xavier de, *Histoire du Paraguay*, 6 vols., Paris, 1757

—— *Journal of a Voyage to North America*, 2 vols., Chicago, 1923

CHINNERY, E. W. P. and BEAVER, W. N., " Notes on the Initiation Ceremonies of the Koko, Papua," *J.R.A.I.*, xlv, 1915

CHRISTIAN, F. W., *The Caroline Islands*, New York, 1899

CHRISTOL, Frederic, *Au Sud de l'Afrique*, Paris, Nancy, 1900

CHURCHILL, William, " The Duk-Duk Ceremonies," *Popular Science Monthly*, xxxviii, 1891

CLODD, Edward, *Magic in Names, and Other Things*, London, 1920

CLOZEL, P. J., *Les Bayas*, Paris, 1896

CODRINGTON, R. H., *The Melanesians*, Oxford, 1891

—— " On Social Regulations in Melanesia," *J.R.A.I.*, xviii, 1889

COLE, H., " Notes on the Wagogo of German East Africa," *J.R.A.I.*, xxxii, 1902

COLENSO, W., " Contributions toward a better Knowledge of the Maori Race, *Transactions and Proceedings of the New Zealand Institute*, xi-xiv, 1879-1882

—— " Historical Incidents and Traditions of the Olden Times pertaining to the Maoris of the North Island," *Transactions and Proceedings of the New Zealand Institute*, xiii, 1881

—— " On the Maori Races of New Zealand," *Transactions and Proceedings of the New Zealand Institute*, i, 1875

COLLE, R. P., " Les Baluba," *Collection de Monographies ethnographiques*, Bruxelles, 1913

COLLINS, David, *An Account of the English Colony in New South Wales* 2nd ed., London, 1804

CONDON, M. A., " Contributions to the Ethnography of the Baosga-Batambe Protectorate, British East Africa," *Anthropos*, vi, 1911

COOK, Capt. James, " A Voyage to the Pacific Ocean . . . in the Years, 1776-1780," *General History and Collections of Voyages and Travels*, xv-xvi, Edinburgh, 1815

COWAN, James, *The Maoris of New Zealand*, Christchurch, Wellington, and Dunedin, 1910

CRANTZ David, *The History of Greenland*, 2 vols., London, 1820

CRAWFORD, John, *History of the Indian Archipelago*, 3 vols., Edinburgh, 1820

CREMONY, John G., *Life among the Apaches*, San Francisco, 1868

CRUICKSHANK, Brodie, *Eighteen Years on the Gold Coast of Africa*, 2 vols., London, 1853

DE LA CRUZ, Luis, " Descripción de la Naturaleza de los Terrenos que se comprenden en los Andes por los Peguenches," *Colección de Obras y Documentos relativos a la Historia Antigua de los Provincios del Rio de la Plata*, i, Buenos Aires, 1835

CUREAU, Adolphe Louis, *Savage Man in Central Africa*, London, 1915

CURR, Edward M., *The Australian Race*, 4 vols., Melbourne, London, 1886-1887

CZAPLICA, M. A., *Aboriginal Siberia*, Oxford, 1914

DALE, Godfrey, "An Account of the Principal Customs and Habits of the Natives inhabiting the Bondei Country," *J.R.A.I.*, xxv, 1896

DALL, William H., *Alaska and Its Resources*, Boston, 1870

DANKS, Benjamin H., "Marriage Customs of the New Britain Group," *J.R.A.I.*, xviii, 1889

DEANE, Lionel, *Fijian Society*, London, 1921

DECLE, W., *Three Years in Savage Africa*, London, 1900

DELAFOSSE, Maurice, "Le Peuple Sienao ou Senoufo," *Revue des Etudes ethnographiques et sociologiques*, i, 1908

DELHAISE, Charles, "Ethnographie congolaise. Chez les Wabemba," *Bulletin de la société royale belge de Géographie*, xxxii, 1908

—— "Chez les Warundi et les Wahorohorro," *Bulletin société royale belge de Géographie*, xxxii, 1908

—— "Chez les Wasongola du Sud," *Bulletin société royale belge de Géographie*, xxxiii, 1909

—— *Les Warega*, Bruxelles, 1909

DOBRIZHOFFER, Martin, *An Account of the Abipones, an Equestrian People of Paraguay*, London, 1822

D'ORBIGNY, Alcide, *L'Homme Americain*, 2 vols., Paris, 1839

DORMAN, S. S., "The Tati Bushmen (Masarwas) and their Language," *J.R.A.I.*, xlvii, 1907

DORSEY, George A., "Caddo Customs of Childhood," *Journal of American Folklore*, xviii, 1895

DORSEY, J. Owen, "Omaha Sociology," 3rd *A.R.B.A.E.*, 1884

—— "Siouan Sociology," 15th *A.R.B.A.E.*, 1897

—— "A Study of the Siouan Cults," 11th *A.R.B.A.E.*, 1894

DU CHAILLU, Paul B., *Explorations and Adventures in Equatorial Africa*, London, 1861

DUNDAS, Charles, "History of the Kitui," *J.R.A.I.*, xliii, 1903

—— "The Organisation and Laws of some Bantu Tribes in East Africa," *J.R.A.I.*, xlv, 1915

DUNDAS, Kenneth R., "The Wawanga and other Tribes of the Elgon District, British East Africa," *J.R.A.I.*, xliii, 1903

EASTMAN, Charles, *Indian Boyhood*, New York, 1902

EGEDE, Hans, *A Description of Greenland*, London, 1818

EHRENREICH, P., "Beiträge zur Volkenkunde Brasiliens," *Veröffentlichungen aus dem Königlichen Museum für Völkerkunde*, ii, Berlin, 1891

ELIOT, Sir Charles, *The East African Protectorate*, London 1905

ELLIS, A. B., *The Ewe-Speaking Peoples of the Slave Coast of West Africa*, London. 1890

—— *The Tshi-Speaking Peoples of the Gold Coast of West Africa*, London, 1887

—— *The Yoruba-Speaking Peoples of the Slave Coast of West Africa*, London, 1894

ELLIS, William, *History of Madagascar*, 2 vols., London, n.d.

—— *Polynesian Researches*, 4 vols., London, 1859

ELTON, F., "Notes on the Natives of the Solomon Islands," *J.R.A.I.*, xvii, 1888

EMPAIN, A., "Les Bakela de Loto (Congo Belge)," *Bulletin de la société royale belge de Géographie*, xlvi, 1922

ENRIGHT, W. J., "The Initiation Ceremonies of the Aborigines of Port Stephens, New South Wales," *Proceedings of the Royal Society of New South Wales*, xxxiii, 1899

ERDLAND, A., *Die Marshall-Insulaner*, Münster, i, W., 1914

ERMAN, A., "Ethographische Wahrnehmungen und Erfahrungen an den Küsten des Beringmeeres," *Zeitschrift für Ethnologie*, iii, 1871

ESCHLIMANN, Henry, " L'Enfant chez les Kuni," *Anthropos*, vi, 1911

EVANS, Ivor H., *Among Primitive Peoples in Borneo*, London, 1922

EYLMANN, Edward, *Die Eingeborenen der Kolonie Südaustralien*, Berlin, 1908

FELKIN, Robert W., " Notes on the For Tribe of Central Africa," *Proceedings of the Royal Society of Edinburgh*, xiii, 1885

—— " Notes on the Madi or Moru Tribe of Central Africa," *Proceedings of the Royal Society of Edinburgh*, xii, 1884

FEWKES, J. Walter, " Dolls of the Tusayan Indians," *Internationales Archiv für Ethnographie*, vii, 1894

—— " Tusayan Katcinas," 15th *A.R.B.A.E.*, 1897

FINSCH, O., *Ethnologische Erfahrungen und Belegstücke aus der Südsee*, Wien, 1893

—— " Ueber die Bewohner von Ponapé (ostl. Carolinen)," *Zeitschrift für Ethnologie*, xii, 1880

FISCH, Rudolf, " Die Dagbamba," *Baessler-Archiv*, iii, 1913

FISKE, John, *Excursions of an Evolutionist*, Boston, 1892

FISON, Lorimer, " The Nanga, or Sacred Enclosure of Wainimala, Fiji," *J.R.A.I.*, xiv, 1885

FISON, Lorimer, and HOWITT, A. W., *Kamilaroi and Kurnai*, Melbourne, 1880

FLETCHER, Alice C., " Glimpses of Child-Life among the Omaha Tribe of Indians," *Journal of American Folklore*, i, 1868

FLETCHER, Alice C., and LA FLESCHE, Francis, " The Omaha Tribe." 27th *A.R.B.A.E.*, 1911

FORBES, H. O., " On the Ethnology of Timor," *J.R.A.I.*, xiii, 1884

—— " On the Ethnology of Timor-Laut," *J.R A.I.*, xiii, 1884

FRANCOIS, H. VON, *Nama und Demara Deutsch Südwest Africas*, Magdeburg, 1896

FRANKE, Erich, *Die Geistige Entwicklung der Negerkinder*, Leipzig, 1915

FRENCH-SHELDON, Mrs, " Customs among the Natives of East Africa with special reference to their Women and Children," *J.R.A.I.*, xxi, 1892

FRIC, Votjech, and RADIN, Paul, " Contributions to the Study of the Bororó Indians," *J.R.A.I.*, xxxvi, 1906

FRITSCH, Gustav, *Die Eingeborenen Südafrikas*, Breslau, 1872

FURNESS, William Henry, *The Home-Life of the Borneo Head-Hunters*, Philadelphia, 1902

GANN, Thomas W. F., " The Maya Indians of Southern Yucatan and Northern British Honduras," *B.A.E.*, bulletin 64, 1918

GARDINER, J. Stanley, ".The Natives of Rotunda," *J.R.A.I.*, xxvii, 1897

GEISELER, *Der Oster-Insel*, Berlin, 1883

GENNEP, Arnold van, *Les Rites de Passage*, Paris, 1909

GIBBS, George, " Tribes of Western Washington and North-Western Oregon," *Contributions to North American Ethnology*, i, 1877

GIRSCHNER, Max, " Die Karolineninsel Manoluk und ihre Bewohner," *Baessler-Archiv*, ii, 1912

GLAVE, E. J., *Six Years of Adventure in Congo-Land*, London, 1893

GOMES, Edwin H., *The Sea-Dyaks of Borneo*, Westminster, 1907

GOTTSCHLING, E., " The Bawenda : A Sketch of their History and Customs," *J.R.A I*, xxv, 1886

GRAAFLAND, N., *De Minahassa*, 2 vols., Haarlem, 1898

GRABOWSKY, F., " Gebräuche der Dajaken Südost-Borneos bei der Geburt," *Globus*, lxxii, 1897

GREEN, Laura C., and BECKWITH, Martha W., " Hawaiian Customs and Beliefs relating to Birth and Infancy," *A.A.* (n.s.), xxvi, 1924

GREGORY, J. W., *The Great Rift Valley*, London, 1896

GRIMBLE, Arthur, " From Birth to Death in the Gilbert Islands," *J.R.A.I.*, li, 1921

GRINNELL, G. B., *The Cheyenne Indians*, 2 vols., New Haven, 1923

—— " Cheyenne Women Customs," *A.A.* (n.s.), iv, 1902

GRUBB, W. Barbrooke, *An Unknown People in an Unknown Land*, London, 1911

GUEVARA, Thomas, *Historia de la Civilización de Araucanía*, 2 vols., Santiago de Chile, 1898

GUISE, R. E., " On the Tribes inhabiting the Mouth of the Wanigela River, New Guinea," *J.R.A.I.*, xxviii, 1899

GUMILLA, Joseph, *El Orinoco Ilustrado*, Madrid, 1741

GUPPY, H. B., *The Solomon Islands and their Inhabitants*, London, 1887

HADDON, A. C., " The Ethnography of the Western Tribes of Torres Straits," *J.R.A.I.*, xix, 1890

—— " Notes on the Children's Games in British New Guinea," *J.R.A.I.*, xxxviii, 1908

HAGEN, B., " The Orang Kubu auf Sumatra," *Veröffentlichungen aus dem Königlichen Museum*, Frankfort-am-Main, ii, 1906

—— *Unter den Papuas*, Wiesbaden, 1899

HAHL, D., " Mittheilungen über Sitten und rechtlichen Verhältnisse auf Ponapé,' *Ethnologische Notizblatt*, ii, 1901

HAMBLY, W. D., *Origins of Primitive Education*, New York, 1926

Handbook of American Indians, 2 vols,, *B.A.E.*, bulletin 30, 1907

HARTLAND, E. S., *Primitive Paternity*, 2 vols., London, 1910

HAWKES, E. W., " The Labrador Eskimo," *Dept. of Mines, Geological Survey*, Memoir 91, Ottawa, 1916

HAWTREY, Seymour H. C., " The Lengua Indians of the Paraguayan Chaco," *J.R.A.I.*, xxxi, 1901

HELMS, Richard, " Anthropology," *Transactions of the Royal Society of South Australia*. xvi. 1896

HENRY, Joseph, *L'ame d'un Peuple Africain. Les Bambara*. Münster n.d.

HICKSON, Sydney, *A Naturalist in North Celebes*, London, 1899

HILL-TOUT, C., *British North America. I. The Home of the Salish and the Déné*, Toronto, 1907

—— " Ethnological Report on the StsEelis and Sk.aulits Tribes of the Salish of British Columbia," *J.R.A.I.*, xxxiv, 1904

—— " Report on the Siciatl of British Columbia," *J.R.A.I.*, xxxiv, 1904

HINDE, J. L. and H., *The Last of the Masai*, London, 1901

HOBLEY, C W., *Bantu Beliefs and Folklore*, London, 1921

—— *Ethnology of the Akamba and other East African Tribes*, Cambridge, 1910

—— " Further Researches into Kikuyu and Kamba Religious Beliefs and Customs, *J.R.A.I.*, xli, 1921

HOLLANDER, J. J., *Handleiding bij de Boefening der Land-en Volkenkunde van Nederlandsch-Oost-Indië*, 2 vols., Te Breda, 1884

HOLLIS, A. C., " History and Customs of the People of Taveta," *Journal of the African Society*, i, 1901

—— *The Nandi*, Oxford, 1909

HOLMES, J. H., *In Primitive New Guinea*, London, 1924

HOLUB, Emil, *Seven Years in South Africa*, 2 vols, London, 1881

HOOPER, Lucille, ' The Cahuilla Indians," *University of California Publications in American Archeology and Ethnology*, xvi 1920.

HOOPER, W. H., *Ten Months among the Tents of the Tuski*, London, 1853

HOSE, Charles, and McDOUGALL, William, *The Pagan Tribes of Borneo*, 2 vols., London, 1912

HOVELACQUE, Abel, *Les Nègres de l'Afrique sus-Equatorial*, Paris, 1889

HOWITT, A. W., " The Jeraiel, or Initiation Ceremonies of the Kurnai Tribe," *J.R.A.I.*, xiv, 1885

—— *The Native Tribes of South East Australia*, London, 1904

—— " On Some Australian Ceremonies of Initiation," *J.R.A.I.*, xiv, 1884

—— " Presidential Address," *Australian Association for the Advancement of Science*, iii, 1891

HUNT, Archibald E., " Ethnographical Notes on the Murray Islanders, Torres Straits," *J.R.A.I.*, xxviii, 1899

HUREL, Eugene, " Religion et Vie domestique des Bakerewe," *Anthropos*, vi, 1911

HUTUREAU, A., " Les Bakongo," *Bulletin de la société royale belge de Geographie*, xxxiv, 1910

—— " Documents ethnographiques congolais. Les Mafoto," *Bulletin de la société royale belge de Geographie*, xxxiv, 1910

—— " Notes sur la vie familiale et juridique des Mayumbe," *Bulletin de la société royale belge de Géographie*, xxvii, 1909

HYADES, P. et DENIKER, J., " Mission Scientifique au Cap Horn," vii, *Anthropologie et Ethnographie*, Paris, 1891

IM THURN, Everard F., *Among the Indians of Guiana*, London, 1883

INGLIS, John, *A Dictionary of the Aneityumese Language*, London, 1882

JACOBS, Julius, *Het Familie- en Kampongleven op Groot-Atjeh*, 2 vols., Leiden, 1894

JAGOR, F., *Reisen in den Philippinen*, Berlin, 1873

JARVES, James Jackson, *History of the Hawaiian Islands*, Honolulu, 1847

JENKS, Albert Ernest, " The Bontoc Igorot," *Dept. of the Interior. Ethnographical Survey*, Manila, 1905

JENNESS, D., and BALLANTYNE, A., *The Northern D'Entrecasteaux*, Oxford, 1920

JOCHELSON, Waldemar, " Material Culture and Social Organization of the Koryak," *Memoirs of the American Museum of Natural History*, x, 1905

—— " The Yukaghir and the Yukaghirized Tungus," *Memoirs of the American Museum of Natural History*, xiii, 1910

JOHNSTON, H. H., *British Central Africa*, New York, 1897

—— *The River Congo from its Mouth to Bolobo*, 3rd ed., London, 1884

—— *George Grenfell and the Congo*, New York, 1910

—— *Liberia*, 2 vols., London, 1906

—— *The Uganda Protectorate*, 2 vols., 2nd ed., New York, 1904

JOHNSTONE, H. B., " Notes on the Customs of the Tribes occupying Mombasa Sub-District, British East Africa," *J.R.A.I.*, xxxii, 1902

JONGHE, M. de, " Les Sociétés Secretès au Bas-Congo," *Revue des Etudes Scientifiques*, 3 series, xii, Louvain, 1907

JOSKE, Adolphe B., " The Nanga of Viti-Levu," *Internationales Archiv für Ethnographie*, ii, 1899

JUNGHUHN, Franz, *Die Battaländer auf Sumatra*, Berlin, 1847

JUNOD, Henri A., *Les Chants et les Contes des Ba-ronga*, Lausanne, n.d.

—— " Les Conceptions Physiologiques des Bantous Sud-Africains et leurs Tabous," *Revue d'ethnographie et de sociologie*, i, 1910

—— *The Life of a South African Tribe*, 2 vols., London, 1912

KEATE, George, *An Account of the Pelew Islands*, 2nd ed., London, 1788

KELLER, A. G., *Societal Evolution*, New York, 1916

KENNAN, George, *Tent Life in Siberia*, New York, 1870

KIDD, Dudley, *The Essential Kaffir*, London, 1904

—— *Savage Childhood*, London, 1906

KING, P. Parker, and FITZROY, Robert, *Narrative of the Surveying Voyages of His Majesty's Ships, Adventure and Beagle*, 3 vols., London, 1839

KINGSLEY, Mary H., *Travels in West Africa*, London, 1897

—— *West African Studies*, London, 1899

KLOSE, Heinrich, *Togo unter Deutscher Flagge*, Berlin, 1899

KNOCHE, Walter, " Einige Beobachtungen über Geschlechtsleben und Niederkunft auf der Osterinsel," *Zeitschrift für Ethnologie*, xliv, 1912

KOCH-GRUNBERG, Theodor, *Zwei Jahre unter den Indianern*, 2 vols., Berlin, 1910

KOHL, J. G., *Kitchi-Gami*, London, 1860

KOLBEN, Peter, *Beschreibung des Vorgebürges der Guten Hoffnung and derer darauf wohnenden Hottentoten*, Frankfurt, 1745

KOPPERS, Wilhelm, *Unter Feuerland-Indianern*, Stuttgart, 1924

KRÄMER, Augustin, *Die Samoa-Inseln*, 2 vols., Stuttgart, 1903

KRAPF, J. L., *Travels and Missionary Labours in East Africa*, London, 1860

KRAUSE, Aurel, *Die Tlinkit-Indianer*, Jena, 1865

KRIEGER, Maximilian, *Neu-Guinea*, Berlin, 1899

KROPF, A., *A Kaffir-English Dictionary*, Lovedale, South Africa, 1899

—— *Das Volk der Xosa-Kaffern*, Berlin, 1889

KUBARY, J. S., " Aus dem samoanischen Familienleben," *Globus*, xlvii, 1885

KULISCHER, M., " Die Behandlung der Kinder und der Jugend auf den primitiven Kulturstufen " *Zeitschrift für Ethnologie* xv, 1883

LAFITAU, P., *Moeurs des Sauvages Ameriquains*, 2 vols., Paris, 1724

LAIDLER, P. W., " Bantu Ritual Circumcision," *Man*, xxii, no. 7, 1922

LANDOR, A. H., *Alone with the Hairy Ainu*, London, 1893

LAWSON, John., *History of North Carolina*, Raleigh, 1860

LE HERISSÉ, A., *L'ancien royaume du Dahomey*, Paris, 1911

LETOURNEAU, Ch., *L'Evolution de l'Education dans les diverses Races humains*, Paris, 1898

LE JEUNE, Paul, " Relation de ce qui s'est passé en la nouvelle France en l'année 1634," *Jesuit Relations*, vi, Cleveland, 1897

LESSON, R. P., " Notice sur l'île Routouma," *Nouvelles Annales des Voyages*, xxvii, Paris, 1825

LICHTENSTEIN, H., *Reisen in Südlichen Afrika*, 2 vols., Berlin, 1811-1812

LINDBLOM, Gerhard, *The Akamba*, Upsala, 1916

LIPPERT, Julius, *Die Geschichte der Familie*, Stuttgart, 1884

—— *Kulturgeschichte der Menschheit in ihrem organischen Aufbau*, 2 vols., Stuttgart, 1887

LIVINGSTONE, David, *Missionary Travels and Researches in South Africa*, London, 1857

Low, Hugh, *Natives of Sarawak*, London, 1848

LOWIE, Robert H., " Notes on the Social Organization of the Mandan, Hidatsa, and Crow Indians," *Anthropological Papers, American Museum of Natural History*, xxi, 1917

—— " Social Life of the Crow Indians," *Anthropological Papers*, ix, 1912

LUMHOLTZ, Carl, *In Unknown Mexico*, 2 vols., New York, 1902

MAASS, Alfred, *Durch Zentral-Sumatra*, 2 vols., Berlin, 1910
MACCAULEY, Clay, " The Seminole Indians of Florida," 5th *A.R.B.A.E.*, 1887
McCLINTOCK, *The Old North Trail*, London, 1910
MACDONALD, Duff, *Africana*, 2 vols., London, 1882
MACDONALD, James, " East Central African Customs," *J.R.A.I.*, xxii, 1893
—— " Manners, Customs, Superstitions and Religions of the South African Tribes," *J.R.A.I.*, xix, 1890
McGEE, W. J., " The Seri Indians," 17th *A.R.B.A.E.*, 1898
—— " The Siouan Indians," 15th *A.R.B.A.E.*, 1897
McKIERNAN, Bernard, " Some Notes on the Aborigines of the lower Huter River, New South Wales," *Anthropos*, vi, 1911
MACKILLOP, S. J., " Anthropological Notes on the Aboriginal Tribes of the Daly River, North Australia," *Transactions and Proceedings of the Royal Society of South Australia*, xvii, 1893
MADDOX, John Lee, *The Medicine Man*, New York, 1923
MAGYAR, Ladislaus, *Reisen in den Südlichen Afrika in dem Jahren 1849 bis 1857*, Leipzig, 1859
MALINOWSKI, B., *The Family among the Australian Aborigines*, London, 1913
—— " The Natives of Mailu," *Transactions and Proceedings of the Royal Society of South Australia*, xxxix, 1915
MAN, E. H., *The Andaman Islanders*, London, n.d.
MANGIN, Eugene, " Les Mossi," *Anthropos*, ix, 1914
MARCUSE, Adolf, *Die Hawaiischen Inseln*, Berlin, 1894
MARINER, William, " An Account of the Tonga Islands," *Constable's Miscellany*, xiii-xiv, Edinburgh, 1827
MARQUES, A., " Notes pour servir a une Monographie des Iles Samoa,' *Boletin de Sociedade de Geographica de Lisboa*, viii, 1889
MARSDEN, William, *The History of Sumatra*, 3rd ed., London, 1811
MARTIN, K., *Reisen in den Molukken*, Leiden, 1894
MARTIUS, Carl Friedrich Phil. von, *Zur Ethnographie Amerika's zumal Brasiliens*, 2 vols., Leipzig, 1867
DE MAS, Sinibaldo, *Informe sobre el estado de las Islas Filipinas en 1842*, Madrid, 1843
MASON, Ous Tufton, *Woman's Share in Primitive Culture*, New York, 1894
MATHEWS, R. H., " Aboriginal Bora held at Gundabloui in 1894." *Proceedings of the Royal Society of New South Wales*, xxviii, 1894
—— " The Bora of the Kamilorai Tribes," *Proceedings of the Royal Society of Victoria*, ix (n.s.), 1897
—— " The Bunan Ceremony of New South Wales," *A.A.* (n.s.), 1896
—— " The Burbung of the Darkining Tribes," *Proceedings of the Royal Society of Victoria*, x (n.s.), 1897
—— " The Burbung, or Initiation Ceremonies of the Murrumgidge Tribes," *Proceedings of the Royal Society of New South Wales*, xxxi, 1897
—— " The Burbung of the New England Tribes, New South Wales," *Proceedings of the Royal Society of Victoria*, ix (n.s.), 1897
—— " The Burbung of the Wiradthuri Tribes," *J.R.A.I.*, xxv, 1897
—— " Initiation Ceremonies of the Australian Tribes," *Proceedings of the American Philosophical Society*, xxxvii, 1898
—— " The Keeparra Ceremonies of Initiation," *J.R.A.I.*, xxvi, 1897
—— " The Wandarral of the Richmond and Clarence River Tribes," *Proceedings of the Royal Society of Victoria*, x (n.s.), 1897
MAUGHAM, R. C. P., *Zambezia*, London, 1910

MAYER, L. Th., *Een Blik en het Javaansche Volksleven*, 2 vols., Leiden, 1920

MEDINA, José Toribio, *Los Aborijines de Chile*, Santiago, 1862

MELLAND, F. H., *In Witch-Bound Africa*, London, 1923

MENDEZ, Santiago, " The Maya Indians of Yucatan in 1861," *Indian Notes and Monographs*, ix, no. 3, *Museum of the American Indian, Heye Foundation*, 1921

MERKER, M., *Die Masai*, Berlin, 1904

—— " Rechtsverhältnisse und Sitten der Wadschagga," *Pertermanns Mittheilungen aus Justus Perthes Geographischer Anstalt*, xxx, 1902

MIKLUCHO-MACLAY, N. VON, " Anthropologische Bemerkungen über die Papuas der Maclay Küste in Neu-Guinea," *Natuurkundig Tijdschrift voor Nederlandsch-Indië*, xxxiii, 1873

—— " Ethnologische Bemerkungen über die Papuas," *Natuurkundig Tijdschrift voor Nederlandsch-Indië*, xxv-xxvi, 1873

MOCKLER-FERRYMAN, A. F., *Up the Niger*, London, 1892

MOFFAT, R., *Missionary Labors and Scenes in Southern Africa*, 4th ed., New York, 1853

MONCELON, M. Leon, " Reponse alinea par alinea pour les Neo-Caledoines au Questionnaire de Sociologie et d'ethnographie de la Societe," *Bulletins de la Société d'Anthropologie de Paris*, series 3, ix, 1886

MORGAN, Lewis H., *League of the Ho-Dé-Sau-Nee, or Iroquois*. 2 vols., New York, 1901

MOSZKOWSKI, Max, " Die Völkerstämme am Mamberambo in Holländisch-Neuguinea und auf den vorgelagetten Inseln," *Zeitschrift für Ethnologie*, xliii, 1911

MULLER, Wilhelm, " Yap. Ergebnisse der Südsee Expedition, 1908-1910," *Hamburger Wissenschaftliche Stiftung*, ii, band 2, 1917

MURDOCH, John, " Ethnological Results of the Point Barrow Expedition," 9th *A.R.B.A.E.*, 1892

MUSTERS, George Chaworth, *At Home with the Patagonians*, London, 1871.

NACHTIGAL, Gustaf, *Sahara und Soudan*, 2 vols., Berlin, 1879-1881

NANSEN, Fridtjof, *Eskimo Life*, London, 1893

NASSAU, Robert Hamill, *Fetichism in West Africa*, New York, 1904

NELSON, Edward William, " The Eskimo of Bering Strait," 16th *A.R.B.A.E.*, 1899

NELSON, William, *The Indians of New Jersey*, Paterson, 1894

NIBLACK, Albert P., " The Coast Indians of Southern Alaska and Northern British Columbia," *Report of the United States National Museum*, reprint, 1890

NIEBOER, H. J., " Der ' Malthusianismus ' der Naturvölker," *Zeitschrift für Socialwissenschaft*, vi, 1903

—— *Slavery as an Industrial System*, Gravenhage, 1900

NIEUWENHUIS, A. W., *Quer durch Borneo*, 2 vols., Leipzig, 1913

DE OCA, José Montes, " La Isla de Yap," *Boletin de la Sociedad Geografica de Madrid*, xxxiv, 1893

OLDEN, Sarah Emilia, *The People of Tipi-Sapa*, Milwaukee, 1918

OPHUYSEN, CH. A. VON, *Kikjes en het Huiselijk Leven der Bataks*, Leiden, 1910

OROZCO Y BERRA, MANUEL, *Geografia de las Lenguas y Carta Etnográfica de México*, Mexico, 1864

OWENS, J. G., " Natal Ceremonies of the Hopi Indians," *Journal of American Ethnology and Archeology*, ii, 1892

PARK, MUNGO, " Travels in the Interior Districts of Africa," *Pinkerton's Voyages, and Travels*, xvi, 1814

PARKINSON, R., " Beiträge zur Ethnographie der Gilbertinsulaner," *Internationales Archiv für Ethnologie*, ii, 1889

—— " Die Berlinhafen-Section," *Internationales Archiv für Ethnographie*, xiii, 1900

—— *Dreissig Jahre in der Südsee*, Stuttgart, 1907

PARSONS, ELSIE CLEWS, "Tewa Mothers and Children," *Man*, xxiv, no. 112, 1924

PARTRIDGE, CHARLES, *Cross River Natives*, London, 1905

PATERNO, R. A., *Los Itas*, Manila, 1890

PECHUEL-LOESCHE, E., *Die Loango-Expedition*, Stuttgart, 1907

PERIERO, A. CABEZA, *La Isla de Ponapé*, Manila, 1895

PERELEAR, M. T. H., *Ethnographische Beschrijving der Dajaks*, Zalt-Bommel, 1870

PFEIL, JOACHIM GRAF VON, *Studien und Beobachtungen aus der Südsee*, Braunschweig, 1899

PLEYTE, C. M., " Plechtigheden en gebruiken uit den cyclus van het familieleven der volken van den Indischen Archipel," *Bijdragen tot Taal-, Land- en Volkenkunde van Nederlandsch-Indie*, xli, 1892

PLOSS, H., *Das Kind in Brauch und Sitte der Völker*, 2nd ed., Leipzig, 1884

POUPON, H., " Etude Ethnographique der Baya, *L'Anthropologie*, xxvi, 1915

POWERS, STEPHEN, " Tribes of California," *Contributions to American Ethnology*, iii, 1877

PRITCHARD, W. T., *Polynesian Reminiscences*, London, 1860

PROYART, ABBE, " History of Loango, Kakongo and other Kingdoms in Africa," *Pinkerton's Voyages and Travels*, xvi, 1814

RADIGUET, MAX, *Les Derniers Sauvages*, Paris, n.d.

RADIN, PAUL, " The Autobiography of a Winnebago Indian," *University of California Studies in American Archeology and Ethnology*, xvi, 1920

—— " Some Aspects of Puberty Fasting Among the Ojibwa," *Canada, Dept. of Mines, Geological Survey, Museum Bulletin* 2, 1914

RADLOFF, WILHELM, *Aus Sibirien*, 2 vols., Leipzig, 1893

RAFFLES, T. S., *The History of Java*, 2 vols., 2nd ed., London, 1830

RAWLING, C. G., *The Land of the New Guinea Pgymies*, London, 1913

READ, CARVETH, " No Paternity," *J.R.A.I.*, xlviii, 1918

READE, W. WINWOODE, *Savage Africa*, New York, 1864

RENZ, BARBARA KLARA, " Elernliebe bei amerikanischen Stämmen," *Verhandlungen des XVI Internationalen Amerikanisten-Kongress*, Wien, 1910

RIBBE, CARL, *Zwei Jahre unter den Kannibalen der Salomo-Inseln*, Dresden, 1913

RIDLEY, WILLIAM, *Kamilaroi and other Australian Languages*, 2nd ed., Sydney, 1875

RIEDEL, J. G. F., " Galela und Tobeloresen," *Zeitschrift für Ethnologie*, xvii, 1885

—— *De sluik-en kroesharige rassen tusschen Selebes en Papua*, 's Gravenhage, 1886

—— " De Topanunuasen of Oorspringlijke Volksstammen van Centraal Selebes." *Bijdragen tot de Taal-, Land- en Volkenkunde van Nederlandsch Indië*, xxv, 1886

RIGGS, STEPHEN RETURN, " Dakota Grammar, Texts and Ethno-
graphy," *Contributions to North American Ethnography*, ix, 1893
RINK, HENRY, *Tales and Traditions of the Eskimo*, Edinburgh, 1875
RIVERS, W. H. R., *History of Melanesian Society*, 2 vols., Cambridge,
1914
ROCHEFORT, *Histoire Naturele et Morale des Iles Antilles de l'Amérique*,
Rotterdam, 1665
ROMILLY, H. H., " The Islands of the New Britain Group," *Proceedings
of the Royal Geographical Society* (n.s.), 1887
ROSCOE, JOHN, *The Bagesu*, Cambridge, 1924
—— *The Bakitara*, Cambridge, 1923
—— *The Banyankole*, Cambridge 1923
—— " Notes on the Manners and Customs of the Baganda," *J.R.A.I.*
xxxii, 1901
—— " Further Notes on the Manners and Customs of the Baganda,"
J.R.A.I., xxxiii, 1902
—— " Notes on the Bagesu," *J.R.A.I.*, xxxix, 1909
—— *Twenty-Five Years in East Africa*, Cambridge, 1921
ROSENBERG, H. VON, *Der Malayische Archipel*, Leipzig, 1878
ROTH, H. LING, *The Aborigines of Tasmania*, London, 1890
—— *The Natives of Sarawak and British North Borneo*, 2 vols., London,
1896
—— " On the Significance of the Couvade," *J.R.A.I.*, xxii, 1893
ROTH, WALTER EDWARD, " An Introductory Study of the Arts, Crafts
and Customs of the Guiana Indians," 38th *A.R.B.A.E.*, 1924
—— *North Queensland Ethnography*, Bulletin 4—" Games, Sports and
Amusements," Bulletin 5—" Superstition, Magic and Medicine,"
Brisbane, 1902-1903
ROUTLEDGE, W. SCORESBY AND K., *With a Prehistoric People*, London,
1910
RUIZ, J. M. AND SANCHEZ, FRANCOIS, *Exposicion General de las Islas
Filipinas en Madrid*, Manila, 1887
RUSSELL, FRANK, " The Pima Indians," 26th *A.R.B.A.E.*, 1908
RUST, HORATIO N., " Puberty Ceremony of the Mission Indians,"
A.A. (n.s.), xviii, 1906

SAFFORD, W. E., " Guam and Its People," *A.A.* (n.s.), iv, 1902
ST JOHN, *Life in the Forests of the Far East*, 2 vols., London, 1862
SARASIN, P. AND F., *Die Weddas von Ceylon*, 2 vols., Wiesbaden, 1893
SARFERT, A., " Kusae," *Ergebnisse der Südsee Expedition*, ii, Hamburg,
1920
SCHADENBURG, A., " Uber die Negritos der Philippen," *Zeitschrift für
Ethnologie*, xiii, 1880
SCHMID, K. A., *Geschichte der Erziehung*, 5 vols., Stuttgart, 1884-1902
SCHMIDT, MAX, *Indianerstudien in Zentralbrasilien*, Berlin, 1905
SCHMIDT, ROBERT, *Les Baholoholo*, Bruxelles, 1912
SCHOMBURGK, RICHARD, *Reisen in British Guiana in den Jahren*, 1840-
1844, 2 vols., Leipzig, 1848
SCHOOLCRAFT, HENRY R., *The American Indians*, revised ed., Rochester,
1851
SCHULIEN, MICHEL, " Die Intitiationsceremonien der Mädchen bei den
Atxuabo " (Portugesisch-Ostafrika), *Anthropos*, xviii-xix, 1924
SCHULZE, LOUIS, " Aborigines of the Upper and Lower Finke River,"
Transactions of the Royal Society of South Australia, xiv, 1891
SCHURTZ, HEINRICH, *Altersklassen und Männerbunde*, Berlin, 1902
SCHUSTER, FR., " Die Sozialen Verhältnisse des Banyange-Stammes
(Kamerun)," *Anthropos*, ix, 1914

SCHWEIGER, ALBERT, "Der Ritus der Beschneidung unter den Xosa und den ama Fingo in der Kaffraria, Südafrika," *Anthropos*, ix, 1914

SCHWEINFURTH, GEORGE, *The Heart of Africa*, 2 vols., 3rd ed., London, n.d.

SEBBELOV, GERDE, "The Social Position of Men and Women Among The Natives of East Malekula, New Hebrides," *A.A.* (n.s.), xv, 1913

SEEMANN, BERTHOLD, *Viti ; An Account of a Government Mission to the Vitian or Fijian Islands*, Cambridge, 1862

SELIGMANN, C. G., *The Melanesians of British New Guinea*, Cambridge, 1911

SELIGMANN, C. G. AND BRENDA Z., *The Veddas*, Cambridge, 1911

SEMPER, KARL, *Die Palau-Inseln*, Leipzig, 1873

SERPA PINTO, *How I Crossed Africa*, 2 vols., London, 1881

SHELDON, WILLIAM, "Account of the Caraibs who Inhabited the Antilles," *Transactions and Collections of the American Antiquarian Society*, i, 1820

SHOOTER, JOSEPH, *The Kafirs of Natal, and the Zulu Country*, London, 1857

SIEBOLD, HEINRICH FREIHERRN VON, "Ethnologische Studien über die Aino auf der Insel Yeseo," *Zeitschrift für Ethnologie* (sup.), 1881

SIGAYU, JOSE TENORIO, *Costumbres de los Indios Turuayes*, Manila, 1892

SIMSON, ALFRED, *Travels in the Wilds of Ecuador*, London, 1886

SKEAT, WALTER AND BLAGDEN, CHARLES OTTO, *Pagan Races of the Malay Peninsula*, 2 vols., New York, 1906

SKINNER, ALANSON, "Notes on the Eastern Cree and Northern Salteaux," *Anthropological Papers, American Museum of Natural History*, ix, 1912

—— "Political Organization, Cults and Ceremonies of the Plains-Ojibway and Plains-Cree Indians," *Anthropological Papers*, xi, 1914

—— "Societies of the Iowa, Kansa and Ponca Indians," *Anthropological Papers*," xi, 1914

SKINNER, H. D., "The Morioris of Chatham Islands," *Memoirs of the Bernice T. Bishop Museum*, ix, 1923

SMITH, EDWIN W., AND DALE, A. M., *The Ila-Speaking Peoples of Northern Rhodesia*, 2 vols., London, 1920

SMYTH, R. BROUGH, *The Aborigines of Victoria*, 2 vols., Melbourne 1878

SNOUCK HURGRONJE, C., *De Atjehers*, 2 vols., Batavia, 1895

SOMERVILLE, BOYLE T., "Ethnographical Notes in New Georgia, Solomon Islands," *J.R.A.I.*, xxxvi, 1897

SPECK, F. G., "Family Hunting Territories and Social Life of the Various Algonkian Bands of the Ottawa Valley," *Canada, Dept. of Mines, Geological Survey, Memoir* 70, 1915

SPENCER, BALDWIN AND GILLEN, F. J., "An Account of the Engwarra or Fire Ceremony of Certain Central Australian Tribes," *Proceedings of the Royal Society of Victoria*, x (n.s.), 1897

—— *The Native Tribes of Central Australia*, London, 1899

—— "Notes on Certain of the Initiation Ceremonies of the Arunta Tribes, Central Australia," *Proceedings of the Royal Society öf Victoria*, x (n.s.), 1898

SPENCER, FRANK CLARENCE, *Education of the Pueblo Child* New York, 1899

SPIER, LESLIE, " Southern Digueno Customs," *University of California Publications*, xx, 1923

SPIESS, Carl, " Beiträge zur Kenntnis der Religion und der Kultusformen in Süd Togo," *Baessler-Archiv*, ii, 1912

SPIETH, JAKOB, *Die Ewe-Stämme*, Berlin, 1906

SPIX, J. B. AND MARTIUS, C. F. P. VON, *Reisen in Brasilien*, 3 vols., München, 1823-1831

STADE, HANS, *Captivity of Hans Stade in A.D. 1547-1555, Among the Wild Tribes of Eastern Brazil*, London, 1874

STANNUS, H. S. AND DAVEY, J. B., " The Initiation Ceremony for Boys Among the Yao of Nyasaland," *J.R.A.I.*, xliii, 1913

STARR, FREDERICK, *Notes on the Ethnography of Southern Mexico*, Davenport, Iowa, 1900

STEINEN, KARL VON DEN, *Unter den Naturvölkern Zentral-Brasiliens*, 2nd ed., Berlin, 1897

STEINMETZ, S. R., *Ethnologische Studien zur Ersten Entwicklung der Strafe*, 2 vols., Leiden, 1894

—— " Das Verhältniss zwischen Eltern und Kindern bei den Naturvölkern," *Zeitschrift für Socialwissenschaft*, i, 1898

STELLER, GEORG WILHELM, *Beschreibung von dem Lande Kamtschatka*, Frankfurt-am-Main, 1774

STEVENSON, MATILDA COXE, " The Sia," 11th *A.R.B.A.E.*, 1894

—— " The Zuni Indians," 23rd *A.R.B.A.E.*, 1904

STEVENSON, TILLY, E., " The Religious Life of the Zuni Child," 5th *A.R.B.A.E.*, 1897

STOLL, OTTO, " Die Ethnologie der Indianerstämme von Guatemala, *Internationales Archiv für Ethnologie*, i, 1889

STOW, G. W., *The Native Races of South Africa*, London, 1905

STREHLOW, CARL , " Die Arand- und Loritja-Stämme in Zentral-Australien," *Veröffentlichungen aus dem Städtischen Völker-Museum Frankfurt-am-Main*, i, 1910

STRETTON, W. G., " Customs, Rites and Superstitions of the Aboriginal Tribes of the Gulf of Carpentaria," *Transactions and Proceedings of the Royal Society of South Australia*, xvii, 1893

STUHLMANN, FRANZ, *Mit Emin Pasha ins Herz von Afrika*, Berlin, 1894

SUMNER, W. G., *Folkways*, Boston, 1907

SUMNER, W. G. AND KELLER A. G., *The Science of Society*, 4 vols., New Haven, 1926-1927

SWANTON, JOHN R., " Indians of the Lower Mississippi Valley and Adjacent Coasts of the Gulf of Mexico," *B.A.E.*, bulletin 43, 1911

—— " Social Conditions, Beliefs and Linguistic Relationship of the Tlingit Indians," 26th *A.R.B.A.E.*, 1908

TATE, H. R., " Notes on the Kikuyu and Kamba Tribes of British East Africa," *J.R.A.I.*, xxxiv, 1904

TAUXIER, LOUIS, *Le Noir du Sudan*, Paris, 1912

—— *Le Noir du Yatenga*, Paris, 1917

TAYLOR, RICHARD, *Te Ika a Maui*, London, 1870

TEIT, JAMES, " The Thompson River Indians of British Columbia," *Memoirs of the American Museum of Natural History*, ii, 1900

TESSMANN, GUNTER, *Die Pangwe*, 2 vols., Berlin, 1913

—— *Die Kinderspiele der Pangwe*, Baessler-Archiv, ii, 1912

TESCHAUER, P. C., " Die Caining oder Coroados-Indianer im brasilienischen Staate Rio Grande do Sul," *Anthropos*, ix, 1914

THEAL, G., *The Yellow and Dark-Skinned Peoples South of the Zambesi* London, 1910

THOMSON, BASIL, *The Fijians*, London, 1908
—— " Notes on the Natives of Savage Island, or Niue," *J.R.A.I.*, xxxi, 1901
THOMSON, JOSEPH, *Through Masai-Land*, New York, 1885
THURNWALD, RICHARD, " Ethno-psychologischen Studien an Südsee Völkern auf dem Bismarck-Archipel and den Salomo-Inseln," *Beihefte zur Zeitschrift für angewandte Psychologie und psychologische Sammelforschung*, vi, 1913
—— *Forschungen auf den Salomo-Inseln and dem Bismarck-Archipel*, 3 vols., Berlin, 1912
TODD, ARTHUR JAMES, *The Family as an Educational Institution*, New York, 1913
TORDAY, E., *Camp and Tramp in African Wilds*, London, 1913
—— " Der Tofoke," *Mitteilungen der Anthropologischen Gesellschaft in Wien*, xxxi, 1911
TORDAY, E. AND JOYCE, T. A., " Notes on the Ethnography of the Ba-Huana," *J.R.A.I.*, xxxvi, 1906
—— " Notes on the Ethnography of the Ba-Mbala," *J.R.A.I.*, xxv, 1895
—— " Notes on the Ethnography of the Ba-Yaka," *J.R.A.I.*, xxxvi, 1906
TORREND, J., *Specimens of Bantu Folk-Lore from Northern Rhodesia*, London, 1921
TREAGER, EDWARD, *The Maori Race*, Wanganui, N.Z., 1904
TREMEARNE, A. J. N., " Bori Beliefs and Ceremonies," *J.R.A.I.*, xlv, 1915
—— *Mausa Superstitions and Customs*, London, 1913
TURNER, GEORGE, *Samoa a Hundred Years Ago and Long Before*, London, 1884
TURNER, LUCIEN M., " Ethnology of the Ungava District," 11th *A.R.B.A.E.*, 1894
TYLOR, EDWARD B., *Primitive Culture*, 2 vols., 6th ed., London, 1920
—— " On a Method of Investigating the Origins of Institutions," *J.R.A.I.*, xviii, 1889

URICOCHEA, EZEQUIEL, *Memoria sobre las Antiguedades neo-Granadinas*, Berlin, 1854

VAEINE ET BERNARD, " Ethnographie congolaise, Chez les Lessa," *Bulletin de la société royale belge de Géographie*, xxxiv
LE VAILLANT, *Travels from the Cape of Good Hope into the Interior Parts of Africa*, 2 vols., London, 1790
VAN DE VELDE, LIEVEN, " Le region du Bas-Congo et de Kivilou-Niadi," *Bulletin de la sociéte royale belge de Géographie*, x, 1886
VAN EKRIS, A., "Iets over het Ceramsche Kakian-Verbond," *Tijdschrift voor Taal-, Land- en Volkenkunde Nederlandsch-Indië*, xvi, 1867
VAN OVERBERGH, CYR, *Les Mangbetu*, Bruxelles, 1909
VELTEN, C., *Sitten und Gebräuche der Suaheli*, Gottingen, 1903
VENEGAS, MIGUEL, *A Natural and Civil History of California*, 2 vols., London, 1759
VETH, P. J., *Borneos Wester-Afdeeling*, Zalt-Bommel, 1856
—— *Java*, 4 vols., Haarlem, 1907
VOLKENS, G., *Kilimandscharo*, Berlin, 1897
VON HAGEN, GUNTHER, " Die Bana," *Baessler-Archiv*, ii, 1912
VORMANN, FR., " Die Intitiationsfeiern der Jünglinge und Mädchen bei der Monumbo-Papuas, Deutsch Neuguinea," *Anthropos*, x-xi, 1916

Voth, H. R., " Oraibi Natal Customs and Ceremonies," Field Columbian Musem, *Anthropological Studies*, vi, no. 2, 1905

Wallace, Alfred Russell, *The Malay Archipelago*, New York, 1869
—— *Narrative of Travels on the Amazon and Rio Negro*, London, 1910
Ward, Herbert, *Chez les Cannibales de l'Afrique Centrale*, 2nd ed., Paris, 1910
Weeks, John H., *Among Congo Cannibals*, London, 1923
—— *Among the Primitive Bakongo*, London, 1913
—— " Anthropological Notes on the Bungala of the Upper Congo River," *J.R.A.I.*, xxxix-xl, 1909-1910
—— *Congo Life and Folklore*, London, 1911
Weiss, Max, *Die Volkerstämme im Norden Deutsch Ostafrika*, Berlin, 1910
Werner, A., *The Natives of British Central Africa*, London, 1906
Westermarck, Edward, *The History of Human Marriage*, 3 vols., London, 1921
Weule, K., " Afrikanische Kinderspielzeug," *Ethnologisches Notizblatt*, ii, 1899
—— *Native Life in East Africa*, London, 1915
Wheelwright, C. A., " Native Circumcision Ceremonies in the Zoutpansberg District," *J.R.A.I.*, xxxv, 1905
Whiffen, Thomas, *The North-West Amazons*, London, 1915
White, John, *The Ancient History of the Maori*, 5 vols., Wellington, 1887
Wied-Neuwied, Maximilian, *Travels in Brazil*, 2 vols., London, 1830
Wilhelmi, Charles, " Sitten und Gebräuche der Port-Lincoln Eingeborenen," *Aus Allen Welttheilen* i, 1870
Wilken, G. A., *Handleiding voor de Vergelijkende Volkenkunde van Nederlandsch-Indië*, Leiden, 1893
—— *Verspreide Geschriften*, 4 vols., 's Gravenhage, 1912
Wilkes Charles, *Narrative of the United States Exploring Expedition During the Years* 1838, 1839, 1840, 1841, 1842, 5 vols., Philadelphia, 1845
Williams, Thomas and Calvert, James, *Fiji and Fijians*, New York, 1859
Williamson, R. W., *Some Unrecorded Customs of the Makao People of British New Guinea*, London, 1913
Willoughby, W., *Race Problems of the New Africa*, Oxford, 1923
—— " Notes on the Initiation Ceremonies of the Becwana," *J.R.A.I.*, xxxix, 1909
Wilson, J. Leighton, *West Africa*, New York, 1856
Wollaston, A. F. R., *Pygmies and Papuans*, London, 1912

INDEX